THE DARK SUN

The Dark Sun

A STUDY OF D. H. LAWRENCE

GRAHAM HOUGH

DUCKWORTH

First published 1956
Reprinted 1968
First Paperduck edition 1970
Reprinted 1970, 1975 and 1983

© GRAHAM HOUGH 1956

ISBN 0 7156 0085 0 (cased)
ISBN 0 7156 0547 X (paper)

Printed in Great Britain by
Biddles Ltd, Guildford, Surrey

So one of the gods with hidden faces walked out of the water, and climbed the hill and looked about. He looked up at the sun, and through the sun he saw the dark sun, the same that made the sun and the world, and will swallow it again like a draught of water.

The Plumed Serpent

PREFACE

IN an earlier book, *The Last Romantics*, I tried among other things to trace the fortunes of the religion of art among a number of English writers from Ruskin to Yeats. This set my mind on the many attempts in the last hundred years to find satisfaction for the religious impulse outside Christianity. But as I brooded on the religion of humanity, the religion of evolution, the religion of social and scientific progress, the flesh wearied on my bones. I gradually came to feel that the only recent English writer besides Yeats to break into new spiritual territory outside the Christian boundaries was D. H. Lawrence, and that his vitalism had had something of the same disruptive and fertilising effect in our century as æstheticism did in the nineteenth. So though it seems a far cry from *The Blessed Damozel* to the *The Plumed Serpent*, there was an intelligible transition between the two.

I decided therefore to attempt a study of Lawrence, especially since, as with most readers of my age, he had loomed more or less largely in the imagination since the early thirties. In spite of the large number of books on Lawrence, there was when I began no comprehensive literary study, and I hoped that my book would do something to supply the deficiency. I immediately came up against difficulties of organisation. For a writer whose works are so intimately connected with his life as Lawrence's, a straightforward chronological treatment seemed the obvious one. But that would mean considering novels, short stories, poems and expository works together, and end in the kind of mixed critico-biographical stew of which there were several already. So the following plan was adopted. I assume a knowledge of Lawrence's life such as can be gained from Mr. Aldington's or Mr. Moore's biography. The major novels are treated chronologically, with some slight biographical reference where necessary, so as to outline the development of Lawrence's thought. The short stories and the poems are then treated in separate chapters, and referred to this general scheme of development. The principal object of these exercises, in my own mind, was to make it possible to write the last chapter, which is on Lawrence's philosophy of life. Here I have put discussions of the critical and expository works, with a good deal of reference back to the imaginative writing. I hope in this way to be able to treat the novels as novels, the poems as poems; but also to proceed from them to a general grasp of Lawrence's creative impulse and his system of ideas.

My principal debt to previous writers is to the biographers and writers of reminiscences. I believe I have made use of all of them for background material, but I owe most, and most directly, to Richard Aldington's *Portrait of a Genius, But——*, and to Harry T. Moore's *Life and Works of D. H. Lawrence*. Mr. Moore's fuller biography, *The Intelligent Heart*, did not appear till my work was nearly finished. I found little helpful criticism except that of Dr. Leavis. His book, *D. H. Lawrence, Novelist*, also appeared when my work was nearly complete, but of course I had read much of it beforehand in *Scrutiny* articles. I owe most to his chapters on *The Rainbow* and *Women in Love*, which indeed leave little for a later hand to add. In other places I am conscious of disagreement with his conclusions, and I attach much greater importance to areas of Lawrence's work which he has not touched.

My thanks are due to Dr. E. M. W. Tillyard, Mr. L. J. Potts, Dr. D. Daiches and Dr. J. H. Plumb for lending me books that were hard to come by; to my wife for reading and talking over many parts of the script; to Mrs. Helen Tomlinson for her expert and accurate typing of the whole; and to Mrs. Frieda Lawrence, Messrs. William Heinemann Ltd., and Centaur Books, Philadelphia, for permission to use the many quotations from Lawrence's works.

G. H.

Christ's College,
Cambridge.

CONTENTS

Chapter I

LAWRENCE AND THE NOVEL

THREE years before the First World War Lawrence published his first novel. His last came out in 1930; and in the twenty years between an old world broke up, in violence and suffering greater than any mankind had known before. It is surprising how little of this is reflected in the great imaginative literature of the age. The novel especially is supposed to hold the mirror to the times; yet from the work of Lawrence's great contemporaries—Gide, Proust, Mann and Joyce—a reader from another planet would hardly gather much of the convulsion in Europe. Perhaps it is usually minor literature that reflects history in any immediately recognisable way. The tempests of the imagination are not those which vex the sea of political history. They are generated in another region, and drive their victims to other shores. It is so in the work of Lawrence, too. A chapter of *Kangaroo* and a handful of letters reveal his response to the war—a response so egotistical as to be almost insane. He has an intense private concern with class distinctions, but almost none with the functioning class system and the transformations it was going through in his lifetime. The old social edifice, patched and battered conglomeration of church and palace, factory and slum, was to be swept down the flood before his eyes; but his life as an artist goes on almost independently of all this. The fact is that for him, as for most of the great imaginative writers of the time, the historical catastrophe was only part of a great revolution of sensibility; a revolution that began before the political ones, and may be uncompleted yet, though it seems to have reached at least a temporary point of rest. In this great change of feeling, indescribable while it was taking place, yet cumulatively so distinctive, between the pre-1914 world and our own, Lawrence is surely very near the centre.

Whether he is or is not a great artist, whether he is a true or a false prophet, this remains so; his work will always remain a pretty massive phenomenon and will always have to be taken into account, whatever

1

his ultimate reputation, simply because it is part of a general alteration of the mental and moral landscape—an alteration that has been widely noticed but not yet adequately described.

In England at the moment it seems fashionable to pretend that this change has never taken place, that the storms which perturbed the youth of the century were only storms in tea-cups, or that we knew it all along, and that we are now back where we really always were, among the power politics, the test matches and the perennial *condition humaine*. But this is a confusion of scale. No doubt, in the long run men have always the same things to worry about, and in the light of eternity any shift of interest can be made to appear insignificant. In a shorter perspective changes are real. The distribution of attention alters; the sea submerges formerly frequented valleys; unknown peaks appear above its surface; and though the total quantity of land and water presumably remain the same, the arrangement of the land-scape becomes suddenly unfamiliar. It will surely be recognised by future historians of culture that there was an upheaval in the early part of this century as great as the now familiar Romantic one of a hundred and fifty years ago.

It is as great, but it is not as easy to define. Historians of the Romantic period have had the great advantage of a central figure to whom the leading ideas of the time could attach themselves. Ideas about the individual genius, the private sensibility and the natural man all group themselves around Rousseau. They are not all his ideas, and their expressions vary from the Declaration of Independence to *Prometheus Unbound*. But the figure of Rousseau serves as a portent and a symbol: he takes his place among M. Maritain's *Three Reformers*, and he becomes the eponymous hero of Irving Babbitt's *Rousseau and Romanticism*. Rousseau can, within the limits of all such personal attributions, be made both the political ancestor of the Revolution and the emotional ancestor of the literary Romantic movement. Our recent revolution of feeling is not yet so clearly describable, and it is not possible to find a single figure in whom we can centre our notions. We can ascribe a premonitory vision of the conflicts of capitalism and the political emergence of the proletariat to Marx; but all the time the interior life takes, not an opposite, simply an unrelated path. If we are to find some eminent individual to place behind the imaginative experiments of the early twentieth century, it can only be an *éminence grise*—and the strongest candidate is the ambiguous Freud. Ambiguous because he is not (or is not supposed to be) an imaginative writer, but a scientist, working in the interests of a strict scientific positivism; yet he opened the door to a crowd of gorgons, hydras and chimeras stranger and more frightening than any invented by irresponsible romantic agonists. It was not till quite late that he even came to have much influence on the arts. He is simply the most powerful organiser of a great body of observations and reflections, seen by him chiefly in their clinical aspects, but active also in almost every other department of life. Of course the territory that he mapped had been travelled blindly by artists and mythologists in all ages—why else would he have named one of his prime discoveries after the ancient Œdipus? But in his own lifetime the whole field of unrecognised and irrational motivation, of the divagations of love and their consequences, were being explored with a greater intensity than ever before—not directly under Freud's guidance, but in obedience to some unseen, unknown current of attention that carried artists and scientists along together.

To this stream Lawrence belongs. But when we try to place him within it, it is not so easy. Just where does he belong? Not perhaps with the great European figures we have already mentioned—Gide, Proust, Mann, Joyce. He is too idiosyncratic; he is only intermittently interested in the European cultural tradition; much of it he deliberately repudiates. He does not fit easily into any of the great tributary streams of contemporary European letters; he is not a naturalist, and he does not claim with much conviction his share in the heritage of symbolism. But he certainly does not belong either with his nearest English contemporaries, altogether more local and restricted—Virginia Woolf and E. M. Forster—nor with his immediate seniors—Bennett, Galsworthy and Wells. Quite early in his career he became an international writer. His books were far more read in the United States than in England, and they were widely translated into other languages while they were still making their way with difficulty at home. Nor does he fit more easily into English literary history than into that of Europe. He breaks with the mainly sociological tradition. of the English novel, and does nothing whatever to advance the more rigorous æsthetic definition of the novel's outline that we associate with Henry James. Indeed, in his untidiness, his continual breaking off from whatever he is supposed to be doing to exhort, denounce or explore, he is akin to the Victorian prophets Ruskin or Carlyle. And just as Carlyle, for all his provincialism and eccentricity, gains strength from taking part in a general European movement against mechanism and materialism, so Lawrence, for all his rejections and rootlessness, gains strength from taking part in the great European expedition away from the usual trade-routes into the hinterland of consciousness.

And that is where any consideration of his work as a novelist must ultimately arrive. Lawrence continually enlarges the boundaries of our consciousness, and a judgment of his individual artistic achievement will in the long run probably depend on the extent and the worth of the new territory acquired. Of course with many novelists this kind of inquiry would be pointless. They are concerned with putting in order experiences of a kind we are already quite familiar with. Lawrence (or Dostoevsky or, in his own way, Proust) extends our experience; and to think about a novelist of this kind at once lands us in difficulties. We cannot talk for long about technique, powers of representation or even of moral insight; for we soon find that we are dealing with ideas and mental states that we have never clearly recognised till we meet them in this particular artistic context. Of course we can set Lawrence against traditional moral habits, as Mr. Eliot does in his primer of modern heresy;[1] and of course Lawrence comes out a heretic. To define the limits of his offences against faith and morals may be a useful thing, even highly illuminating. But this net is so wide that the essence of his work simply slips through the mesh, as Mr. Eliot knows well. If we want to do more than provide a prophylactic against infection, this method will hardly do. His books, or some of them, are works of art, and we can discuss them within the æsthetic framework. They are also, like other novels, comments on human experience, and we must say what we can about their range and aptness. But they are also, unlike most novels, deliberate explorations in search of new values; if we are to take Lawrence seriously, we must come to some sort of decision about the worth of what is discovered. There is a good deal of expository writing besides what is implicit in his fiction. Much of what he says at one time he contradicts, at least superficially, at another; and most of what he says arouses a strong reaction of one kind or another; so that to confront him fairly is not an easy task. It is in some ways like tackling Coleridge

or Ruskin: confusion of detail, contradiction, mania, false science—
yet throughout, power, and an intelligence that besides penetrating
to what are called the central problems of the time, casts a brilliant
and arresting light on many facets of experience that have never been
illuminated before.

It is as well to say this at the start, for to some people to-day he
is already an exploded prophet; and the attempt to deal seriously
with him will not seem worth the trouble. It is indeed quite possible
that his doctrine is false, its influence evil. Writers as different as
T. S. Eliot and Bertrand Russell have said so. It is also quite possible
that we owe to him a new insight into matters that very much needed
it. But there is only one way to deal with prophets who are also artists
—and that is to respond to their art. It is only after we have done
this that it is worth while asking the other questions. They are, in
any case, too large and too complicated for a frontal attack. So let
us first look at Lawrence's work when it offers least difficulty, at
prose that does beautifully some of the things that prose has done
before: expressing the spirit of a place and a season, for example,
like this very early passage from *The White Peacock*:

> I was born in September, and love it best of all the months.
> There is no heat, no hurry, no thirst and weariness in corn
> harvest as there is in the hay. If the season is late, as is usual
> with us, then mid-September sees the corn still standing in stook.
> The mornings come slowly. The earth is like a woman married
> and fading; she does not leap up with a laugh for the first fresh
> kiss of dawn, but slowly, quietly, unexpectantly lies watching the
> waking of each new day. The blue mist, like memory in the eyes
> of a neglected wife, never goes from the wooded hill, and only
> at noon creeps from the near hedges. There is no bird to put a
> song in the throat of morning; only the crow's voice speaks during
> the day. Perhaps there is the regular breathing hush of the scythe
> —even the fretful jar of the mowing machine. But next day, in the
> morning, all is still again. The lying corn is wet, and when you
> have bound it, and lift the heavy sheaf to make the stook, the
> tresses of oats wreathe round each other and droop mournfully.
> (Pt. I, Ch. 6.)

Or this from *Lady Chatterley's Lover*—a piece of the common human
feeling in which Lawrence is often supposed to be lacking:

"It must have been terrible for you!" said Connie.
"Oh, my Lady! I never realised at first. I could only say:

5

Oh my lad, what did you want to leave me for!—That was all my cry. But somehow I felt he'd come back."

"But he *didn't* want to leave you," said Connie.

"Oh no, my Lady! That was only my silly cry. And I kept expecting him back. Especially at nights. I kept waking up thinking: Why he's not in bed with me!—It was as if my *feelings* wouldn't believe he'd gone. I just felt he'd *have* to come back and lie against me, so I could feel him with me. That was all I wanted, to feel him there with me, warm. And it took me a thousand shocks before I knew he wouldn't come back, it took me years."

"The touch of him," said Connie.

"That's it, my Lady! the touch of him! I've never got over it to this day, and never shall. And if there's a heaven above, he'll be there, and will lie up against me so I can sleep."

(XI.)

The first piece is quite undramatic. Cyril the narrator is hardly more than a mouthpiece for certain aspects of Lawrence's sensibility, and this passage is not related to any particular situation in the plot. We can judge it quite simply therefore as a piece of evocative description. The essence of the writing is its physical immediacy, conveyed in a variety of ways: auditory, tactile, muscular and synæsthetic as well as visual imagery. The attention is first caught by the beautifully onomatopœic phrases—"the regular breathing hush of the scythe"; "the fretful jar of the mowing machine"; but the effect is completed by impressions that bring all parts of the sensuous apparatus into activity, separately or together; the absence of heat, hurry and thirst; the lingering blue mist; the wetness and weight of the lying corn, and the mournful drooping of the oat tresses.

The metaphors of the woman married and fading and the neglected wife are a little juvenile, a little selfconsciously decorative. Lawrence would not have used them later on. But they are not merely decorative. They do in little what the whole book does on a larger scale—bring together the life of nature and the life of man, see them with the same eyes; just as the crow *speaks*, the earth *lies watching*, and the absence of purely human hurry and weariness in the work of harvesting is equated with the calm and stillness of the season itself. There is no logical or syntactic relation, no progression among the separate items of the description—that is to say, no intellectual pattern is imposed upon it. Unity is given by the merging of the natural and the human, and by a pervading, gently modulated rhythm. It is a beautiful example of a kind of writing which starts with the individual sensibility ("I was born in September and love it best of all the months"), and then, instead of exploiting an egotistical pathetic fallacy, submerges the individual completely in the object of contemplation.

The second passage speaks almost with the common voice of the English novel: its pathos contains hints of Dickens, of Emily Brontë and of Hardy; but again there is a physical immediacy that the Victorians did not commonly allow themselves. It recalls fleetingly Cathie's cry after Heathcliff; but it also recalls an older world:

> Is there any room at your head, Saunders,
> Is there any room at your feet,
> Is there any room at your twa sides
> Where fain, fain, I would sleep.

There is a point in quoting the ballad, with its utter impersonality. Lawrence is often an egotistical and opinionated writer, and this passage, as it happens, is closely linked with the thesis of *Lady Chatterley*; yet it is completely free from any imported tendentiousness; it shows the artistic integrity that effaces all personal assertion before the demands of the material itself.

These are both passages of sympathetic comprehension, where we are asked to share, as we generally are in the traditional English novel, in emotions familiar to the writer and to ourselves. They are commoner in Lawrence than is supposed. And of course they must form the staple of any fiction. A novel that dealt entirely in unfamiliar and unidentifiable feelings would be incomprehensible. But the special Laurentian quality is something different: it is to present, with equal directness and conviction, persons and states of mind that we are not familiar with, that we do not understand, that are outside the range of our more or less rational daily intercourse: Rosalino, the Mozo, for instance, in *Mornings in Mexico*.

> We settled in, and Rosalino seemed to like doing things for us. He liked learning his monkey-tricks from the white monkeys. And since we started feeding him from our own meals, and for the first time in his life he had real soups, meat-stews, or a fried egg, he loved to do things in the kitchen. He would come with sparkling black eyes: "*Hé comido el caldo. Grazias!*" ("I have eaten the soup. Thank you.")—And he would give a strange, excited little yelp of a laugh.

Came the day when we walked to Huayapa, on the Sunday, and he was very thrilled. But at night, in the evening when we got home, he lay mute on his bench—not that he was really tired. The Indian gloom, which settles on them like a black marsh-fog, had settled on him. He did not bring in the water—let me carry it by myself.

Monday morning, the same black, reptilian gloom, and a sense of hatred. He hated us. This was a bit flabbergasting, because he had been so thrilled and happy the day before. But the revulsion had come. He didn't forgive himself for having felt free and happy with us. He had eaten what we had eaten, hard-boiled eggs and sardine sandwiches and cheese ; he had drunk out of the orange-peel *taza*, which delighted him so much. He had had a bottle of *gazoosa*, fizz, with us, on the way home, in San Felipe.

And now, the reaction. The flint knife. He had been happy, *therefore* we were scheming to take another advantage of him. We had some devilish white monkey-trick up our sleeve; we wanted to get at his *soul*, no doubt, and do it the white monkey's damage. We wanted to get at his heart, did we ? But his heart was an obsidian knife.

The bright, sharp phrases, the particularity of detail, the colloquial carelessness of expression are all spontaneous flashes of penetration into something that is still recognised as fundamentally a mystery. One would like to illustrate further Lawrence's sheer intuitive intelligence, the power to get at something essential in a writer or a situation with a swift X-ray glance. It is at its best in his critical prose, and of that in its place. But we find it everywhere—in the loose verse of *Pansies*, for example—the ability to penetrate a complex subject with an observation that is brief, pungent and compelling. I can hardly imagine any other two hundred words that could say more about one of the great crises of our century than these :

> One cannot now help thinking
> how much better it would have been
> if Vronsky and Anna Karenin
> had stood up for themselves, and seen
> Russia across her crisis,
> instead of leaving it to Lenin.
>
> The big, flamboyant Russia
> might have been saved, if a pair
> of rebels like Anna and Vronsky
> had blasted the sickly air
> of Dostoevsky and Tchekov,
> and spy-government everywhere.

But Tolstoi was a traitor
to the Russia that needed him most,
the clumsy, bewildered Russia
so worried by the Holy Ghost.
He shifted his job on to the peasants
and landed them all on toast.

Dostoevsky, the Judas,
with his sham christianity
epileptically ruined
the last bit of sanity
left in the hefty bodies
of the Russian nobility.

So our goody-good men betray us
and our sainty-saints let us down,
and a sickly people will slay us
if we touch the sob-stuff crown
of such martyrs; while Marxian tenets
naturally take hold of the town.

Too much of the humble Willy wet-leg
and the holy can't-help-it touch,
till you've ruined a nation's fibre
and they loathe all feeling as such,
and want to be cold and devilish hard
like machines—and you can't wonder much.[2]

Many good novelists have got on very well without the sort of
intensity and sensitiveness in detail that these passages reveal.
The quality of a novel can be curiously independent of detail; the
total impression is often quite different from what an examination
of the smaller parts would suggest. But Lawrence cannot be treated
in this way, as a maker of myths and stories, grandiose in their
totality, but heavy and insensitive in their parts. He is a poet who
happens to write in prose; and the special quality of his imagination
needs to penetrate every fibre of the work. When this does not occur,
the failure is more complete than with most novelists. "The business
of art", he says, "is to reveal the relation between man and his
circumambient universe, at the living moment. As mankind is always
struggling in the toils of old relationships, art is always ahead of the
times, which themselves are far in the rear of the living moment. . . ."[3]
Art conceived in this way needs sensitiveness at every point, if it is
to respond to the immediate flow of life before it has hardened into a

formula or been analysed into separate components. The word "flow" is the one Lawrence actually uses in another place to describe the material on which the novel works.

> It is the way our sympathy flows and recoils that really determines our lives. And here lies the vast importance of the novel, properly handled. It can inform and lead into new places the flow of our sympathetic consciousness and it can lead our sympathy away in recoil from things gone dead.[4]

Any tendency towards fixity and definition is death to the novel.

> Now here we see the beauty and great value of the novel. Philosophy, religion, science, they are all of them busy nailing things down, to get a stable equilibrium. . . . But the novel, no. The novel is the highest example of subtle interrelatedness that man has discovered. Everything is true in its own time, place, circumstance, and untrue outside of its own time, place, circumstance. If you try to nail anything down, in the novel, either it kills the novel, or the novel gets up and walks away with the nail.[5]

Definition divides and analyses, and it is the business of the novel to be concerned with the whole of man's experience. The saint decides that man is a soul, the philosopher that he is a mind, the scientist that he is a body. For Lawrence none of these is true, and they are not true for the novel either.

> Now I absolutely flatly deny that I am a soul, or a body, or a mind, or an intelligence, or a brain, or a nervous system, or a bunch of glands, or any of the rest of these bits of me. The whole is greater than the part. And therefore I, who am man alive, am greater than my soul, or spirit, or body, or mind, or consciousness or anything else that is merely a part of me. I am a man and alive. I am man alive, and as long as I can, I intend to go on being man alive.
>
> For this reason I am a novelist. And being a novelist, I consider myself superior to the saint, the scientist, the philosopher, and the poet, who are all great masters of different bits of man alive, but never get the whole hog.
>
> The novel is the one bright book of life. Books are not life, they are only tremulations on the ether. But the novel as a tremulation can make the whole man alive tremble, which is more than poetry, philosophy, science, or any other book-tremulation can do.[6]

This is one of Lawrence's rather slack bits of journalism, and it is not a very exact differentiation of the novel from other forms of art; but in a loose way it is saying something significant. Poetry can also deal with the totality of experience; but it does so at a higher level of abstraction—what might be rather than what is. Poetry has always found it embarrassing to deal with some aspects of the actual and the immediate; and it is always difficult for it to build up the rounded actualisation of an individual figure with its background. Expository writing tends towards the abstract in a different way; not the myth, not the lyric moment, but the generalisation; not—this is what actually happened, but—this is the sort of thing that goes on.

The novel presents what actually occurs: particularly in its modern form, where the scene, immediate dramatic presentation is more important than summary or retrospect. What the novel has to say about ultimate things, about the human condition in general, can only be said through incidents, scenes and characters which must all be particular and actual. Lawrence is primarily drawn to this manner of presentation: not man alone with his destiny, but a particular man in a particular situation, with his own body, mind and heart jostled by the bodies, minds and hearts of those around him, rooted in a particular soil, or uprooted from it and transplanted to some other spot. That is why so much of his work is autobiographical; his own experience is the most concrete and immediate thing of which a man can be aware. It is the unforced impress of life that Lawrence's writing can convey most naturally and with the greatest power.

But, then, that is not the whole story. From these particular notes of experience a pattern begins to appear—often a repeating pattern. The same points are formally stressed in different situations. The same relations between man and man, or between man and his natural soil, appear again and again, though with different individual characters and different material circumstances. The 'pure' novelist like Henry James would be content to present these uncommented appearances, and let the beholder piece out the figure in the carpet as best he might. But Lawrence does not leave it at that. He is not only a sensibility and a revealing instrument, and his art is not only (in the literal sense) a passion, something experienced and transmitted as directly as may be—it is also a deliberate exploration and analysis of discoveries.

The novels and poems come unwatched out of one's pen. And then the absolute need one has for some sort of satisfactory mental attitude towards oneself and things in general makes one try to abstract some definite conclusions from one's experience as a writer and a man. The novels and poems are pure passionate experience. These 'pollyanalytics' are inferences made afterwards from the experience.[7]

In fact, he does not keep these two modes of expression as separate as he suggests. It is not true that the novels are pure passionate experience and that the inferences are kept elsewhere, for the two strands are continually mixed and interwoven within the novels themselves. *Aaron's Rod* and *Kangaroo* in particular are an odd mixture of autobiography, speculation and fiction. It is in the *nouvelles*, the long-short stories, such as *The Fox* or *The Woman Who Rode Away* that the pure passionate experience emerges in its most refined form. Of the long books it is perhaps only *Sons and Lovers* that shows an unmixed inspiration worked out complete and uncontaminated. Lawrence was bitterly contemptuous of 'form' and of the critics who wanted him to have more of it. Considering the unreal pedantry that the concept of form in the novel has often generated, you can hardly blame him. But in practice he is equally contemptuous of consistency and keeping: quite different modes of conception and presentation appear side by side in the same book; and perhaps the best way of looking at some of his books is to regard them as works of mixed purpose like *Sartor Resartus*, where autobiography, fantasy and doctrine interpenetrate.

The autobiographical element in his work is unusually large. *Sons and Lovers* is unique in being completely founded on his own experience; *The White Peacock* runs it close, though with some social transpositions; and *Aaron's Rod*, *Kangaroo* and *The Plumed Serpent* include long sections drawn directly from Lawrence's own life. *Women in Love* is full of recognisable (and malicious) portraits. And the same sort of thing turns up constantly in the short stories. Lawrence was incapable of writing straight autobiography, or said he was; but he was also incapable of keeping himself and his friends out of his books. The degree of adaptation to his artistic purpose varies. The real Miriam's account of the events that gave rise to *Sons and Lovers* differs a good deal from the novel; but Lawrence probably thought he was telling the story as it was. Aaron's experiences in Italy are often as close as possible to Lawrence's, as we can see from the letters:

though it is Lilly, not Aaron, who is the chief mouth-piece of the author in this book. The domestic life of Somers and Harriet in *Kangaroo* seems to be a close study of that of Lawrence and Frieda in Australia, though the attendant political events are pure fantasy. The chapter "The Nightmare" in the same book is an almost hysterically exaggerated account of Lawrence's own experiences during the war; the letters of the war years tell the same story, but the resentment and the outraged egotism are kept more nearly within the bounds of sanity.

Personally and socially Lawrence was often to blame in matters of this kind. Artistically they are irrelevant, but they have had a curious result. The correspondence between Lawrence's books and his life is often so close that his whole *œuvre* tends to be treated as disguised autobiography. What purport to be biographical studies turn out to be based largely on his novels: and literary analyses turn out to be commentaries on his life. It is hard to keep the two considerations entirely apart, and there is no reason why one should; of course the work and the life illuminate one another. But this does not mean that they can be identified, and the more reckless combinations of fact and fiction lead only to muddle and distortion. The climax of methodological absurdity is reached by Middleton Murry, who begins his *Son of Woman* by saying that "there is and can be but one true life of Lawrence; and it is contained in his works"; and then proceeds throughout to blame the works for not telling the story right. No doubt Lawrence often caused pain to his friends by telling the truth about situations in which they were involved, or by telling something rather different from the truth. As well as reproducing experience, no doubt he compensates for failures in experience in his work. But surely we should know by now that relations between *Erlebnis* and *Dichtung* are infinitely varied and complex. A poet writes about what happened, or what he thinks happened; but also about what nearly happened, what he hoped or feared might happen. Lawrence is like Byron in being a writer whose person can never be successfully dissociated from his works. But his writing cannot be properly read or judged simply as a long series of self-revelations. One could wish it were still possible to read *Sons and Lovers* and *Aaron's Rod* as some of their earlier readers must have done, knowing nothing of the writer or his circumstances.

However, we are only too well-informed; and this inevitably affects our view of the works: we cannot help seeing how the natural development of a character, or the expected relation between two persons is sometimes distorted to fit the current bit of Laurentian doctrine, or the need to say something about a pressing, immediate experience. One way of putting this is to say that Lawrence is not much interested in character in the ordinary sense. This is partly true, and he makes a good deal of it himself. A letter to Garnett on *The Rainbow* brings this out: "But somehow—that which is physic— non-human, in humanity, is more interesting to me than the old-fashioned human element—which causes one to conceive a character in a certain moral scheme and make him consistent. . . . You mustn't look in my novel for the old stable *ego* of the character. There is another ego according to whose action the individual is unrecognisable, and passes through, as it were, allotropic states which it needs a deeper sense than any that we are used to exercise, to discover are states of the same single radically unchanged element."[8] This fits *The Rainbow* well enough, and may even be a bit of special pleading for some of its inconsistencies and failures in realisation. And it points to a permanent interest of Lawrence in themes and states of consciousness rather than in the persons who move through them. It is for this reason that we so often fail to feel sympathy or identification with Lawrence's personages. But when the element of autobiography or portraiture becomes strong, this attitude breaks down, and his people become subsistent individuals, with individual, even social personalities. No doubt Lawrence's speciality is the study of certain obscure states of the human soul. Over large areas of his work, however, he is portraying character in action in the same way as any other novelist. We remember that he is capable of social realism, even of social satire; that the beginning of *The Lost Girl* reminds us of Arnold Bennett; the beginning of *The Captain's Doll* of Somerset Maugham; and that almost everyone Lawrence knew turns up somewhere in his work in a brilliant and personally recognisable vignette.

Hence some of the mysterious shifts and modulations of key that occur in his work: the change in *Kangaroo* from an assured and vivid presentation of Australia, its geographical and social atmosphere; the fine placing within it of the very objective and actual Somers and Harriet—the change from all this to the strange figure of Kangaroo himself, quite incredible on the plane of naturalism on which the book begins. Or the change in *The Plumed Serpent* from the Mexico City of bullfights and tourists to the mysterious evocation of the ancient gods. There is a great deal of sheer wanton carelessness, or deliberate defiance of the ordinary canons, in Lawrence's sudden switches from one kind of narrative to another. But there is also a consistent movement in his writing from naturalism to symbol, from actuality to myth; and if the reader is really to swallow his work, he must be ready to swallow both. One detects two schools among his admirers. There are those who love the Lawrence of the Midlands, of the travel books, the incomparable evocator of the spirit of place or the spirit of a particular society; and they are often impatient of the mythology and of much of the philosophising. To this school Mr. Aldington seems to belong; it is appropriate therefore that of all those who knew him he should have written the most honest and objective biography of Lawrence. Then there are those whose real interest is in Lawrence the prophet, the mystic *à rebours*. They want to find in Lawrence a guide to life, and are commonly impatient of his presentation of actualities, complain of cruelty and falsification in his dealings with persons. To this school Mr. Murry belongs; and his contribution to our understanding of Lawrence, buried as it is beneath emotionalism and obscure resentments, is an intuitive understanding of the darker side of a very complex character. But if Lawrence is an artist at all, he is an artist of both kinds. Neither standpoint alone will enable us to see him whole, and we must somehow continue to take both sides of his work into account, even if possible to reconcile them.

A few sentences of Aldous Huxley's probably give us the best clue to how this is to be done.

> Lawrence's special gift was an extraordinary sensitiveness to what Wordsworth calls "unknown modes of being". He was always aware of the mystery of the world, and the mystery was always for him a *numen*, divine. Lawrence could never forget, as most of us continually forget, the dark presence of the otherness that lies beyond man's conscious mind. This special sensibility was accompanied by a prodigious power of rendering this immediately experienced otherness in terms of conscious literary art.[9]

But not only in terms of literary art—in terms of the concrete, the visible and palpable. From the streets of Eastwood to one of the central tangles of human relationships; from the visible Australian landscape to the whole status of man in an ancient and empty world; from the sensible ferocities of the Mexican scene to the gods of violence and terror who lurk in the background of all human life; from the actual snake drinking at the water-trough to the whole mystery of non-human consciousness. If we want to do justice to Lawrence's fundamentally consistent vision of life, it is this movement that we must look for.

Chapter II

THE MAJOR NOVELS

I. EARLY BACKGROUND

THROUGHOUT his life Lawrence returned to his native Midlands for the themes of his novels and stories. But only the two early books, *The White Peacock* and *Sons and Lovers* (*The Trespasser*, of the same period, is almost an irrelevance), are firmly rooted in the soil of his youth. In everything written after he left England in 1912 he sees Nottingham in the light of Germany, Italy or Mexico. The grime of industrial England seems not only a distress and a problem, but something willed and unnecessary, a cause for anger rather than pity or comprehension. It is hard to believe that anyone need continue to endure what one has personally succeeded in escaping: and that is the feeling that very soon begins to appear in the letters written on his first Continental journey.

> No, I don't believe England need be so grubby. What does it matter if one is poor, and risks one's livelihood and reputation. One can have the necessary things, life, and love, and clean warmth.[10]

Up to this time he never seems to have found England grubby at all, or to have longed for any landscape beyond that around Nethermere. But the mere experience of richer and larger scenes begins to make the image of England shrink and wither.

> I only talk about my poverty so as not to seem to swank. I can always afford what I want. Indeed the Villa Leonardi is quite gorgeous and palatial. The figs they send up, fresh gathered out of the garden, are a dream of bliss. Grapes and peaches are ripe— there are miles of vineyards and olive woods. The lake is dark blue, purple and clear as a jewel, with swarms of fishes. And the boats have lemon-coloured sails.[11]

After this he is never again going to see his Midland childhood exactly as it was. Conscious criticism from another standpoint begins to affect even *Sons and Lovers*, for though it was experienced, con-

17

ceived and mostly written before Lawrence had met Frieda and shaken the dust of England from his feet, it was finished in Italy in the early days of his marriage.

But at heart it belongs to Eastwood; and the greatest help to understanding Lawrence's early work would be to forget his later wanderings, social and geographical, and feel Eastwood as it was, from the inside, when the only openings to other worlds were through books or the imagination. A great deal of nonsense has been talked about Lawrence's background and education. The contrast between the provincial childhood and the cosmopolitan later life has been over-played. Childhood is always provincial, and its horizon is always restricted—the particular circumstances that make it so are not important. A rather hoity-toity concept of culture has been used to show that Lawrence had a hole-and-corner upbringing, and remained therefore an inspired barbarian, ignorant of the grand calm expanses of properly certified European civilisation. But the only people who ever inhabit this kind of European civilisation are cultivated Americans, like Henry James or Mr. Eliot; Europeans live in Nottingham or Nancy, Paris or Piacenza, Frankfurt or Fenny Stratford, and the actual life of any of these places has always seemed a poor and disappointing affair to visitors from the platonic New England heights. To Mr. Eliot, therefore, Lawrence is a wild man: he suffers from a "lack of intellectual and social training".[12] Dr. Leavis counters with some indignation, by presenting Lawrence as the product of a rich, vigorous and morally admirable English working-class culture.

Mr. Eliot's strictures on Lawrence in *After Strange Gods* are accompanied, as he admits, by a very imperfect acquaintance with Lawrence's work: perhaps also with his life; and Dr. Leavis does well to remind us of the opportunities for reading and study that Lawrence's youth afforded, and the admirable use of them that Lawrence and Jessie Chambers made. He goes on, however, to present them as enjoying the advantage of "a still persistent cultural tradition that had as its main drive the religious tradition that Mr. Eliot speaks of so contemptuously"[13]; of "a family life quite finely civilised, though pressed on by immediate economic and practical exigencies".[13] And here, surely, the facts simply revolt. We have only to recall a few aspects of the oft-recorded actuality: Mrs. Lawrence using her Band of Hope piety as a weapon against her disappointing husband;

she and her 'superior' children ganging up against the coarse father on whose sweat they nevertheless lived; Jessie Chambers turned into a drudge and sneered at by her clumsy brothers—all this is far from the sober paradise of Dr. Leavis's polemic. As for the finely civilised family life, its chief flower was the hateful possessive bullying which killed Lawrence's richest and most beautiful friendship.

Mr. Eliot finds it convenient to discount Lawrence's inconvenient views by referring them to his unfortunate origins. No product of Eastwood Congregationalism and Nottingham High School, even if accidentally endowed with Individual Talent, could possibly be in proper relation to Tradition. Dr. Leavis replies by producing a proletarian-nonconformist tradition to square up to Mr. Eliot's. Even if this tradition existed in the form that Dr. Leavis ascribes to it, it would be more adapted to producing the high-minded lecturer at a teacher's training college that Lawrence so signally refused to become; but in fact both the ignorant barbarism and the tradition are largely mythical. The fact is that from Elizabethan times intellectual ability and education, however acquired, have been a passport to the central stream of English culture. The reason that the English provincial tradition is so weak is that hardly anyone of first-rate ability ever stays in it; and they do not stay in it because it is so easy to get out. England is the land of snobbery, but not of rigid snobbery: class boundaries are shifting and often transcended. The upper bourgeoisie remains culturally dominant because it makes itself so accessible to all who have anything to bring to it, and thus attracts to itself all real outside talent. The inspired barbarian is not likely to remain a barbarian for long: if he is really inspired someone will soon make it his (or more probably her) business to civilise him; and the talented provincial is not likely to remain long in his province: if he is really talented he will soon be drawn into the stream of metropolitan or cosmopolitan culture. The only door Samuel Johnson from Lichfield ultimately found closed to him was Lord Chesterfield's. It is Lord Chesterfield who is generally held to have been the loser. And Herbert Lawrence from Nottingham soon found that he was able to move, geographically, socially and intellectually, pretty well where he liked.

Of all the snobberies in England, the educational is the strongest and the most absurd, and the pother about Lawrence's background is largely a consequence of it. It is of course very recent; but the nineteenth-century public-school and university complex has so successfully bemused both its admirers and its detractors that any intellectual success not achieved by way of Eton and King's, or Winchester and New College, is felt to stand in need of explanation, as though a Trobriand islander were to write *The Golden Bough*. The classic case is Shakespeare's. But the truth is that from Shakespeare's day on the majority of educated people in England have received their education at small, local grammar schools. When Oxford and Cambridge were the only universities, the youth of outstanding talent generally managed to get there. From the foundation of the provincial University Colleges, still more people managed to get a higher education. Though they were cut off from most of the graces and amenities of English culture, to suppose that they were deprived of any vital intellectual opportunities is the result either of ignorance or prejudice. Sufficient is given for the man of real powers to take what he needs. And Dr. Leavis rightly maintains that Lawrence at twenty-one had as sound an intellectual training as most.

But this does not imply the existence of a provincial intellectual tradition, except in an extremely impoverished and attenuated form; for as soon as the provinces produce a man of outstanding quality, he moves elsewhere. There are no Weimars in England—the reasons are complex, and in any case are not our business—and the result is that local intellectual life is constantly drained of its most creative spirits—the best gift their education could give them was the means of escape.

But for Lawrence as a boy there was nothing particularly constricting about Eastwood. It was a normal place to live. If his family were poor, so were most others that they knew. There is no evidence that the ugliness and meanness of a mining district oppressed him; and it would be surprising if there were. They oppress people who have seen something else, not those who have lived there all their lives. There was much lovely, unspoiled country close at hand, and the dwellers in the smaller industrial districts are not cut off from the rhythm and the freshness of nature. There is no evidence that he felt his educational chances restricted, and there is no reason why he should. The tools of learning were put into his hands. He could get all the books he needed. He began French and German at thirteen; some Latin came later. (He was reading the *Georgics* at the time *The White Peacock* was taking shape.) If he had less classics, he had a far wider range of English literature than the contemporary public-school boy. He was always successful academically: in the ordinary exam-passing, scholarship-winning sense he was a very clever boy; and there was absolutely nothing to prevent him becoming a well-educated successful minor professional man in his own part of the country. Nothing: except that the whole code of educational self-improvement in which he and his contemporaries were brought up could only have the effect of driving the most successful away.

The economic foundation of Eastwood life was the pit, and the young Lawrences were brought up to despise the pit and all it stood for. Mrs. Lawrence was superior, and they were to become superior, too, to be white-collar workers. The moral and religious foundations were generally Nonconformist, in the case of the Lawrences Congregational; sincere rather than merely formal; intelligent rather than merely emotional, though not without richness of feeling. Lawrence has more than once recorded his deep response to the hymns of his childhood; and Jessie Chambers has recorded the contempt felt by her family for the Anglican curate's "string of platitudes that did duty for a sermon", in contrast to the "reasoned discourse" they were used to in the Congregational chapel. A tradition certainly not to be despised. But there is no use pretending that by the beginning of the century there was much life left in English Nonconformity. It had already split, into an untenable fundamentalism on the one hand, and on the other a vague liberal piety without positive content. The High School and the University College made the first impossible for Lawrence; that he remained faithful to the other for longer than is commonly supposed we can see from a letter written to his sister in 1911, six months after their mother's death:

> I am sorry more than I can tell to find you going through the torment of religious unbelief: it is so hard to bear, especially now. However, it seems to me like this: Jehovah is the Jew's idea of God, not ours. Christ was infinitely good, but mortal as we. There still remains a God, but not a personal God: a vast, shimmering impulse which waves onward towards some end, I don't know what—taking no regard of the little individual, but taking regard for humanity. When we die, like rain-drops falling back into the sea, we fall back into the big, shimmering sea of unorganised life we call God. We are lost as individuals, yet we count in the whole.

It requires a lot of pain and courage to come to discover one's own creed, and quite as much to continue in lonely faith. . . . I would still go to chapel if it did me any good. I shall go myself, when I am married. Whatever name one gives Him in worship we all strive towards the same God, so we be generous-hearted: Christians, Buddhists, Mrs. Dax, me, we all stretch our hands in the same direction. What does it matter what name we cry? It is a fine thing to establish one's own religion in one's own heart, not to be dependent on tradition and second-hand ideals.[14]

That is the true voice of the religious tradition to which Dr. Leavis refers. It is startlingly unlike anything really personal to Lawrence: it might have come from Mark Rutherford, or Butler's Ernest Pontifex after he had lost his faith. To hear Lawrence using their accents is almost laughable. This is the familiar late-Victorian landscape, vague, lifeless and unexacting.

<blockquote>
That is why, I suppose,
The best and worst never stayed here long but sought
Immoderate soils . . .
       . . . "Come!" cried the granite wastes,
"How evasive is your humour, how accidental
Your kindest kiss, how permanent is death." (Saints-to-be
Slipped away sighing.) "Come!" purred the clays and gravels.
"On our plains there is room for armies to drill; rivers
Wait to be tamed and slaves to construct you a tomb
In the grand manner: soft as the earth is mankind and both
Need to be altered." (Intendant Cæsars rose and
Left, slamming the door.) But the really reckless were fetched
By an older colder voice, the oceanic whisper:
"I am the solitude that asks and promises nothing;
That is how I shall set you free. There is no love;
There are only the various envies, all of them sad."[15]
</blockquote>

In one way or another Lawrence was to hear all these voices before the end; but they were not heard at Eastwood. For the present Lawrence and Jessie Chambers, that eager, sensitive and touching pair of adolescents, were reading everything they could lay their hands on. There is no need to repeat the list given in her memoirs—and it would be impossible to reproduce the feeling of excitement and absorption which she conveys with such beautiful sincerity. Together they went through most of the great English novelists of the nineteenth century: Ruskin, Carlyle and the essayists; a good deal of poetry, mostly Romantic; and a fair selection of the French novel, too. For Lawrence the nineteenth-century rationalists soon followed, and a good introduction to English empirical philosophy— Locke, Berkeley and Mill. Of the Germans he read some Kant, Nietzsche and Schopenhauer.[16] It would be hard to say that a youth with this background had not a very fair idea of the general lay-out of the intellectual map; and harder still to believe that anyone with Lawrence's devouring moral and intellectual energy, so equipped, would stay long in the orbit of family life and Dissenting piety that Dr. Leavis has made much of.

In the meantime, that is where he was; and in the meantime, and from the inside, it was doubtless a far richer and more varied affair than is apt to appear to the outside critic. The emotional and personal adventures of youth are much the same whatever their setting: the varieties of human character are as great, the complications of human relations as intricate in a small town as in a big, in a poor society as in a rich one; and Lawrence's fears, hopes and inquiries were as much stirred by Eastwood and Nottingham as Proust's by the Faubourg St. Germain. With all this in mind, we can begin to look at *The White Peacock*.

II. THE WHITE PEACOCK

The White Peacock contains more of Lawrence's youth than any of his other novels. *Sons and Lovers* is directly autobiographical (and of course a far greater achievement); but it is experience at least partly digested, and some of it is wisdom after the event. The conflict it deals with has come out into the open. Above all, it was begun only just before his mother's death, and in the last stages of the relation with Miriam which his mother had ruined. *The White Peacock* is the actual contemporary product of the period which *Sons and Lovers* describes. Together they represent the flowering and the exhaustion of Lawrence's youth.

It was a very literary youth, as we have seen. The idea of writing was first mentioned between Lawrence and Jessie Chambers when he was seventeen, but *The White Peacock* was not begun till two years later. By that time Lawrence had read most of the classic English novels and a good many of the French. They had all been eagerly discussed, too; so that however inexperienced, Lawrence was by no means an unsophisticated student of fiction, and he had plenty of available literary models. The presiding genius at the birth of *The White Peacock* seems, in fact, to have been George Eliot. She stands prominently among his early reading; he regarded her as the first novelist to start "putting all the action inside";[17] and when he first thought clearly of writing a novel, her practice was in his mind.

"The usual plan is to take two couples and develop their relationships," he said. "Most of George Eliot's are on that plan. Anyhow, I don't want a plot, I should be bored with it. I shall try two couples for a start."[18]

George Eliot was likely to have a special appeal to Lawrence and Jessie because her country was so close to theirs; and personal relations in a Midland setting seemed the predestined theme for Lawrence's first work. The tone of the lines just quoted suggests that Lawrence began by wanting to write a novel, rather than this or that particular novel; but from the start of his literary projects he had wanted to get himself and his friends into his work. Very early we find him saying to Jessie: "I'm sure we could do something if we tried. Lots of the things we say, the things you say, would go ever so well into a book."[19] They didn't particularly; and most of the references to the genesis of *The White Peacock* make it sound a little factitious. But the absorption in his own immediate environment and the desire to do something with it is real enough.

In fact, the book is made up of a medley of autobiography and portraiture, with fiction which at first seems rather contrived. George Saxton owes a little to Gabriel Oak, and more than a little to Tom Tulliver; Lettie something to Hardy's capricious and unsatisfied ladies. The original plot was quite different, with a story-book falsity which Jessie Chambers objected to. In the present revised version the main theme comes authentically to life, largely because of the solid placing and portrayal of George Saxton. But not all the plot nor all the characters are successfully transmuted. There are loose ends, themes started and not developed, and the ordinary social genre-painting, on which a good deal of the novel appears to depend, is often uncertain. Yet there is a freshness and sensitiveness about the whole that quite transcends objections of this kind. Lawrence begins his career as he is to go on, by writing a novel with many and obvious technical faults, yet nevertheless achieving something that makes the faults almost irrelevant. In *The White Peacock* it is not immediately obvious what the achievement is.

As with most of Lawrence's creations, the starting-point, the grit in the oyster, is autobiography. The setting is Lawrence's own country and the places are all identifiable. Cyril Beardsall the narrator is, rather feebly, Lawrence himself as a youth. Beardsall was his mother's maiden name. Even in his nomenclature Lawrence wishes to deny the share of the father in his being, just as, by a simple piece of wish-fulfilment, he removes him from the plot. Emily is the Jessie Chambers of real life and George is her brother. Lettie is Lawrence's own sister. All these people and their relationships are studied far more fully and intensely later on—in their proper setting. Here the impulse to contrivance and novel-making is suggested by a social transposition. The Beardsalls and their friends—except for the farming Saxtons—are transported into the comfortable middle class. This is partly due to a conventional view of the necessities of fiction. The whole conception demands that Cyril and Lettie should be selfconscious, and articulate; to portray working people in this light was still a fairly bold enterprise for the novel, and Lawrence shirks it—as many of his contemporaries shirked their non-genteel characters. On the other hand, the transformation of the Lawrences corresponds to their aspiration if not to the actuality. An entry into the professional class was precisely what Mrs. Lawrence desired for her sons, and *The White Peacock* effects it. The untranslatable father is simply removed.

Lawrence later believed that there was an essential gulf between middle-class and working-class life; and his later acute consciousness of class differences would never have allowed him to switch his characters from one part of the social system to another. Here the social transposition makes for a rather feeble and pallid picture of the Beardsall-Tempest world. Mrs. Beardsall becomes a shadow. Lettie is rather lightly drawn and loosely attached to her setting; the treatment contrasts strongly with the solid establishment of her farmer-lover George. And Cyril's only real attribute is a rather girlish sensibility. More serious in what appears to be, and in part is, a regional novel of manners, the strong outlines of a clearly defined social system which give such a sturdy framework to most English novels become wavering and uncertain. Not that the result is wholly false. The pretentious and often vulgar talk of the young Beardsalls' student friends is bad because the author wishes one to accept it as clever rather than because it is improbable. In the Midlands and the North, where industry and commerce have made for rapid rises and rapid falls, the boundaries are really less defined; and that Lettie should be courted by both Leslie and George is a real social possibility. Lawrence loves to take advantage of all the places where the classes can meet and mingle—a small half country, half industrial town, or a literary-social Bohemia. He wants these juxtapositions. And he wants, though less consistently, to preserve a reasonable air of social actuality. However, he is always willing to sacrifice this for the sake of bringing widely differing types into contact. Hence the social ambiguities and improbabilities in which, side by side with extremely penetrating observations, his works abound.

But of course the suggestion that this is a realistic novel is not the whole truth. A variety of themes and motives are stirring vaguely in *The White Peacock*; some are hinted at and dropped, some are partly developed, and almost all reappear in Lawrence's maturer writing. Because of their very naïvety at this stage some themes that were extremely important to Lawrence appear here more simply and with less distortion than they are ever to do again. There is very little deliberate exploration of the unknown. *The White Peacock* is like a dream before it is interpreted, or before the possibility of interpretation has been entertained. Many of the classic Laurentian motives which he was later to drag out into consciousness and expound and comment on here appear unanalysed and unaware of their own significance. We need only enumerate them briefly: the relationship with Jessie Chambers, to be elaborated and finally exorcised in *Sons and Lovers*; the hostility to the father, and hence to the principle of authority in general; the conflict for a woman between a selfconscious, civilised man and an earth-bound, inarticulate one; the degeneration of the man who denies his own potentialities; the gamekeeper, with his violent hatred of modern women and their standards; the lady who gives herself to a more primitive kind of man; the love-relation between man and man, almost overtly homosexual in the 'Poem of Friendship' chapter of *The White Peacock*, later concealed and distorted in *Women in Love, Aaron's Rod, Kangaroo* and *The Plumed Serpent*.

There is enough here for a dozen stories, and they were duly written later on. Their co-presence in *The White Peacock* suggests a certain confusion of purpose. But although Lawrence is bursting with all this rich stock of material, he knows quite enough about conventional novel structure to subordinate most of it to a single central plot—the story of Lettie and her two suitors. They are Leslie Tempest, the smart, rich, selfconscious, moderately sensitive but ultimately rather empty manufacturer's son; and George Saxton, the slow, earth-bound, inarticulate young farmer. It is in this part of the book that Lawrence approaches most nearly to George Eliot or Hardy—to the traditional novel of English provincial life; and it is in the Saxton family that all the rich, solid evocation of character and background is concentrated. Anywhere in later Lawrence, George would have represented primary and valid feeling against the etiolated Leslie, and he would have been victorious. But Lawrence had not yet developed this myth. At the time when his own conscious intelligence was awakening, he was not so apt to deny its claims as he later became. Here George's inarticulateness and unawareness tell against him. He has not yet reached the stage of full human consciousness. "You are blind; you are only half-born," Lettie says to him. He cannot act out his emotions because he has not yet realised them to himself. A good deal is made of George's awkwardness among the suburban refinements of the Beardsall household; the note is a little false, and on the social plane the presentation is barely adequate. But very subtly, in the middle of this, the conviction is allowed to grow up that George's failure is a failure of will. Lettie's feeling for George is at one time as deep as his for her; yet he allows it all to slip away. And he could have done otherwise. "You should have insisted and made your own destiny," Cyril tells him. "You should have had the courage to risk yourself." He deals, or fails to deal, with the degeneration of the farm and his own future in the same way—merely drifts. He has denied his manhood, not in the familiar way of later Laurentian characters, by starving the passions and the senses, but by allowing consciousness and will to rot unused.

The result for both George and Lettie is something near to tragedy. The latter part of the book shows his consequent degeneration. His marriage to a soft, sensual, mindless woman, Meg of the Ram, is a direct consequence of his refusal of the responsibility of consciousness. By the perverse law of compensation, it is only after he has chosen this course and committed himself to a dulled, half-bestialised existence, that his need for an individual assertion of the will awakens. He makes a success of his business, becomes in his way a power in the town, takes pleasure in opposing Lettie's husband. But it is too late. He is unsatisfied, unhappy, takes to drink, and ends in hopeless mental and physical degradation—the outward and visible result of his interior refusal. Lettie marries Leslie, with his superficial social attractions, and becomes absorbed into a bourgeois world of surface values. She extinguishes herself in social life and her children. "Having reached that point in a woman's career when most, perhaps all, of the things in life seem worthless and insipid, she had determined to put up with it, to ignore her own self, to empty her own potentialities into the vessel of another or others, and to live her life at second hand. This peculiar abnegation of self is the resource of a woman for escaping the responsibilities of her own development." Like George, Lettie has failed herself; and though the failure is not dramatic or externally obvious, it too is irreclaimable.

The secondary plot, much slighter and less conclusive, deals with the relation of Cyril the narrator to George's sister Emily; and at bottom it presents the same kind of failure. It is an uncompleted sketch of the complex frustrations of *Sons and Lovers*. But the maternal possessiveness is little stressed. Cyril is merely childish, mentally clever but emotionally undeveloped. He is deeply drawn to Emily, but cannot make up his mind to any determinate relation with her. He is sensitive in a rather girlish way—one of his mocking girl friends always calls him Sibyl instead of Cyril, and a good deal is made of this. He fails to live up to a real emotional exigency, and when Emily becomes engaged to another man he merely lets her go. The only strong feeling that possesses him is a passive one for George.

This relation with George represents a complex of feeling that Lawrence was never to realise clearly. But it exercises a strong intermittent influence on his later work. The "Poem of Friendship" chapter in Part II is specially devoted to it. George and Cyril bathe in a pond before a day's haymaking. They dry themselves in the sun and compare their physique.

> He saw that I had forgotten to continue my rubbing, and laughing he took hold of me and began to rub me briskly, as if I were a child, or rather a woman he loved and did not fear. I left

myself quite limply in his hands, and, to get a better grip of me, he put his arm round me and pressed me against him, and the sweetness of the touch of our naked bodies one against the other was superb. It satisfied in some measure, the vague, indecipherable yearning of my soul; and it was the same with him. When he had rubbed me all warm, he let me go, and we looked at each other with eyes of still laughter, and our love was perfect for a moment, more perfect than any love I have known since, either for man or woman.

(Pt. I, Ch. 8.)

Cyril is the passive, feminine partner, at least in the physical relation. Mentally he is dominant. This situation is partly echoed in the relation between Birkin, the physically frail yet spiritually powerful protagonist of *Women in Love*, and Gerald Crich, physically splendid yet spiritually without direction. Later this mode of feeling suffers some strange transformations. There is the feminine tenderness with which Lilly succours Aaron in *Aaron's Rod*; and tries to dominate him mentally at the same time. Yet Aaron remains sturdily masculine and refuses to be dominated in either sense. Lilly is neither lover nor beloved, he is more like a mother attempting to possess her son by tenderness and moral authority combined. And Aaron rejects the offer, just as Somers later rejects a similar offer by Kangaroo. This is an area of the map of love which Lawrence never became familiar with, though he is always trying to explore it. In *The White Peacock* the failure in realisation is not in the relation of Cyril and George itself: it is that it is never integrated with the rest of the story. Cyril's feeling for George is never related to his failure with Miriam, or to his own childishness and irresponsibility. It remains an unassimilated episode.

There are other such episodes, too. They are distinguishable because they are separate entities, each discovered and dismissed in a single chapter, without effect on the rest of the plot. It is possible to see them all as simply naïveties of construction. But they are something more—they are attempts at saying or symbolising something that Lawrence knew to be important, whose bearing and relevance he cannot yet see. The most striking example is the lost father theme. The Beardsall children are discovered living alone with their mother: and the missing father is accounted for and disposed of in Chapter IV by a bit of absurd novelese complication which is never developed and never has any consequences. In *Sons and Lovers* the whole question of the father's relation to the family is faced; in *The White Peacock* Lawrence is not yet ready: he simply shirks the problem, and substitutes a bit of wish-fulfilment. The coarse, drunken but very solid and vital father of actuality who proved such a disturbance to the mother and son idyll is reduced to a faded and permanently absent waster who obligingly dies and allows the author to get on with the part of the story that he has more fully understood. The same disposal of the unwanted recurs, with a fuller sense of its tragic implications, in *The Widowing of Mrs. Holroyd*.

The third episode, that of the gamekeeper Annable, is less easy to account for. It is powerfully felt and powerfully written, but it remains an excrescence on the main story. And if we cannot relate it to the design of the book as a whole, we cannot relate it either to the more heterogeneous mass of experience from which the book sprang. Annable's savagery and bitterness, his hatred of his dead wife, extending itself to all women, his whole tone of violence and sexual disgust, are clearly beyond anything that Lawrence either knew or could have known in life at this time. Annable is one of the characters, to become more numerous as time goes on, whose genesis is not in social experience but in deeper psychological recesses. His embittered masculine protest recurs again and again in later stories: his profession, part of his life-history and much of his sexual experience, come up again in *Lady Chatterley's Lover*. More important, he is the first sign of the recurrent movement in Lawrence's work from character conceived naturalistically to character conceived as part of a mythology. He is the first bearer of the Laurentian philosophy.

Annable believes only in the physical: he scorns all spirituality and other-worldliness. "Be a good animal, true to your animal instincts" is his motto. He has run away from his socially superior wife because she became soulful, a poet got hold of her, and she took up with Pre-Raphaelitism. She is one embodiment of the peacock symbol in the title of the book. While Cyril is talking with Annable in the churchyard an actual peacock comes and perches on the angel's head of a gravestone, and Annable sees it as "the very soul of a lady". The bird befouls the angel's head, and Annable comments: "A woman to the end, I tell you, all vanity and screech and defilement." A peacock perching on a gravestone in the form of an angel—it represents the unanchored, unsatisfied, unliving woman who is to appear so often in Lawrence's later fiction. Lettie, by her rejection of George, becomes such a one: she is a peacock, too. Annable, the representative of elemental male force, stands aside and hates them all.

He is violent, brutish, coarse and immensely strong; yet, like Lawrence's other gamekeeper, he is really a sort of gentleman in disguise. He has been to Cambridge, was a curate once and has chosen the life he now leads; just as Lady Chatterley's lover has been an officer in the war, can speak the King's English when he wants to and has chosen to return to his former status. To find this naïve snobbery at the heart of Lawrence's symbolism is disconcerting, especially as it does not even begin to be plausible as a piece of ordinary social realism. But one does not escape from the English social system by being born in Eastwood; and many of Lawrence's elemental forces have to establish their credentials by first making it clear that they could have been a success in middle-class society if they had wanted to. And, anyway, Annable has to be killed. He bears his testimony, he interferes where he can with sentimental flower-picking and courting, and then he falls down the quarry and is crushed. He and the forces that he represents are not to be allowed at this stage to interfere with the normal texture of life.

Annable asserts his manhood, flouts idealism and society, and is killed. George fails to assert his, and sinks into a sodden wreck. Cyril has none to assert, and ends as ineffectual as he began. Emily remains elusive and Lettie unsatisfied. No one finds fulfilment, no one even points the way to it. To judge in the conventional terms of a plot acted out by characters, the book is a pattern of disappointments. Yet there is a paradox here, for the prevailing impression it leaves behind is one of tenderness, freshness and young growth. How is this contradiction to be explained? Perhaps we should return to the letter to Edward Garnett quoted in the first chapter. "But somehow that which is physic—non-human—in humanity is more interesting to me than the human element." *The White Peacock* is not at bottom what we have so far made it appear—a naturalist novel with incompletenesses and inconsistencies. Lawrence's profoundest interest is not in the human and social destiny of his characters. This is where the life of most novels is centred; but in *The White Peacock* it is not so: the centre is displaced. The centre is displaced so that the circumference of the book includes, not only the characters and their personal fates, but the whole life of nature which surrounds and flows through them. The characters are only forms into which this universal *mana* transitorily flows, and it is *mana* that is Lawrence's real subject.

Annable is killed, and his funeral takes place on a magnificent morning in early spring.

> The upper air was woven with the music of the larks, and my whole world thrilled with the conception of summer. The young pale wind-flowers had arisen by the wood-gate, and under the hazels, where perchance the hot sun pushed his way, new little suns dawned, and blazed with real light. There was a certain thrill and quickening everywhere, as a woman must feel when she has conceived. A sallow tree in a favoured spot looked like a pale gold cloud of summer dawn; nearer it had poised a golden, fairy busby on every twig, and was voiced with a hum of bees, like any sacred golden bush, uttering its gladness in the thrilling murmur of bees, and in warm scent. Birds called and flashed on every hand; they made off exultant with streaming strands of grass, or wisps of fleece, plunging into the dark spaces of the wood, and out again into the blue.
>
> (Pt. II, Ch. 2.)

The whole passage, with its sense of quivering, delicate vitality, is remarkable; coming on the heels of the gamekeeper's horrible death, it suggests that the life of a man is in itself a small thing: it is only an expression of a force that is everywhere, quick, tender and strong. Human life is only significant so far as it perceives and participates in this; and it is more complex only because it has so many opportunities of turning away from and denying the authentic life that is everywhere. How to share in it without denying the claims of the specifically human situation—that is the eternal problem of man's existence. Lawrence at this point has no easy answer; but he has already posed the question that was to occupy him for the rest of his days. From the point of view of traditional European ethics, his later answers were to be highly eccentric, but there is no hint of this in *The White Peacock*. Where George fails, for instance, he fails not only by the Laurentian code but also by a quite central and normal moral code: he hides his light under a bushel; his will refuses to accept the responsibilities of consciousness. The same is true, less markedly, of Cyril. Lawrence is not for the most part thinking in traditional moral terms, but so far his presentation has nothing repugnant to them.

Annable's case could be put more strongly. He is the first bearer of what later became an important part of the Laurentian philosophy, and as such is clearly an object of fascination to his creator. He has repudiated, not only the ordinary social bonds and duties but all the decency and gentleness of ordinary human intercourse. All has been sacrificed to his own code—"Be a good animal"—to *mana* in its crudest and least differentiated form. He is an extreme example of the heresy of feeling which Mr. Eliot detects in Lawrence's work. But what we should notice here is that his heresy is not allowed to prevail: the event unequivocally condemns him. His violent death is directly due to his own over-confident physical self-assertion—his persistence in using a quarry path that he had always been told was dangerous. So, at any rate, it was decided at the inquest. But he was hated throughout the countryside for his violence and harshness; and there were rumours in the village that it was not an accident, that it was revenge that had overtaken him. In either case, the implication is the same. The Annable philosophy is avenged, either by nature itself or by other men. It is no way of life for man to identify himself with the blindest and harshest of natural forces.

Lettie's situation is different. The choice that faces her is not in any ordinary sense a moral one at all. She is perfectly free to take either of her suitors. She takes Leslie, and the choice leaves her unhappy and unsatisfied. But there is nothing in traditional ethics to tell her why. Lawrence later weakened this kind of case by approximating it (of course in his own peculiar terms) to the old conflict between love and duty. We all know that love is much more fun. But here there is no question of duty: it is a conflict between two kinds of love—affection and compatibility on the one hand, and a far deeper stirring of the instinctual forces on the other. This has not yet been elevated to the plane of quasi-religious intensity it later reached and Lawrence is able to deal with it unemphatically and without strain. He was never to do it again with more delicacy and truth.

The White Peacock leads one to wonder what would have become of Lawrence the novelist if he had not found it necessary also to become a prophet. Most of his later themes and ideas are found here in something more than embryonic form. But they have not yet become articles of faith. Leaving aside some youthful (and on the whole unimportant) immaturities, *The White Peacock* has a singularly pure and untrammelled kind of discernment. But this pure vision is not enough for Lawrence; the impulse to theorise and expound on what he had seen was always strong in him; and having achieved what he could with the candid gaze of his youth, he immediately gives it up, in pursuit of something more turbid and more difficult.

* * * * *

Lawrence's second novel, *The Trespasser*, need not detain us long. In the first place it is not entirely his own, but a revision of some work by Helen Corke, the friend of his London school-teaching days. A good deal of it is pretty close to conventional novelese, both in plot and in details. I suspect that it has been strongly influenced by George Moore's *Evelyn Innes*; and Moore's brand of worldly æstheticism sits very ill on Lawrence. The story of Siegmund and Helena and their frustrated love-affair is not substantially different from a hundred other such situations in fiction. Even if we did not know that it had no very deep roots in Lawrence's experience, we should divine it from the uncertain quality of the writing. It never manages to be modestly undistinguished: in parts it is extremely good, but in other parts it is grossly and flamingly bad, not with the prophetic over-emphasis of Lawrence's later bad writing, but with the second-hand poetry of the woman's magazine.

> They are all still—gorse and the stars and the sea and the trees, are all kissing, Siegmund. The sea has its mouth on the earth, and the gorse and the trees press together, and they all look up at the moon, they put up their faces in a kiss, my darling. But they haven't you—and it all centres in you, my dear, all the wonder-love is in you, more than in them all, Siegmund—Siegmund.

(XI.)

Well, well; it is kinder to turn to the more purely descriptive passages. Most of this frustrated idyll takes place in the Isle of Wight, and the enchanting picture of a white, sunny, salty landscape does more than provide the setting for Siegmund's and Helena's affairs, it conditions and flavours their whole relationship during the few days of the story. Even when he is working on second-hand and second-rate material, nothing can dull Lawrence's sense of the inter-penetration of man's life and the life of nature. And it survives even when his own relation with his theme is slight. Lawrence was in the

Isle of Wight only for a short holiday, yet the spirit of the place is as keenly and clearly felt as that of the other landscape with which he was far more deeply involved. And this kind of sensibility is the only certain thing in Lawrence's writing at this stage. As far as human experiences are concerned, he is quite uncertain, without any standard of taste or judgment—perceptive, delicate and sure when he is on his own ground, quite capable of being false and second-hand when he is off it; and apparently unaware of the difference. *The Trespasser* is the product of a brief taste of London literary life after the appearance of *The White Peacock*. This kind of society never did Lawrence much good; and in *Sons and Lovers* he is to return to his own country.

III. SONS AND LOVERS

The novels and poems come unwatched out of one's pen. And then the absolute need one has for some sort of satisfactory mental attitude towards oneself and things in general makes one try to abstract some definite conclusions from one's experience.[20]

So Lawrence accounts for the relation between his imaginative and his expository writing. One of the clearest examples of the relation seems to be *Sons and Lovers*. We have the novel, the most complete and integrated of Lawrence's works; and we have his own excellent analysis of it, quite the best that has ever been done, in a letter to Garnett.

A woman of character and refinement goes into the lower class, and has no satisfaction in her own life. She has had a passion for her husband, so the children are born of passion, and have heaps of vitality. But as her sons grow up, she selects them as lovers—first the eldest, then the second. These sons are *urged* into life by their reciprocal love of their mother—urged on and on. But when they come to manhood, they can't love, because their mother is the strongest power in their lives, and holds them. . . . As soon as the young men come into contact with women there is a split. William gives his sex to a fribble, and his mother holds his soul. But the split kills him, because he doesn't know where he is. The next son gets a woman who fights for his soul—fights his mother. The son loves the mother—all the sons hate and are jealous of the father. The battle goes on between the mother and the girl, with the son as object. The mother gradually proves the stronger, because of the tie of blood. The son decides to leave his soul in his mother's hands, and, like his elder brother, go for passion. Then the split begins to tell again. But, almost unconsciously,

35

the mother realises what is the matter and begins to die. The son casts off his mistress, attends to his mother dying. He is left in the end naked of everything, with the drift towards death.[21]

The broad psychological outlines emerge more clearly in this exposition, which is evidently the fruit of later reflection, than in the novel as it stands. But the matter is not quite as simple as that, for both elements are present in the novel itself. There are several layers of experience in *Sons and Lovers*, some very close to biographical actuality, some more remote. The element of autobiography constantly obtrudes itself in Lawrence's fiction. It does not always repay minute inquiry, and external evidence is often lacking. But *Sons and Lovers* is a special case, and its relation to reality is a peculiar one. The book is a catharsis, achieved by re-living an actual experience—re-living it over and over again; and the achievement is a necessary preliminary to all the later work. As it happens, we have more detailed information about its genesis, from several sources, than we have for any other novel of Lawrence; both the means and the incentive to make the biographical connection present themselves. So there is something to be said for standing for a time outside the completed work to observe how it arose from its matrix in Lawrence's early life.

The first version was begun some time in 1910, before his mother's death, in the ambience of the conflict which it describes. Miriam was created under the direct supervision of her actual prototype; and as we can see from her memoir, her pressure was constantly exercised towards presenting things just as they were. Like *The White Peacock*, *Sons and Lovers* began with a contrived and conventional plot, and it was at Jessie Chambers' suggestion that Lawrence re-wrote it as a far more direct embodiment of the actuality. We first hear of the book in October 1910, under the name of *Paul Morel*, which it long retained. Lawrence wrote to Sydney Pawling at the time he was negotiating with Heinemann over *The Trespasser* about "my third novel, *Paul Morel*, which is plotted out very interestingly (to me), and about one-eighth of which is written. *Paul Morel* will be a novel—not a florid prose-poem, or a decorated idyll running to seed in realism."

The antitheses in the last phrase are of course with *The Trespasser*—the florid prose-poem, and *The White Peacock*—the decorated idyll. It is not quite clear what is meant by saying that *Paul Morel*, by contrast, will be a novel, but probably that it had something like a regular and conventional novelist's plot. The earliest surviving manuscript is described by L. C. Powell, and in it "the father accidentally kills Paul's brother, is jailed, and dies on his release".[22] Even this early version was, it appears, re-worked, for Helen Corke says that Lawrence was re-writing the early chapters about Whitsun 1911.[23] Then in the autumn of that year he showed the manuscript to Jessie Chambers. This was evidently not the same as the manuscript described above, for she says that the brother Ernest does not appear in the story at all. She found the writing strained and tired. "He was telling the story of his mother's married life, but the telling seemed to be at second-hand and lacked the living touch."[24] She herself was presented as Miriam in the story, but placed in a bourgeois setting—in the same family from which the Alvina of *The Lost Girl* was taken. The theme of the mother's hostility to Paul's love for Miriam was explicit from the start; among the sentences she quotes from this early draft are these:

> What was it he wanted of her? Did he want her to break his mother down in him? . . . Mrs. Morel saw that if Miriam could win her son's sex sympathy there would be nothing left for her.[25]

But the mother-and-son relationship was presented with a storybook falsity verging on sentimentalism. She said that "what had really happened was much more poignant and interesting than the situations he had invented". Finally she suggested, as she had done about *The White Peacock*, that he should cut out the fiction, and tell the story of his mother, his home life and his adolescence as simply as possible.

Lawrence appealed to her to help him, because of her much clearer recollection of their early days together, and a second re-writing began, under her influence, and with passages for the Paul and Miriam relationship supplied by her. Lawrence worked on this version at Eastwood, in late 1911 and early 1912. It was immediately after the serious illness that followed his mother's death. He had left his teaching job in Croydon, and was writing again on his home ground, again under Miriam's guidance, but with the being of his mother almost more vivid to him than it had been in her life. He is thus back in the thick of the conflict that *Sons and Lovers* describes.

The passages supplied by Jessie Chambers, or as many of them as survive, are recorded in Appendix D to Moore's *Life and Works of D. H. Lawrence*. Lawrence took them over pretty well wholesale, and the existing evidence goes far to suggest that the whole of the "Lad and Girl Love" chapter and parts of "Strife in Love" and "Defeat of Miriam" may have been written up from notes supplied by her. However, things did not progress as she wished. When she saw the new version, she was greatly impressed by the force and truth of the home life of the Morels but "bewildered and dismayed" at the Paul and Miriam portion. The hero's bondage to his mother, she felt, was "glorified and made absolute".[26] "His mother had to be supreme, and for the sake of that supremacy every disloyalty was permissible."[27] Worse still, she felt he had betrayed the essential nature of their young relationship. Fragments of a commentary by her, also recorded by Moore, show us how. It was by the premature introduction of sexual conflict, the attribution to her of a sexual selfconsciousness and a desire for kisses to which Paul was unable to respond. She feels in essence that Lawrence is complicating and distorting a deep, innocent and unselfconscious adolescent tenderness, which in fact was only crossed by his mother's hostility, and that he is doing this in the interests of his mother's point of view. She wrote bitterly to Helen Corke: "The Miriam part of the novel is a slander—a fearful treachery. David has interpreted her every word, action and thought in the light of 'Mrs. Morel's' hatred of her."[28]

It can be argued, and with a good deal of truth, that Jessie obstinately regarded the work as biography not fiction, and every departure from actuality as a falsification. And Lawrence was writing a novel. But this is not the whole story. In the last stages of his relation with Jessie Chambers, Lawrence was endeavouring to convince her, not only of the artistic appropriateness of his version, but of its truth.[29] Inspired by maturer understanding or the need for self-justification, or whatever it might be, he was imposing his own interpretation on events, giving his own interpretation of the failure of their love, and desperately seeking to make it finally convincing to himself by persuading Jessie to accept it, too. The biographical situation is a moving and complicated one, but this is not our concern. Critically speaking, two points of importance become clear. First, the extraordinarily intimate connection between Lawrence's writing and his experience; what he writes as fiction must be retrospectively accepted as fact.

And secondly, the co-presence in the Paul and Miriam parts of *Sons and Lovers* of two different kinds of experience—more or less simple recollection, checked and assisted by Jessie Chambers; and a later interpretation of the whole sequence of events. Jessie, as we have seen, believed that this interpretation was a posthumous assertion of his mother's power.

She is unlikely to have been wholly right—but the temptation to biographical speculation must be resisted. The effect of this literary episode on their personal life was a pathetic failure, and it led directly to the ultimate breach between them. The last stage of Lawrence's love for Jessie Chambers was crossed and broken by relations with other women, and then all these were decisively interrupted by the meeting with Frieda. This was the end of his youthful pilgrimage. He left England with Frieda in 1912. For a time they were together in Metz. Then Frieda remained there with her relatives, and Lawrence went off to cousins of his own in Waldbröl. There, unsettled, uprooted but free, utterly severed from all former ties and associations, he took up *Paul Morel* again and worked on a further revision. When he and Frieda were together again at Icking, the work continued with furious intensity. "I lived and suffered that book, and even wrote bits of it,"[30] she says, thus fulfilling the rôle that Jessie Chambers had first assumed. On November 11th, 1912, the novel, now called *Sons and Lovers*, was finished, and the manuscript sent to Garnett.

Since the whole situation presents the Freudian Œdipus imbroglio in almost classic completeness, it has naturally raised the question of Freudian influence on the composition of *Sons and Lovers*. The first thing to be said about this is that the situation was there in actuality, and was pretty well recognised for what it was at the time. Jessie herself wrote:

> The day before his mother's funeral we went a walk together. . . . At the end of that same walk, as we stood within a stone's throw of the house where his mother lay dead, he said to me: "You know, J., I've always loved mother."
> "I know you have," I replied.
> "I don't mean that," he answered. "I've loved her—like a lover—that's why I could never love you."[31]

At this time (1910), the general diffusion of Freudian ideas was of course still far distant, and it is exceedingly unlikely that Lawrence had ever heard Freud's name. Later on Lawrence said that he had not read Freud in the *Sons and Lovers* period, but had heard of him.[32] He does not say when or from whom. But there need be no mystery about this. It was in 1912, and from Frieda. Freud's name occurs on the first page of her memoir *Not I but the Wind*: "I had met a remarkable disciple of Freud and was full of undigested theories"; and on the day of their first meeting she and Lawrence "talked about Œdipus and understanding leaped through our words".[33] Later she wrote that she was a great admirer of Freud when she met Lawrence in 1912, and that he and she had long arguments about Freud together.[34] And of course the final draft of *Sons and Lovers* was written as strongly under Frieda's influence as the earlier ones had been under Miriam's. *Sons and Lovers* is indeed the first Freudian novel in English, but its Freudianism is mediated not by a text-book but by a person—a person, moreover, who was at the same time offering an object-lesson in many of the matters with which Freud deals.

It cannot be supposed that Frieda Lawrence's Freudianism (which s unlikely to have been very scholastically complete) materially altered the conception of the story, most of which, in any case, was in being before she came on the scene. What it could and almost certainly did do is set a theoretical seal on a situation that had been very thoroughly explored in actuality. Its influence can surely be detected in the analysis of the novel sent to Garnett. Frieda herself says nothing about this. But she does say that the bits she wrote or suggested are, curiously enough, passages presenting the mother's point of view. Or perhaps it is not curious. By this time she had taken possession of Lawrence's soul, masterless since his mother's death. She had given up her own children to do so. She had renounced her maternal rôle in life, but can play it over again in the book. Lawrence had at last renounced his mother, but had found someone who could still present her point of view. So the last fragment needed to make the experience behind *Sons and Lovers* into an intelligible whole was added. But Frieda's rôle does not appear directly in the book, and it is right that it should not. It says more for Lawrence's restraint and sense of form than we can generally say that he is able to keep out of *Sons and Lovers* the emancipation, geographical, physical and mental, that Frieda brought him; that he can see it artistically in its proper place—as the external standpoint which made the whole vision possible, without the temptation to drag it between the covers.

So much for the genesis of *Sons and Lovers*. To indicate, as we have just done, different strata of composition in a single work usually leads to a process of disintegration, to the perception of some failure in unity and wholeness. With *Sons and Lovers* it is quite otherwise. It is the very presence of these several points of view, differing in time, in degree of maturity and in kind, that gives the book its depth and richness. The solid establishment of character and setting in the early part would be incomplete without its flowering in the Miriam idyll: and the puzzled groping of the later relations with Miriam would be nebulous without its firm, realistic foundation. Lawrence was quite incapable of the sort of conscious æsthetic planning that gives their form to the novels of Henry James. Form for him was the embodiment of an experience, and a form not lived through in experience was impossible to him. This is why even a formal criticism of *Sons and Lovers* must be in part a discussion of the actuality, as far as that can be discovered, or of Lawrence's changing attitudes to it. Certainly the analysis sent to Garnett in November 1912 represents far more than was in Lawrence's mind at the outset.

Even quite late in its composition Lawrence refers to *Sons and Lovers* as "the colliery novel", and it seems quite likely that the original idea was a well-made story of colliery life, to get away from the shapelessness of *The White Peacock* and the factitious emotionalism of *The Trespasser*. Then by Jessie Chambers' advice he abandons the attempt at strength through plot, at any rate plot of the contrived, deliberate kind, and reverts at first to pure naturalism. The whole of Part I up to the death of William is of this kind—strong, straightforward, deeply felt, the best picture of industrial, working-class life in English, probably the only one written completely from the inside. Lawrence describes, as he does again in *Women in Love*, two stages of English industrial development—the small-scale, manageable, quasi-paternalist system, which still allowed some scope for human feelings and genuine human relations; and its supersession by huge mechanistic organisations that inevitably negate the life of the men who are engaged in them. It is the beginning of a lifelong preoccupation with the effects of industrialism, though in *Sons and Lovers* the element of social protest is not strong; there is simply the direct presentation of an intimately known and accepted reality. The very fully developed picture of colliery life is neither an intrusion into the novel nor a mere background; it is integrally connected with the plot. The life of East-wood offers nothing to a vital, instinctive, unambitious man like Walter Morel, except the pit and the public-house. To Lydia his wife, with her intelligence and her longing for refinement, it offers nothing but the chapel and the hope of getting up into the middle class—through her children if not through her disappointing husband. Their marriage, therefore, after the first flush of passion has died down, can be nothing but a sterile conflict; on the one hand, brutal toil and the relief from it in brutal drinking; on the other, pinched material struggle and the aspiration after a meagre superiority. This is Paul Morel's heritage, and the neurotic refusal of life engendered in him is the direct result of his parents' failure. And the parents' failure is the direct result of the pressure of an inhuman system. Their strong, disparate personalities make conflict inevitable; it might in another setting have been fruitful conflict: in Eastwood it can only be life-destroying.

With the advent of Miriam, the nature of the novel changes. It is no longer a decisive setting down of experience that has been thoroughly understood. There is no need to apply Jessie Chambers' criticisms, which are essentially of an ethical and personal nature, to the novel as a novel. That Lawrence's treatment of this story was a personal tragedy for her is true and demands our sympathy; but that is another matter. The essential literary point is that here Law-rence begins to do something new and something that is far more peculiar to himself than the admirable first part of *Sons and Lovers*— to use the novel as a deliberate means of exploring an experience that has not been fully understood. "It is the way our sympathy flows and recoils that determines our lives"; and the central Paul and Miriam section of *Sons and Lovers* is a study of the way Paul's sympathies flowed and recoiled. It is not possible that such a study should be true to Miriam's different experience of the same events or to objective fact. Or rather, the only objective fact that is in question is the fluctuation of feeling in Paul-Lawrence's own mind. And leaving aside, as we must, her sense of pain and betrayal, all we can say is that Jessie Chambers was right, and showed acute literary, as well as personal, judgment in feeling the contrast between the first part of the book and the second. For it is here that Lawrence begins to turn the novel to his own purpose, to use it as a means of coming to understand a situation where understanding had not been achieved in ordinary experience.

Any judgment of Lawrence as an artist must depend in some measure on how this process is viewed. "The only way of representing emotion in the form of art", writes Mr. Eliot, "is by finding an 'objective correlative'; in other words, a set of objects, a situation, a chain of events which shall be the formula of that *particular* emotion; such that when the external facts, which must terminate in sensory experience, are given, the emotion is immediately evoked." For those who hold this view much of Lawrence's most characteristic writing must fail. We recall, however, that from this point of view *Hamlet* was also an artistic failure. Of course in what many people consider his best—his descriptive—writing, Lawrence is superbly successful at finding in landscapes, beasts and flowers objective equivalents for emotion. But in writing of human relations he often leaves a residue of the unobjectified. A situation is suggested, it is illuminated in one or two brilliant flashes, and for the rest—a frank confession of the residual mystery.

> And gradually the intimacy with the family concentrated for Paul on three persons—the mother, Edgar, and Miriam. To the mother he went for that sympathy and that appeal which seemed to draw him out. Edgar was his very close friend. And to Miriam he more or less condescended, because she seemed so humble.
>
> But the girl gradually sought him out. If he brought up his sketch-book, it was she who pondered longest over the last picture. Then she would look up at him. Suddenly, her dark eyes alight like water that shakes with a stream of gold in the dark, she would ask:
>
> "Why do I like this so?"
>
> Always something in his breast shrank from these close, intimate, dazzled looks of hers.
>
> "Why *do* you?" he asked.
>
> "I don't know. It seems so true."
>
> "It's because—it's because there is scarcely any shadow in it; it's more shimmery, as if I'd painted the shimmering protoplasm in the leaves and everywhere, and not the stiffness of the shape. That seems dead to me. Only this shimmeriness is the real living. The shape is a dead crust. The shimmer is inside really."
>
> And she, with her little finger in her mouth, would ponder these sayings. They gave her a feeling of life again, and vivified things which had meant nothing to her. She managed to find some

meaning in his struggling, abstract speeches. And they were the medium through which she came distinctly at her beloved objects.

Another day she sat at sunset whilst he was painting some pine-trees which caught the red glare from the west. He had been quiet.

"There you are!" he said suddenly. "I wanted that. Now, look at them and tell me, are they pine-trunks or are they red coals, standing-up pieces of fire in that darkness? There's God's burning bush for you, that burned not away."

Miriam looked, and was frightened. But the pine-trunks were wonderful to her, and distinct. He packed his box and rose. Suddenly he looked at her.

"Why are you always sad?" he asked her.

"Sad!" she exclaimed, looking up at him with startled, wonderful brown eyes.

"Yes," he replied. "You are always, always sad."

"I am not—oh, not a bit!" she cried.

"But even your joy is like a flame coming off of sadness," he persisted. "You're never jolly or even just all right."

"No," she pondered. "I wonder—why."

"Because you're not; because you're different inside, like a pine-tree, and then you flare up; but you're not just like an ordinary tree, with fidgety leaves and jolly——"

He got tangled up in his own speech; but she brooded on it, and he had a strange, roused sensation, as if his feelings were new. She got so near him. It was a strange stimulant.

Then sometimes he hated her. Her youngest brother was only five. He was a frail lad, with immense brown eyes in his quaint, fragile face—one of Reynolds' "Choir of Angels," with a touch of elf. Often Miriam knelt to the child and drew him to her.

"Eh, my Hubert!" she sang, in a voice heavy and surcharged with love. "Eh, my Hubert!"

And, folding him in her arms, she swayed slightly from side to side with love, her face half lifted, her eyes half closed, her voice drenched with love.

"Don't!" said the child, uneasy—"don't, Miriam!"

"Yes; you love me, don't you?" she murmured deep in her throat, almost as if she were in a trance, and swaying also as if she were swooned in an ecstasy of love.

"Don't!" repeated the child, a frown on his clear brow.

"You love me, don't you?" she murmured.

"What do you make such a *fuss* for?" cried Paul, all in suffering because of her extreme emotion. "Why can't you be ordinary with him?"

She let the child go, and rose, and said nothing. Her intensity, which would leave no emotion on a normal plane, irritated the youth into a frenzy. And this fearful, naked contact of her on small occasions shocked him. He was used to his mother's reserve. And on such occasions he was thankful in his heart and soul that he had his mother, so sane and wholesome.

(VII.)

This is a typical passage from the central part of *Sons and Lovers*. It defines with extraordinary sensitiveness the nature of the girl, with her deep intelligence and feeling, only just awaking to consciousness, newly aware of the possibilities of sympathy and communication; and the boy, slightly arrogant and cocksure, deeply attracted, but unwilling to submit to the demands of her emotional intensity. Yet a great deal of the effect is gained by the admission of the unrealised, the uncomprehended.

"Always something in his breast shrank from this close, intimate, dazzled look of hers." Miriam *"doesn't know"* why she likes Paul's sketches. She would *"ponder* his sayings"; "She *managed* to find some meaning in his *struggling* abstract speeches". She *wonders why* she always appears to be sad. And Paul for his part "gets *tangled up* in his own speech"; "experiences a *strange* roused sensation. It was a *strange* stimulant". And all this disturbing, ill-understood emotion is placed by contrasting it with his mother's sanity and reserve.

It might be said that a good deal of this is an evasion of real difficulties, a mere token payment, a gesture towards defining a relationship, but an uncompleted gesture. This is true of the word *strange*, which Lawrence constantly overworks and makes into a mere rubber stamp for the undefinable. Otherwise, however, the passage is remarkable for the precision with which it establishes the situation. The actors in the scene are faintly bewildered, unaware of what is happening to them; and the writing refrains from going beyond their actual awareness; yet the material for a fuller understanding is there. It is there in the contrast between her feeling and his, and in the use of the mother as a point of reference. Another writer would have had to make use of the tape-recorder, stream of consciousness technique, or endow the characters with preternatural insight and self-consciousness, or provide a commentary of his own. Lawrence's method gives the actual process of living, with all the groping, the intermittence of vision associated with life as it is lived.

Later in the same chapter comes the episode of the algebra lesson. Miriam hates her status as a household drudge, and is eager for learning. Paul offers to teach her. But she is slow and self-conscious, and too anxious to be able to learn with ease.

> She was poring over the book, seemed absorbed in it, yet trembling lest she could not get at it. It made him cross. She was ruddy and beautiful. Yet her soul seemed to be intensely supplicating. The algebra-book she closed, shrinking, knowing he was angered; and at the same instant he grew gentle, seeing her hurt because she did not understand.
>
> But things came slowly to her. And when she held herself in a grip, seemed so utterly humble before the lesson, it made his blood rouse. He stormed at her, got ashamed, continued the lesson, and grew furious again, abusing her. She listened in silence. Occasionally, very rarely, she defended herself. Her liquid dark eyes blazed at him.
>
> "You don't give me time to learn it," she said.
>
> "All right," he answered, throwing the book on the table and lighting a cigarette. Then, after awhile, he went back to her, repentant. So the lessons went. He was always either in a rage or very gentle.
>
> "What do you tremble your soul before it for?" he cried. "You don't learn algebra with your blessed soul. Can't you look at it with your clear simple wits?"

(VII.)

The scene is repeated again and again; and always Paul is ashamed of his anger. All that appears on the surface is her humility, his arrogance and impatience. Yet what appears between the lines is different. Miriam puts her soul and its complexities into the algebra lesson because to her it stands for learning and the life of the mind, all that has been denied her. It has been granted to Paul: this is his world, and learning is a means of access to him; she is timid and self-conscious because she already loves him, and already with prophetic insight fears that he will go beyond her. Paul is angry with her hesitation, her slowness and her emotional intensity because it already begins to constitute a claim on him. Strongly drawn to Miriam, he cannot and will not give himself to her; he wants to keep their encounter, all her life that touches him, on the level of her "clear simple wits", where he knows he is safe and knows he is her master.

"Then he often avoided her and went with Edgar. Miriam and her brother were naturally antagonistic. Edgar was a rationalist, who was curious and had a sort of scientific interest in life." Here Paul feels secure.

Most of this material is already present in one of the earliest written portions of *Sons and Lovers*. None of the explanation of Paul's and Miriam's motives suggested above is in the book at any stage. It is doubtful whether Lawrence could have explained them at the time this part of the book was written. He is not writing an interpretation of the Paul-Miriam relation in the light of full psychological knowledge. He is portraying it from the inside, as it seemed at the time. If he is deluded about it, he portrays the delusions. But he puts their grounds and causes into the picture, too. Paul thinks he is a clear-headed, rational creature, irritated by the obscure complexities of Miriam's nature. But in fact he is in a far more complex emotional tangle than she; and the matter for such a reading of the situation is presented quite fully at the same time as his own quite different view. This is not a common achievement—to give the false judgment of a participant in a situation, to give it almost entirely through his eyes, yet to incorporate in it the grounds of a true judgment. It is not a necessary part of the novelist's business to give a final omniscient judgment; but it is his business to give the material on which a final judgment could be based.

The Paul and Miriam chapters are the essential core of *Sons and Lovers*. Adolescent love has been treated in fiction both before and since, tenderly or ironically; but never with such penetration, so little sentimentality or such honest determination to show its nature and the corruptions to which it is subject. Lawrence takes it seriously, and this is rarely done; and he treats it, under the pressure of an urgent personal necessity, from the inside. But quantitatively the Miriam relationship occupies only about a third of the book. The letter to Garnett, after describing the battle between the mother and Miriam for the soul of Paul, continues: "The son decides to leave his soul in his mother's hands, and like his elder brother, go for passion." But this, with other passages in the commentary, is not quite borne out by the text. It is wisdom after the event. At the end of the "Defeat of Miriam" chapter Paul recognises that he cannot love her physically, but he does not know why. He does not clearly recognise the power of the mother-image. It is true that he returns to his mother; the seal is set on his return by their trip to Lincoln together, in which he treats her like "a fellow taking his girl for an outing". But he thinks that he is still faithful to Miriam, that she still holds him in the depths of his soul. Yet her possession of his soul comes to matter less and less, for at the same time another woman is arousing his physical passion.

Clara Dawes represents all that Miriam does not. She is independent, emancipated, experienced and physically uninhibited. She is also separated from her husband, whom she has written off as an insensitive brute. While Miriam trespasses on the sanctities that had been the mother's preserve, Clara Dawes stands freely on unoccupied ground. Miriam wants a completely committed love—with all its concomitants of fidelity, tenderness and understanding. This Paul cannot give; his fidelity and tenderness are already bespoken; and Miriam is condemned to sterile conflict. But Clara's is a frank, physical appeal. The temperamental difference is subtly emphasised. Shortly before his first meeting with Clara, Paul has been reading the Bible to Miriam, and he boggles at a passage about a woman in travail. Anything suggesting the physical relation of man and woman is taboo between them. Not long after, when they are walking with Clara, they meet an elderly spinster lovingly caressing a great horse. They find her odd, and Clara blurts out flatly, "I suppose she wants a man". Immediately after as he sees Clara striding ahead, Paul feels a hot wave of excitement run through him.

The excitement grows. Paul drifts away from Miriam into a Socialist-Suffragette-Unitarian group around Clara. She comes to work under Paul in the factory where he is employed, and her husband also works there. The development of their relation is wholly without the tender pastoral glow of the farmhouse idyll with Miriam, but also, in spite of obvious complications, without the hidden obstacles and inhibitions. He does not even realise at first that he desires her sexually.

> Sex had become so complicated in him that he would have denied that he ever could want Clara or Miriam or any woman whom he *knew*. Sex desire was a sort of detached thing, that did not belong to a woman. He loved Miriam with his soul. He grew warm at the thought of Clara, he battled with her, he knew the curves of her breast and shoulders as if they had been moulded inside him; and yet he did not positively desire her. He would have denied it for ever.

(X.)

His mother is not displeased; she thinks he is getting away from Miriam. And even Miriam is little disturbed by the new situation; she is sure there is nothing in it.

> Miriam knew how strong was the attraction of Clara for him; but still she was certain that the best in him would triumph. His feeling for Mrs. Dawes—who, moreover, was a married woman—was shallow and temporal, compared with his love for herself. He would come back to her, she was sure.
>
> (X.)

Yet she is afraid to let Paul become her lover, and he can never bring himself to push things to a crisis. The situation between them grows steadily more unsatisfactory. Paul's physical desires are becoming more importunate, and it seems on the face of things that it is Miriam's reluctance which stands in the way. We may read between the lines that her reluctance is the consequence of his earlier inhibitions; but this is never said. And from this time on the suspicion obtrudes itself that the author is identifying himself too closely with Paul's point of view. The truth of the presentation is not impaired, as far as it goes; but less than justice is done to Miriam's side, and Paul's *ex parte* explanations have it too much their own way, as they did not in the earlier chapters of the story. Eventually he breaks with her, after eight years of friendship and love.

Of course he goes straight to Clara; and easily, naturally, without forethought or complication, he has of her what he has wanted for years. Their first encounter is not even described. Paul has not yet realised that women need to be satisfied as well as men relieved, and at the time of writing Lawrence probably shared his ignorance. At any rate, he is not at the stage when he wishes to analyse and differentiate sexual experience. The mere fact of its occurrence is enough. Paul is immensely elated. He takes Clara to tea with his mother, without embarrassment, and his mother thinks, "What a man he seems". He is growing up, and the mists that clung round the Miriam relationship have cleared. Even on Clara's visits to the Morel household "it was a clear, cool atmosphere, where everyone was himself and in harmony". Paul still sees Miriam, but now his bitter comment on the affair is that it was only talk—"There never *was* a great deal more than talk between us." The sense of tension relieved is vivid enough; but we are obstinately left with the impression that

Lawrence does not want to convey—that the relation with Miriam was far the stronger and more meaningful of the two. There is a slightly smug satisfaction about Paul, for having got what he wants without forfeiting his mother's approval, in which the author seems at least partly implicated. It is not the women whom their sons sleep with that possessive mothers hate—it is the women whom they love; and it is not hard to see here the cause for Jessie Chambers' charge of capitulation to the mother's point of view.

Paul has at last succeeded in finding pleasure without the sense of guilt; and his need for this is probably the key to another curious episode, otherwise hard to explain. Baxter Dawes, Clara's husband, has degenerated into a drunken bully. He wants his revenge on Paul, waylays him and beats him up. Paul is severely hurt and becomes ill as a result. Pneumonia follows, and while his mother nurses him, both Clara and Miriam are rejected. Paul has had his pleasure, allowed himself to be punished for it, and now returns safely to his mother's care. But it is too late. Immediately afterwards his mother's illness declares itself; it is a fatal cancer. Paul is prostrated with grief. While visiting his mother in hospital, he learns that Dawes is there, too, and he goes to visit him. Between typhoid and drink, Dawes is brought pretty low, and the two meet on the ground of their common misery. A sort of friendship develops between them, and a little later we have the curious situation of Paul's suggesting to Clara that she has used her husband badly. Clara is even inclined to agree with him. Paul is so broken by his mother's illness that he becomes indifferent to Clara, and she begins to tire of him. He tells Dawes that she has finished with him. During the last days of his mother's illness he sees little of Clara and Miriam, and they mean nothing to him when he does; but his rôle as Dawes' friend and protector continues to develop. He visits him in a convalescent home, tries to cheer him up and give him the courage to start in life again. Paul says that he feels in a worse mess than Dawes—"in a tangled sort of hole, rather dark and dreary, and no road anywhere". Paul indeed is withering away. Clara joins them, and she finds Paul paltry and insignificant, finds that her husband in his defeat has more manly dignity—even a certain nobility. Paul is convinced that he is finished, and in a final act of self-negation he slips away and leaves the two together. And it does not take Clara long to recognise her real mate.

"Take me back!" she whispered, ecstatic. "Take me back, take me back!" And she put her fingers through his fine, thin dark hair, as if she were only semi-conscious. He tightened his grasp on her.

(XIV.)

So Paul is cleared of his only real sexual relation, and the bond with the dead mother is unimpaired.

A last effort with Miriam fails. They meet again, with all the old tension. She suggests marriage, and in a scene of tortured, enigmatic confusion he rejects it. The situation hardly explains itself—or rather, two inconsistent explanations are offered. Paul says: "You love me so much, you want to put me in your pocket. And I should die there, smothered." But we are also told that he longs for the comfort and understanding she could give him, and wants her to take possession of him, as it were by force; she will not take that initiative, and as long as the decision rests with him he cannot make it. Again we are placed at the centre of the entanglement, with all the blindness and lack of comprehension that this implies. It is hard to resist the conviction that there is some impurity of motive here. It is as though Lawrence himself is forcing the blame on Miriam for refusing to live Paul's life for him. Paul has been growing weaker and less positive since his first rejection of Miriam. This is the climax of his nullity, and invites the final condemnation of his neurotic refusal of responsibility for his own existence.

Lawrence studiously avoids all attempts at such a final judgment. We are familiar, in the more developed kinds of novel, with the spectator character who stands apart from the action and serves as a vehicle for the novelist's point of view. There is no such character in *Sons and Lovers*. No one is right. No one can claim a superior insight to the others. All the main characters—Paul, Miriam, Mrs. Morel, Clara Dawes—make extremely penetrating remarks on each other. All are blind to much that is going on around them. Even Lawrence the author, whom we must distinguish from his own portrait of himself in Paul, is not in this position. Lawrence's exposition of the novel closes with these words: "He is left in the end naked of everything, with the drift towards death." But never trust the author, trust the tale, as Dr. Leavis puts it. What does the tale actually tell us? It has not often been observed (Anthony West, I believe, is alone in calling attention to it) that at the ghastly climax of his mother's illness Paul, with the connivance of his sister, kills her with an overdose of sleeping tablets to spare her further agony. Realistically considered, it is simply an act of despairing mercy. Symbolically, it has another significance. Here, where the regression of Paul's character has reached its farthest point, there is still something within him which is capable of decisive action—capable even of killing the mother to whom he is bound, to liberate both of them and to end her agony and his. And this prepares us for the actual end of the novel, which is not as Lawrence describes it, but as follows:

> "Mother!" he whimpered—"mother!"
> She was the only thing that held him up, himself, amid all this. And she was gone, intermingled herself. He wanted her to touch him, have him alongside with her.
> But no, he would not give in. Turning sharply, he walked towards the city's gold phosphorescence. His fists were shut, his mouth set fast. He would not take that direction, to the darkness, to follow her. He walked towards the faintly humming, glowing town, quickly.

In fact, he refuses to give in and the final motion is towards life. Paul, whose vacillations and refusals have worn him away till he has reached something like nonentity, proves in the end capable of a regenerating spark. At whatever cost to himself and others he has kept his frail independence alive. And then he puts the whole imbroglio behind him as Lawrence was putting it behind him by writing the book.

"The novels and stories come unwatched out of one's pen." And Lawrence the man is not clearly aware of what has come from the pen of Lawrence the writer. Lawrence the writer, at any rate at this stage, fulfils the conditions demanded by Keats: he is "capable of being in uncertainties, mysteries, doubts, without any irritable reaching after fact and reason". The part of the book which is most contrived, most written to a thesis, is the love-affair with Clara Dawes. It represents, or is supposed to represent, Paul's attempt at a simple physical relationship as a relief from the obscure psychic complexities of the love between himself and Miriam. Yet it is far less powerful, far less successful, in expressing the essential nature of love than the unfulfilled and tormented passages with Miriam.

Lawrence, in fact, is at his strongest when he is exploring a state of affairs which is obscure, which he has not exhausted in life. The writing is a catharsis. When a situation has been lived through and completed, his best and most characteristic powers are not called out. Lawrence's limited experience of mere physiological satisfaction without any stronger bond seems to have been completed before 1912; it never seems to have interested him much in life, and it provides no lasting satisfaction and no solution to the conflict in the novel. Indeed, the emptiness of the affair with Clara Dawes makes it an inadequate counterpoise to the relation with Miriam.

Again, like *The White Peacock*, a novel about frustration and failure and contradictions that are never reconciled. But in *The White Peacock* the human failures are almost absorbed in the quivering joy of earth, the vibration of the non-human world that surrounds them. In *Sons and Lovers* the human conflicts have become more intense and more pressing, and the necessity for following them to a conclusion more absolute. The idyllic passages are not a diversion from the plot; they occur only in the Miriam episodes, and they are strictly subordinated to Miriam herself. They are the necessary setting for her character, and the shared love of Paul and Miriam for flowers, birds'-eggs and trees is only a pathetic extension of their feeling for each other. The intense realisation of personal forces burns away all the minor social falsities that impairs the reality of *The White Peacock*; and it also burns away most of the lyrical tenderness that makes that novel a springtime story in spite of the frustrations of the plot. So that *Sons and Lovers* becomes incidentally a full, intimate, sympathetic, but also a harsh and unrelieved presentation of working-class life—the oppressively close-knit family system, the narrow play for the individual sensibilities; the strength of individual development when it manages to survive among the massive forces that press upon it. Lawrence never captures this continuous sense of actuality in a novel again, though he does in some of the shorter tales. For this reason *Sons and Lovers* remains his masterpiece to those who abide by the central tradition of the novel. Possibly they are right, but those who hold this view are still not penetrating to what is essential in Lawrence. The naturalistic success of *Sons and Lovers* is only incidental; the growing point of the book is the psychological adventurousness, the resolute beginning of an exploration into the tangled

relations between men and women. In his next two novels this is to
be Lawrence's only theme.

As soon as Lawrence finished *Sons and Lovers* in 1912, he began
working on another novel which was at first called *The Sisters*. As
usual, there was much re-writing and rearrangement. The material
was too copious for one book, and it very soon split into two. Of these
the first, after a period in which it was called *The Wedding Ring*,
ultimately became *The Rainbow*, and the second became *Women in
Love*. The connection between them is less close than their common
origin would suggest; but they do represent a continuous development, and an important one—the beginning, in fact, of Lawrence's
adult philosophy and of his mature way of writing. To some of his
critics this is a decline from the solidity and the assured presentation
of *Sons and Lovers*; but to hold this view involves dismissing what
is most characteristic in Lawrence's work, and giving up any real
inquiry into the quality of his creative imagination. *The Rainbow*
marks the transition from books which others might have written to
books which no one but Lawrence could write.

The advent of Frieda had not only transformed Lawrence's outward circumstances, it had effected an interior transformation, too.
But the last re-writing of *Sons and Lovers*, though done so strongly
under Frieda's influence, does not reveal the transformation very
clearly. The mould of the work was already fixed, its essence determined long ago, and it remains for the most part a book written from
within the experience it describes. *The Rainbow* looks back on the
old Midland scene, but from other countries and other ways of life.
Emotionally, as well as socially and geographically, Lawrence begins
to stand in a different relation to his material. In the earlier books
Lawrence had been groping, not so much for the solution as for the
formulation of a problem—that of the growth of love and its obstacles
and frustrations. The early psycho-analytical principle that to understand the genesis of a problem is to make it disappear may have been
over-optimistic, but it seems to have applied to Lawrence's case well
enough. There is no more need now for the continual re-living of his
own experience. *The Rainbow* is perhaps the least autobiographical

of Lawrence's major novels. It is still pre-eminently a novel of exploration; but the need is no longer to come to terms with a pressing personal imbroglio: it is rather to clarify and develop a philosophy of life which is present only in embryo. And the degree of imaginative intensity (which does not necessarily imply artistic success) is greater in that Lawrence does this not by placing himself in the centre of the picture—there is no one in *The Rainbow* who directly represents Lawrence—but by means of situations dramatically conceived. It is notable that the principal characters are women, and the two novels which sprang from *The Sisters* represents a shift of Lawrence's attention to the feminine point of view.

Sons and Lovers ends with a defeat and the hint of a new beginning. Paul is "left naked of everything", but he walks off in the direction of the humming town. And with that gesture he walks out of his author's life. Lawrence is no longer the youth of the early novels. The letters from Germany and Italy in the early days of his marriage are full of the excitement of escape—and it is not only escape from an environment, but escape from an old self. The moral and intellectual struggles of his youth had led to an impasse; an act done on impulse, the elopement with Frieda—by normal standards both unreasonable and wrong—had brought him happiness and an access of new life. A natural result is the attempt to develop a non-moral and anti-intellectualist philosophy. Early in 1913 Lawrence wrote to Ernest Collings: "My great religion is a belief in the blood, the flesh, as being wiser than the intellect. We can go wrong in our minds. But what our blood feels, believes and says is always true. . . . All I want is to answer to my blood, direct, without fribbling intervention of mind or moral or what not."[35] Which means of course that he had just discovered how to do so. And this is all it means. We can go wrong in our minds because our minds can formulate propositions which may be false. What the blood says is always true—but the blood does not formulate any propositions at all; like the poet in Sidney's *Apology* it "nothing affirmeth and therefore never lieth". The alleged utterances of the blood are merely physico-psychological facts, and of course leave the moral problem exactly where it was. They are merely data to be taken into account; and the age-old question of how much authority is to be given to them still remains. But a man who has just discovered, rather belatedly, the existence of his body, and that it is possible to obey the voice of the blood directly, is likely enough to forget this. What Lawrence now proceeds to do is to evolve both a faith and a code of behaviour on the basis of his new-found experience.

Early in 1913 Lawrence wrote a foreword to *Sons and Lovers*.[36] It was sent to Garnett, but never published with the book; and indeed it is not a foreword to *Sons and Lovers* at all, hardly even an epilogue. Though it is related to the theme of *Sons and Lovers* in the last paragraph, the bulk of the text (it extends to seven pages) is a doctrine which could not be deduced from the earlier books: it springs from a later experience, and is far more closely connected with the complex of feelings that was going to make up *The Sisters*. It is the first formal exposition of the Lawrence ethos, and a remarkably compact one; and it is the best commentary on the novels of this period.

Characteristically it is couched in Biblical language. Lawrence's search for a philosophy of life was always conducted with religious intensity. Its expression was more often in gnomic and categorical terms than in the language of discursive reasoning. And there is another reason for the use of the language of Scripture besides its numinous and authoritative quality. Lawrence's religion always starts as a kind of Christian heresy. Unlike Yeats, who seems never to have had any particular orientation to Christianity, Lawrence is haunted by it; he has always to confute it or to get it out of the way first.

The foreword begins: "John the beloved disciple, says 'The Word was made Flesh'. But why should he turn things round? . . . 'The Flesh was made Word'." And it goes on to a thoroughgoing assertion of the primacy of the Flesh, temporally, logically and ontologically. The Word is only the creation of the Flesh, its product, a work of art. To make the Word primary is to reverse the proper order of things; and it occurred "because the Son, struggling to utter the word, took for his God the accomplishment of his work, the Uttered Word". Christ did so, worshipped his own uttered word as the principle of his being; and all men have done so since, worshipping their own works as the Word, in the guise of the Truth, the Law, the Idea. But none of these things is the principle of man's being: the principle of his being is the Flesh. We are not the Flesh itself: the Flesh is God the

Father and transcends us. We are only the Flesh made Word—as
Adam was, as Christ was—the eternal principle, the Flesh, made
into a mouthpiece through which the word may be uttered.

The ultimate Godhead, then, is physical, unselfconscious, inarticulate. Man is created that God's being may be made explicit
in the uttered word. The Word is not the inner principle of anything.
It is only an image that must pass or be worn out. To worship it is
idolatry, to worship the icon instead of the Godhead.

When we say 'I' we mean 'the Word that I am': when we love
our neighbour we love the Word our neighbour. That is, when we
are aware of ourselves or of others, all we are aware of is the ego,
the conscious, the expressed personality. We can only love this
personal self. Our Flesh cannot *love* the Flesh of another: for the
Flesh is the portion of the Godhead in each of us, and is absolute, and
cannot be subordinated to or serve any other portion of itself. The
relation of Flesh to Flesh is something beyond love. Its claims are
above those of charity or fellow-feeling. Love or charity in the
Christian sense is not an ultimate, it is only an affair of the Word,
and does not touch the ultimate, the Flesh.

How do we know the Flesh, the Godhead, if it is ultimate and
inexpressible, and knowledge is only an affair of the Word? We know
the Flesh in woman. This is our approach to the Godhead. The right
way of life is for the man to find his fulfilment, his approach to the
Godhead, in woman; and nourished and strengthened by this to go
out and produce his work, the Word—which is God the Flesh realising
himself in a moment of forgetfulness. We cannot choose or reject
what woman we will, the Flesh must choose for us. Any attempt to
frustrate this means impoverishment and death. So does any refusal
of consummation or any submission of it to the Law. The woman
whose man does not find fulfilment in her is to leave him. For in the
flesh of woman does God exact himself. Man is the go-between from
woman to production, to Art and Work. Woman is the principle of
continuance, and the door by which Man re-enters into the Flesh, the
Godhead, and finds new strength.

If a man chooses his mother to be his woman, he is her lover only
in part and wastes away in the flesh; nor will he if he marries ever be
the true lover of his wife, and she in turn will hope for sons to be her
lovers.

The relevance of this to Lawrence's own situation is evident enough. Only the statement at the end refers directly to the theme of *Sons and Lovers*. The rest of the discourse is partly descriptive and partly prescriptive, and we shall have to return to it, or to the ideas contained in it, later and in another context. At the moment it is enough to observe that out of his private discovery of fulfilment in marriage, Lawrence has done nothing less than manufacture a new religion—a religion of the Flesh, with a devotion and a discipline of its own. Its implications are possibly different from what he intended —but it would be out of place to discuss it further until we have looked at the novels and stories in which its operation is displayed. Of these *The Rainbow* is the first.

The Rainbow is in the first place a novel about marriage, as its original title suggests. It is also a family chronicle—showing the continuity from one generation to another, and the same eternal situations to be faced with individual variations, by a succession of young people watched over by their elders who have themselves passed through to a later stage of the process. It is not a great novel of character, for Lawrence is more interested in the phases than in the people who enact them. The great novels of character are stories about some kind of personal fulfilment, private or social happiness or disaster. There is another less common kind of novel (less common because the task has usually been undertaken by poetry) which is conceived rather with relation to the great, unseen, impersonal forces, however they may be imagined. *The Rainbow* is a novel of this kind, and if we look at Lawrence's imaginative life as a continuous development, *The White Peacock* and *Sons and Lovers* are only propædeutics to this undertaking. Later, especially in *The Plumed Serpent*, this religious quest almost overpowers the element of representation, of mimesis, on which the novel ultimately depends. This is not so in *The Rainbow*, and a great deal of the book is presented with a rich naturalism as complete and as decisive as anything in *Sons and Lovers*. But something else is always struggling to break through and to find a new form of expression; and just as in *Sons and Lovers* the movement is from the known and the comprehensible to the unknown and the obscure, so in *The Rainbow*. Only here the incomprehensible is represented not by an obscure personal problem but by the search which is conducted by all the principal characters—most clearly and most consciously by Ursula—for that which is symbolised by the rainbow itself—the harmony of seen and unseen, "the world built up in a living fabric of Truth, fitting to the over-arching heaven".

We think first of the rainbow symbol because it appears in the title; but in fact the symbol of the Church is just as important. It comes up in the opening paragraph:

> The Brangwens had lived for generations on the Marsh Farm, in the meadows where the Erewash twisted sluggishly through alder trees, separating Derbyshire from Nottinghamshire. Two miles away, a church-tower stood on a hill, the houses of the little country town climbing assiduously up to it. Whenever one of the Brangwens in the fields lifted his head from his work, he saw the church-tower at Ilkeston in the empty sky. So that as he turned again to the horizontal land, he was aware of something standing above him and beyond him in the distance.
>
> (I.)

Will Brangwen's passion for the church and church architecture is perpetually emphasised, and is almost the only constant element in his character; the crisis in his relations with his wife (Chapter VII) occurs in Lincoln Cathedral, and is directly concerned with their different attitudes towards the building. Much of Ursula's growing up is presented by describing her changing attitudes towards the pieties of her childhood. Ursula and her lover Skrebensky have one of their earliest meetings in a church, and Ursula defiantly remarks that she thinks it right to make love in a cathedral. So that the almost ritualistic sense of something standing above and beyond human life is always kept before our minds. Immediately after the opening paragraph quoted above, however, it gives way to something else— to the flood of teeming physical life in which the Brangwen men really lived.

> They felt the rush of the sap in spring, they knew the wave which cannot halt, but every year throws forward the seed to begetting, and, falling back, leaves the young-born on the earth. They knew the intercourse between heaven and earth, sunshine drawn into the breast and bowels, the rain sucked up in the day-time, nakedness that comes under the wind in autumn, showing the birds' nests no longer worth hiding. Their life and interrelations were such; feeling the pulse and body of the soil, that opened to their furrow for the grain, and became smooth and supple after their ploughing, and clung to their feet with a weight

that pulled like desire, lying hard and unresponsive when the crops were to be shorn away. The young corn waved and was silken, and the lustre slid along the limbs of the men who saw it. They took the udder of the cows, the cows yielded milk and pulse against the hands of the men, the pulse of the blood of the teats of the cows beat into the pulse of the hands of the men. They mounted their horses, and held life between the grip of their knees, they harnessed their horses at the wagon, and, with hand on the bridle-rings, draw the heaving of the horses after their will.

(I.)

Almost a return to the mood and manner of *The White Peacock*, but with the idyllic and pictorial element in the background and a far deeper sense of physical and organic life.

The Brangwen women are not satisfied with this—they aspire to the world of activity and organisation:

But the woman wanted another form of life than this, something that was not blood-intimacy. Her house faced out from the farm-buildings and fields, looked out to the road and the village with church and Hall and the world beyond. She stood to see the far-off world of cities and governments and the active scope of man, the magic land to her, where secrets were made known and desires fulfilled. She faced outwards to where men moved dominant and creative, having turned their back on the pulsing heat of creation, and with this behind them, were set out to discover what was beyond, to enlarge their own scope and range and freedom; whereas the Brangwen men faced inwards to the teeming life of creation, which poured unresolved into their veins.

(I.)

Then, as so often and so disconcertingly in Lawrence from this time on, the theme apparently announced here disappears and we are concerned with Tom Brangwen's marriage to a Polish lady, It is beautifully and solidly done. The countryside, the social and individual backgrounds are firmly and truly established; and the fascination and difficulty of the alliance between the slow inarticulate farmer and the infinitely foreign, far more complicated Lydia Lensky are in themselves beautifully related to their background. Tom Brangwen is a more successful George Saxton; and the contrast between his rustic solidity and the different nature of "fine-textured, well-mannered people" is made much of. But Lawrence's experience has widened since *The White Peacock*, and his sense of refinement and complexity is a less pallid and suburban affair. In fact, this part of the book is most remarkable as a piece of closely studied, superbly textured social painting. The attempt to represent sexual love directly, obviously important to Lawrence, is no more successful than it generally is—that is, not successful at all. We may pause to note in Tom Brangwen the first appearance of a centre of consciousness in the bowels (Ch. I); and there are a number of other tortured and tortuous efforts at making the man-woman relationship explicit; but in fact the work of realising the particular quality of this marriage is done almost entirely by more orthodox methods of presentation. And perhaps the best part of it is the growth of a new bond between Tom Brangwen and his stepchild Anna. All this is as good as George Eliot and not so very different, except that a far livelier sense of the physical sympathies is conveyed—not so much in passages which make a direct attempt at presenting them, but by the nature and quality of the writing throughout. At the end of the third chapter a family has been created. The solid but uncompleted Tom Brangwen; the solitary foreigner Lydia and the vivid waif Anna have become a triple unity.

> Anna's soul was put at peace between them. She looked from one to the other and she saw them established to her safety, and she was free. . . . She was no longer called on to uphold with her childish might the broken end of the arch. Her father and her mother now met to the span of the heavens, and she, the child, was free to play in the space beneath, between.
>
> (III.)

As Anna grows up the figures of Tom and Lydia Brangwen grow fainter, and for a time she grows fainter, too. The courtship of Anna by her cousin Will and the preparations for their wedding are rather weak and conventional by comparison with that of their elders; though there is a return of the old warmth and authority in Brangwen's jealousy and distress when Anna prepares to leave him, and in the Brueghel-like wedding scene Tom Brangwen's drunken speech is a half-comic sketch of Lawrence's philosophy of marriage:

> "*If* we've got to be Angels," went on Tom Brangwen, haranguing the company at large, "and if there is no such thing as a

man nor a woman amongst them, then it seems to me as a married couple makes one Angel."

"It's the brandy," said Alfred Brangwen wearily.

"For," said Tom Brangwen, and the company was listening to the conundrum, "an Angel can't be *less* than a human being. And if it was only the soul of a man *minus* the man, then it would be less than a human being."

"Decidedly," said Alfred.

And a laugh went round the table. But Tom Brangwen was inspired.

"An Angel's got to be more than a human being," he continued. "So I say, an Angel is the soul of man and woman in one: they rise united at the Judgment Day, as one Angel——"

"Praising the Lord," said Frank.

"Praising the Lord," repeated Tom.

(V.)

But Lawrence cannot rest long in this gross and tender earthiness. In the succeeding chapter, "Anna Victrix", he returns to his central theme, the attempt to present directly the shifting facets of the relationship between a man and a woman in marriage. For Will Brangwen the honeymoon is the entry into another world, silent and remote from everyday concerns.

So suddenly, everything that had been before was shed away and gone. One day, he was a bachelor, living with the world. The next day, he was with her, as remote from the world as if the two of them were buried like a seed in darkness. Suddenly, like a chestnut falling out of a burr, he was shed naked and glistening on to a soft, fecund earth, leaving behind him the hard rind of worldly knowledge and experience. He heard it in the huckster's cries, the noise of carts, the calling of children. And it was all like the hard, shed rind, discarded. Inside, in the softness and stillness of the room, was the naked kernel, that palpitated in silent activity, absorbed in reality.

Inside the room was a great steadiness, a core of living eternity. Only far outside, at the rim, went on the noise and the destruction. Here at the centre the great wheel was motionless, centred upon itself. Here was a poised, unflawed stillness that was beyond time, because it remained the same, inexhaustible, unchanging, unexhausted.

As they lay close together, complete and beyond the touch of time or change, it was as if they were at the very centre of all the slow wheeling of space and the rapid agitation of life, deep, deep inside them all, at the centre where there is utter radiance,

and eternal being, and the silence absorbed in praise: the steady
core of all movements, the unawakened sleep of all wakefulness.
They found themselves there, and they lay still, in each other's
arms; for their moment they were at the heart of eternity, whilst
time roared far off, for ever far off, towards the rim.

(VI.)

This entranced unity is succeeded by a reassertion of separateness.
Each begins to resent the other and the dependence on the other, and
there are two black, ghastly days of estrangement—then again a
blind rush of tenderness. No one has excelled Lawrence in presenting
these irrational and pointless fluxes and revulsions of feeling. At the
moments of highest tension the language is often strained and frantic:

And at last she began to draw near to him, she nestled to him.
His limbs, his body, took fire and beat up in flames. She clung to
him, she cleaved to his body. The flames swept him, he held her
in sinews of fire. If she would kiss him! He bent his mouth down.
And her mouth, soft and moist, received him. He felt his veins
would burst with anguish of thankfulness, his heart was mad
with gratefulness, he could pour himself out upon her for ever.

(VI.)

Anyone who wants to make the worst of Lawrence has plenty of
material in passages like these. In fact, they do not matter much,
for the real work has been done by quite other means—scraps of
dialogue, the close imaginative following of changing trains of feeling,
a fiery fidelity to the actual which transcends all conventional views
of what men, women and marriage are like. As for physical passion,
Lawrence's equivalents for it are often factitious, tortured and
inflated; of course, no one should try to present it as he does, and
traditional literary good sense has always known it. But no one has
equalled him, no one has ever got so near the bone in presenting the
experience of two people of different sexes living together in one
house.

Gradually a conception of the differing natures of Anna and Will
begins to emerge, and they are defined by reference to a common
symbol, the Church. Lydia's ultimate allegiance had been defined in
the same way (Chapter III). Brought up as a Catholic, she had turned
to the Church of England for protection—the outward form was good
enough for her. "Yet she had some fundamental religion. It was as

if she worshipped God as a mystery, never seeking in the least to define what he was." So she lived perpetually in the presence of this ultimate mystery, and her husband shared it with her. But with the young people, with Will and Anna, it is different. Will, too, feels the mystery and lives in it, but for him it is centred in the visible fabric and symbolism of the Church. He never cares to translate this into conceptual terms, and it makes his personal conscious being unimportant to him. Anna feels an uncomprehending resentment of all this. Her religion is a religion of the ego. "The thought of her soul was intimately mixed up with the thought of her own self. Indeed, her soul and her own self were one and the same in her." And she is filled with a mad impulse to insult the symbols he adores. One is shocked by the callousness and cruelty of this, and by his retaliations; yet even in protesting one is driven to realise how many threads in the fabric of life are of this kind; how much that we slur over as thoughtlessness or fortuitous ill-temper is really a purposeful malignancy. '*Odi et amo*' we all know as a concomitant of enslaving *amour-passion*: Lawrence has most uncomfortably brought out the element of hate that is inextricably entwined with a normal love. There is something shocking in the nakedness and intensity with which he presents it. But he is not insulting love or trying to degrade his characters. Neither love nor his characters are his primary interest. He is trying to show how two people bound together in the Flesh, opposed in the Word, contrive to live together and ultimately to find in it some sort of salvation.

The happiness of Anna in her pregnancy affords another point of rest, her drowsy, enchanted, self-sufficient contentment. Yet this very self-sufficiency generates fresh conflicts; for Will is excluded by it, and his bitter jealousy and anger is poisonous. This again passes as her time draws near, and when the child is born Anna has a sense of complete fulfilment and victory. Soon she is with child again, and lapses again into a vague content. Her personal assertions and ambitions disappear. If she cannot travel herself to the rainbow, her doors opened under its arch:

> She was a door and a threshold, she herself. Through her another soul was coming, to stand upon her as upon the threshold, looking out, shading its eyes for the direction to take.

(VI.)

But no satisfaction is ever complete. For all her satisfied maternity Anna begins to want "her own old sharp self" back again, detached, separate. And this her husband never does want. The enveloping Brangwen intimacy has taken in him a devotional form—-the longing to be absorbed into the great bosom of the Church, something outside and beyond life. In the chapter called "The Cathedral", the Church and the rainbow image are brought together, and the opposed nature of Will's and Anna's religious experiences are made clear:

> Away from time, always outside of time! Between east and west, between dawn and sunset, the church lay like a seed in silence, dark before germination, silenced after death. Containing birth and death, potential with all the noise and transition of life, the cathedral remained hushed, a great, involved seed, whereof the flower would be radiant life inconceivable, but whose beginning and whose end were the circle of silence. Spanned round with the rainbow, the jewelled gloom folded music upon silence, light upon darkness, fecundity upon death, as a seed folds leaf upon leaf and silence upon the root and the flower, hushing up the secret of all between its parts, the death out of which it fell, the life into which it has dropped, the immortality it involves, and the death it will embrace again.
>
> Here in the church, "before" and "after" were folded together, all was contained in oneness. Brangwen came to his consummation.
>
> (VII.)

And Anna hates it. She deliberately destroys his devout absorption by brightly comparing the sculpture with everyday reality, she deliberately brings the cathedral down to earth. And Will is forced to see that his absolute was not an absolute, that included in his ecstasy was much mere desire for a safe absorption, much mere reverence for ancient sanctities. "He listened to the thrushes in the gardens, and heard a note which the Cathedrals did not include, something free and careless and joyous. . . . There was life outside the Church. There was much that the Church did not include. He thought of God, and the whole blue rotunda of the day. . . . Still he loved the Church. As a symbol he loved it. He tended it for what it tried to represent, rather than for that which it did represent." And again there is peace in the house. They are deeply divided in belief and ultimate allegiance: but she loves him because he is the father of her children; he loves to serve the little household; and both are sustained by a mutual physical passion. So a second generation has made its adventures, and through desire, conflict, pain and joy reached a sort of fulfilment and completeness that is beyond any of these things. As the saints found rest in spiritual communion with their God and through their God with each other, so in Lawrence's curious analogical mysticism his unsaintly characters, however torn and divided in the Word, find rest in their absolute, the Flesh, and through the Flesh in each other.

Again the focus shifts: the elders grow faint and the children come into the foreground. The rest of the book, more than half of it, is occupied with Anna's first-born daughter Ursula. She is a manifest continuation of the Brangwen line, but more differentiated, more individual, more demanding. From her wayward, independent child-hood it is evident that her satisfactions will not be easy; that she will not find her fulfilment as naturally and as near at home as her elders. Anyway, the world around her is changing. She is to grow up into circumstances very different from the pastoral simplicities of Marsh Farm. Her childhood and the bond between the father and the child are exquisitely done; here, as in other places, Lawrence shows a singular ability to portray the power of a relation between persons, its enduring vitality, even though it breaks down at times into crass-ness, incomprehension or cruelty. His peculiar view of the polarity between human beings enables him to give their bonds a toughness, an elasticity and a survival value that they notoriously have in life but rarely have to test in fiction.

As Ursula grows up, the old background of traditional pieties is symbolised by the succession of Sundays and the children's feelings about them, the ancient cycle of the Christian year:

The cycle of creation still wheeled in the Church year. After Christmas, the ecstasy slowly sank and changed. Sunday followed Sunday, trailing a fine movement, a finely developed transforma-tion over the heart of the family. The heart that was big with joy, that had seen the star and had followed to the inner walls of the Nativity, that there had swooned in the great light, must now feel the light slowly withdrawing, a shadow falling, darkening. The chill crept in, silence came over the earth, and then all was darkness. The veil of the temple was rent, each heart gave up the ghost, and sank dead.

They moved quietly, a little wanness on the lips of the children,

at Good Friday, feeling the shadow upon their hearts. Then, pale
with a deathly scent, came the lilies of resurrection, that shone
coldly till the Comforter was given.

(X.)

And Ursula's individual development is defined by showing the
development of her private religious sense against this background.
She is enthralled by the idea of salvation, but she resents its means;
she revolts against the humanity of Christ just as she revolts against
her mother's absorption in babies and muddled domesticity. For her
Jesus is of another world, and she is always for the ultimate, the
remote. She is thrilled by the text "The Sons of God saw the daughters
of men that they were fair; and they took to them wives of all which
they chose". But who were the Sons of God? Adam, the only man
directly created by God, or Jesus the only-begotten son? Perhaps
God had other offspring besides Adam and Jesus—and perhaps these
other sons had known no expulsion and no fall. It is in the form of one
of these that Ursula feels that salvation must come to her. As a
man finds his salvation in a woman, so a woman must find it in a man.
Her salvation must be brought by a man, but a man who appears to
her as one of the authentic sons of God. Ursula is very willing to use
the language of Scripture, but the content of the words is transformed. Nor can her unchristened heart accept the gospel ethics.

Nor could one turn the other cheek. Theresa slapped Ursula
on the face. Ursula, in a mood of Christianity humility, silently
presented the other side of her face. Which Theresa, in exasperation at the challenge, also hit. Whereupon Ursula, with boiling
heart, went meekly away.
But anger, and deep, writhing shame tortured her, so she was
not easy till she had again quarrelled with Theresa and had
almost shaken her sister's head off.
"That'll teach you," she said, grimly.
And she went away, unchristian but clean.

(XI.)

Yet she continues to crave for the Sunday world, for the peace that
is promised by the symbols of her childhood.

The passion rose in her for Christ, for the gathering under the
wings of security and warmth. But how did it apply to the weekday
world? What could it mean, but that Christ should clasp her to
his breast, as a mother clasps her child?

67

Yet she *must* have it in weekday terms—she must. For all
her life was a weekday life, now this was the whole. So he must
gather her body to his breast, that was strong with a broad bone,
and which sounded with the beating of the heart, and which was
warm with the life of which she partook, the life of the running
blood.

(XI.)

Much of Ursula's subsequent experience is Lawrence's own,
imaginatively transferred to a young woman—the school-teaching
episode, for example. It is brilliantly done, and helps to keep this
increasingly difficult part of the book firmly rooted in actuality. But
we must pass it by, as we have passed by earlier episodes, to follow
the main thematic line. This continues in Ursula's love for Skrebensky,
a young Pole, connected with the Lenskys of the earlier part of the
book, and, like them, representing a more refined and socially complex
world than that of the Brangwens. So that in this meeting the wheel
has come full circle: Ursula, the intelligent, articulate scion of the
rustic Brangwen world, newly arrived at education and self-consciousness, meets a representative of the old aristocratic Europe, with
long-rooted complications of habit and breeding that the Brangwens
have never known. But the Brangwen women have always aspired
to it, as we were told in the first chapter. At first, as a young girl
Ursula is fascinated by Skrebensky's air of nonchalance and his
physical distinction. Then other things intervene, he goes away, and
she leaves home to find her place in the world. Then he comes back,
and we return to the central motif of Ursula's story. It cannot be said
that it is altogether clear. Many threads, only a few of which are
distinctly discernible in the earlier part of the book, are here at last
woven together; and it is possible that Lawrence, in his efforts to
explain the inexplicable has (for the first time, as it seems to me, in
this book) made some false combinations. Let us try to follow the
pattern as best we may.

In the first place we are made to understand that Ursula will
need a more individual, less generally accessible, fulfilment than her
forebears. Her grandmother Lydia and her mother Anna were not
lacking in personal distinction and the power of choice. Yet the whole
condition of their world draws them to settle, to root themselves, in
their immediate physical environment. Lydia transfers easily from
the Roman to the Anglican Church; Anna accepts her new father and

becomes a Brangwen; they were plants ready to take root, and it was a soil in which rooting was easy. Ursula is not a plant at all, and she is not rooted anywhere. She has the essentially modern attribute of *disponibilité*, and it is one of Lawrence's distinctions that without any hackneyed palaver about 'the new woman', he successfully conveys this change of period. Secondly, we are to realise a change in the class situation. In early days it is the gentry, the Skrebenskys and their English counterparts, who have freedom and subtlety. Now it gradually becomes plain that Skrebensky has only the appearance of those qualities—the reality of them has passed to Ursula, the newly emancipated daughter of the working class.

For all his apparent ease and nonchalance Skrebensky, the young Sapper officer, is enclosed within the bounds of his class and his profession, and cannot look outside them; while Ursula, who has by now entirely convinced us that she is a bold and eager spirit—neither good nor comfortable, but a creature of inescapable distinction—Ursula cannot be content with him. We may be repelled (though Lawrence does not seem to have been) by the callous cruelty with which she takes what he has to give and then casts him off; but we never doubt that her decision is inevitable and right.

However, there are puzzling features in the case. Lawrence makes a more than usually frenzied attempt to describe the sexual relations between Ursula and Skrebensky; and, as in other places, there is stylistic failure. But in the other places this has been a local failure, and not very important (the novel can stand a good many local failures) because the real work has been done by other means. But here it is not. In describing the physical relations of these two, Lawrence is trying to convey something further, something of deep importance to him, as is plain from the agonised contortions of his style. But it never comes through. The attraction and the failure between Ursula and Skrebensky *ought* to be a mystery, but in fact it becomes a muddle. It would appear that Lawrence is trying to make some equation between the limitations of Skrebensky's mind and his physical failure as a lover. Such an equivalence would be a convenient article for the new creed; but there is of course no reason to suppose that it is valid, nor does Lawrence make it real to us. Very early in the acquaintance Ursula had discovered her contempt for Skrebensky's army-officer outlook:

"I belong to the nation and must do my duty by the nation."
"But when it didn't need your services in particular—when there *is* no fighting? What would you do then?"
He was irritated.
"I would do what everybody else does."
"What?"
"Nothing. I would be in readiness for when I was needed."
The answer came in exasperation.
"It seems to me," she answered, "as if you weren't anybody—as if there weren't anybody there, where you are. Are you anybody, really? You seem like nothing to me."

(XI.)

It is one of the many scenes of successful female bullying in Lawrence; a man of character would be likely to leave Ursula to herself after that. But Skrebensky does not, and there are recurrences of the same feeling on Ursula's part. They become lovers (I am not quite sure when; the style in which sexual encounters are described in this book is so fuliginous that it is impossible to tell just what is going on), and it appears that they enjoy the fullest and completest sexual satisfaction. Ursula's doubts about the conventional Anglo-Indian life to which Skrebensky is about to take her continue to grow. Yet the actual occasion of their parting seems due to a failure in the physical relation. They have a violent and passionate encounter on sand-hills in the moonlight, from which Ursula emerges bitterly dissatisfied, and the next morning they know that all is over between them.

"Well, what have I done?" he asked, in a rather querulous voice.
"I don't know," she said, in the same dull, feelingless voice. "It is finished. It has been a failure."
He was silent. The words still burned his bowels.
"Is it my fault?" he said, looking up at length, challenging the last stroke.
"You couldn't——" she began. But she broke down.
He turned away, afraid to hear more. She began to gather her bag, her handkerchief, her umbrella. She must be gone now. He was waiting for her to be gone.

(XV.)

This seems unequivocal enough, yet it also seems inconsistent with what has gone before. That she loved him physically but found him inadequate spiritually and socially is intelligible enough; that she

found him inadequate in both respects makes their love wholly un-
intelligible, merely makes one wonder what the basis of the affair can
ever have been.

But I think the reason for Lawrence's failure here is clear. He has
evolved a faith in which sexual fulfilment is the ultimate. In Will and
Anna he has shown sexual fulfilment victorious over other temperamental incompatibilities. And surely this duality, and the possibility
of this precarious harmony, is real. Now he has changed his mind and
wants to go further. He wants to maintain that sexual compatibility,
and compatibility of mind and spirit are indissolubly linked. But if
this were so life would surely be a very different business from anything we know; and among the results would be that love affairs would
either be perfect or non-existent. The tragedy (and also the opportunity) of human love is that it is so rarely complete, and that harmony on one plane must, by the exertion of will and character, be
used to compensate for defects on another: and that this process
sometimes fails. On Lawrence's new theory of the monolithic in-
divisibility of human relationships, it is hard to see how a love like
Ursula's and Skrebensky's, which fails on all planes, can ever have
begun—except as an idle diversion, which it clearly was not. We are
not yet in a position to say what has gone wrong with Lawrence's
thought here; but it is at least possible that he has mistaken his
ultimate: that sexual fulfilment stands to Lawrence for some other
more inclusive kind of integration whose nature he does not know;
that he has mistaken the part for the whole.

The confusion and failure in presenting Ursula's relation with
Skrebensky mean that the book can have no proper ending. In rejecting
Skrebensky Ursula feels that she has rejected a whole dead, brittle
kind of civilisation; and enough has been suggested both of his nature
and of her social attitudes to make this identification plausible. But
when Ursula, as a mere result of this rejection, has an intuition of
regenerating power in her visionary encounter with the wild horses,
when she sees the vision of the rainbow with which the book ends,
sees it as a sign of "the earth's new architecture, the old, brittle
corruption of houses and factories swept away, the world built up in
a living fabric of Truth, fitting to the over-arching heaven"—we can
only feel that this is quite insufficiently based, nothing in the book up
to now has led up to it. Regenerations are not achieved by mere

71

rejection; the only positive value consistently represented in the text has been fulfilment in the bond between man and woman; and this Ursula has just signally failed to achieve. The new religion has not really proved itself on the pulses; and all that the end of *The Rainbow* ultimately expresses is a vague hope and the need to end somehow.

There are other causes of disquiet throughout the book. The chief of these is the violence, the ill-temper, amounting at times to positive cruelty, with which the characters treat each other. Some of this is a real extension of the novel's range of vision, a recognition of the very real shadow side of daily life that both social and literary conventions are apt to ignore. But some of it goes beyond this. We are sometimes told that Lawrence was not such an angry and bitter man as he is often made to appear: but there is an increasing tendency for these qualities to appear to excess in his fiction; and apart from any objection we may have to this tendency in itself, it goes far to spoil the reality of the social world which Lawrence in other ways so brilliantly evokes. Dr. Leavis has rightly emphasised the range and grasp of Lawrence's picture of early twentieth-century England; but this is continually vitiated by presenting it as a place of vile tempers and no manners at all. And this is only a part of a growing inability or unwillingness to render the texture of ordinary life, of unimpassioned daily living. It is too often passed over in a paragraph or two, often beautiful—but from the time of *The Rainbow* on, Lawrence's characters spend too much of their time in unnaturally heightened states of consciousness.

Yet for all this *The Rainbow* remains a very fine novel. It is Lawrence's farewell to the England of his youth; it has the solidity, the penetration and the warm glow of George Eliot's *scènes de la vie de province*, with an added physical vitality that she could not command. And this added physical vitality brings with it a deeper and more intimate exploration of the obscure side of human relationships, to be pursued still further in *Women in Love*.

V. WOMEN IN LOVE

It is often denied that *Women in Love* is a sequel to *The Rainbow*, but both, at any rate, sprang out of the same conception; the continuity of character in Ursula is real, and the later book does depend to some slight extent on knowledge of the earlier. I first read *Women in Love* without knowing of the existence of *The Rainbow*, and I found the social setting and status of the Brangwen girls so difficult to grasp that it seriously interfered with the reality of their presentation. But Ursula and Gudrun (the latter was only a child in *The Rainbow*) have behind them the whole Brangwen family history; we remember how their mother wanted to be a 'lady' and then sank contentedly into a laborious muddle of babies and housework; we remember how the earlier Ursula had alternated between dialect and the language of the intelligentsia; we remember' her education and the fight she had to get it—and the disparity between these free and flashing creatures and their drab provincial background appears less startling—a calculated contrast, not a breakdown of consistency. The two girls are newly emancipated members of a class that has hitherto been tied to the narrow local scene. They are now wholly out of touch with it, and are free to dispose of themselves as they like— Ursula a teacher and Gudrun an artist. And the book begins with a conversation between them about marriage. This is still the central theme, as in *The Rainbow*; but here it is not marriage as an accomplished fact—it is the attempt of two adventurous, highly individualised young women to find it possible at all. *Women in Love*, in fact, questions the whole institution of marriage, which *The Rainbow* takes for granted.

The theme is established early. Gudrun sees Gerald Crich, the young colliery owner, in the first scene of the book, and knows at once that she is to be deeply involved with him. Ursula meets Birkin, the inspector of schools, in her class-room not long after; and the rest of the book works out the relationships of the two couples. A great deal else is done besides—in fact, the content of the book is so rich, the themes so numerous, that it is only possible to give an intelligible account of it by missing a good deal out. But the chief subsidiary theme—so powerful at times that it is hardly subsidiary—is a criticism of modern industrial society. It has already made its appearance in the latter part of *The Rainbow*, and Ursula has already rejected the world of mining and machinery.

> No more would she subscribe to the great colliery, to the great machine which has taken us all captives. In her soul, she was against it, she disowned even its power. It had only to be forsaken to be inane, meaningless. And she knew it was meaningless. But

it needed a great, passionate effort of will on her part, seeing the colliery, still to maintain her knowledge that it was meaningless.

(XII.)

Ursula rejects it, and it is not an accident that the Lesbian schoolmistress for whom Ursula has had a passion—the sterile, devouring woman, marries into this world. And Ursula's final vision of the rainbow is an opposition to it all.

They were all in prison, they were all going mad. She saw the stiffened bodies of the colliers, which seemed already enclosed in a coffin, she saw their unchanging eyes, the eyes of those who are buried alive: she saw the hard, cutting edges of the new houses, which seemed to spread over the hillside in their insentient triumph, the triumph of horrible, amorphous angles and straight lines, the expression of corruption triumphant and unopposed.

(XVI.)

But in the rainbow she sees a promise that all this will be changed; not so much the houses and factories as the essential qualities of people's lives must change. "She knew that the sordid people who crept hard-scaled and separate on the face of the world's corruption were living still, that the rainbow was arched in their blood and would quiver to life in their spirit." So that personal regeneration and the regeneration of society are intimately connected; the coal-pits and the squalid houses are only the outward expression of the 'hard-scaled separateness' that Lawrence's positive characters are trying to escape in their personal lives. Gerald Crich, rich, adventurous, physically splendid, is not only a mine-owner but a modern production expert as well. He is quite willing to accept the awfulness of the pits; and he does worse. For the pits, hideous as they are, have at least generated a kind of tradition, a way of life of their own; and Gerald is perfectly prepared to upset even this in the interests of efficiency and industrial progress. He thus becomes the representative both of a deadly social system and of a ruthless life-destroying energy in the personal sphere. In the end he destroys himself. He is perhaps a more extreme and considerably more developed attempt at presenting all that Skrebensky stood for in the earlier book. But this time he is left to the younger sister Gudrun, and Ursula is seen in relation to another kind of man altogether, Birkin, physically frail yet spiritually powerful, life-giving where Crich is life-destroying—the embodiment of

Lawrence's ideas; in fact, the first of many self-dramatisations of Lawrence the prophet.

I think that most readers, while feeling an obscure symbolical power, will find it hard to be convinced by the complicated relations of Gudrun and Gerald, Ursula and Birkin, on the plane of ordinary human action and character; and I think it possible that some impurity of motive, some private compensation and self-justification on Lawrence's part has entered into the picture, as Middleton Murry suggests in *Son of Woman*. The frail and invalidish Birkin is not only to be spiritually dominant over the superb Gerald, he must also be a sexual success, while Gerald in the end is a sexual failure. Let us face this charge here and be done with it. The element of compensation for his own failures and deficiencies is present in most of Lawrence's novels. It is almost bound to appear, in some measure, in any intensely subjective writer. He dramatises his own conflicts and is tempted to fake or distort the outcome. This is a weakness; but it is only part of the essential weakness of being a human being at all; and it has been built into the structure of imaginative writing from the folk-tale of the youngest brother onwards. In Lawrence the element of self-justification shows itself sometimes in stridency, sometimes in obscurity. Both are serious limitations. But to make this element central to all Lawrence's work, as Murry does, is to make the limitations crippling and absolute. It is to deny, in effect, that Lawrence can have anything of general and objective importance to say about human experience. And this, I think, is sufficiently disproved by any serious survey of the whole range of his work, unprejudiced by biographical irrelevancies.

On the obscurity and mystery of the relations of the four central characters of *Women in Love* there are two other things to be said. One is that they lessen on re-reading. All Lawrence's novels tend to carry more conviction in the ordinary social-naturalist sense the more familiar they become. Which only means that his idiom has to be learnt. The second point is that the obscurities, the breaches of ordinary continuity, are an essential part of his method. "You mustn't look in my novel for the old stable *ego* of the character. There is another ego according to whose action the individual is unrecognisable, and passes through, as it were, allotropic states which it needs a deeper sense than any that we are accustomed to exercise, to discover are states of the same radically unchanged element." This obviously applies to *The Rainbow*. Ursula's experiences are extremely vivid, but it sometimes takes an effort to realise that they are experiences of the same person. Will Brangwen seems to exist in two different states—as a lover and as a devout craftsman, and they hardly seem states of the same man. But it is undoubtedly true that the novel in general, owing to the importance commonly attributed to the 'creation of character', has concentrated to excess on the stable ego, on motives that can be explained and understood. And Lawrence, by attending to actual states of body, mind and soul, rather than to consistent motivation, has greatly extended its range, has done more justice than anyone before him to the irrationalities, the inexplicable fluxes and refluxes of feeling with which life is obviously chequered, but which fiction is commonly shy of dealing with.

These qualities are intensified in *Women in Love*, for it is a much more complex piece of work. There is only one conscious seeker after fulfilment in *The Rainbow*. In *Women in Love* there is Gudrun, too, and the two men, who are not only looking for something from their womenfolk, but from each other. So that there is a very involved pattern of both individual and related aspirations; and as the individual fragments alter their positions the whole is transformed, like the patterns in a kaleidoscope. There are so many of these shifting designs that it would be impossible to discuss them all, and since the historic and genealogical thread of *The Rainbow* is lacking, we must simply attempt to seize some of the principal recurrent themes.

Like many other novels, as Lawrence had previously observed, *Women in Love* "takes two couples and develops their relationships". The affairs of one go wrong and those of the other go right. "What I feel strongly about is the relation between men and women," he wrote in 1913. Indeed, as he had already committed himself to a philosophy of life in which the relation between men and women is central, the protagonists here have to illustrate a thesis as well as to work out their own destinies, and there are plenty of indications that the two couples are there to illustrate a right and a wrong way of love. But just what the rights and wrongs are is less easy to determine, and many readers of the book, while feeling an obscure power, have remained doubtful about the direction in which it is exercised. Power is the right word here, for Lawrence is extremely concerned about dominance and submission in love, and the relation between men and women is more like a fight than a friendship. We have already noticed the growing strain of violence in *The Rainbow*. It appears more nakedly in *Women in Love* because the characters are no longer rooted in any settled ground. In *The Rainbow* the farm and the church, the twin cycles of the agricultural and the Christian year, provide an element of permanence and therefore of rest. Marriage, until Ursula begins to grow up, means a family and children; but the chief actors of *Women in Love* are both professionally emancipated and spiritually uprooted, so that a correspondingly greater strain is thrown on their private relations. All are aware of this, all are in search of something: and the leader is Birkin, the representative of Lawrence himself.

Quite early in the book, in the conversation with Ursula and Hermione in the class-room, Birkin makes his position, if not clear, at least definite:

> "But do you really *want* sensuality?" she asked, puzzled.
> Birkin looked at her, and became intent in his explanation.
> "Yes," he said, "that and nothing else, at this point. It is a fulfilment—the great dark knowledge you can't have in your head—the dark involuntary being. It is death to one's self—but it is the coming into being of another."
> "But how? How can you have knowledge not in your head?" she asked, quite unable to interpret his phrases.
> "In the blood," he answered; "when the mind and the known world is drowned in darkness—everything must go—there must be the deluge. Then you find yourself a palpable body of darkness, a demon——"
>
> (III.)

Of course Ursula hasn't read D. H. Lawrence, and some of the phrases Birkin has used, with their negation of the conscious ego, might well puzzle her, for they might well have come from many purely spiritual mystics, both Eastern and Western. And fairly clearly, this is not what Birkin is talking about. It soon becomes apparent that while Birkin shares the mystic's desire for the dissolution of the ego, the daily conscious self, he looks for it, not in any of the traditional disciplines, but in the man-woman relationship alone.

Later, in conversation with Gerald, Birkin says:

> The old ideals are dead as nails—nothing there. It seems to me that there remains only this perfect union with a woman—sort of ultimate marriage—and there isn't anything else.
>
> (V.)

But this sort of ultimate marriage is not a matter of love—it is to be something beyond love. Ursula at first feels like any ordinary girl and wants love. She sees Birkin's desire for something more as a mere lust for bullying and domination, and the fight between them begins because she will not accept his notions. Love gives out in the end, he says; he does not want a meeting and mingling, but an equilibrium, a balance of opposites. And this balance is permanent, it excludes irrelevant wanderings and must give direction to the whole life. When Ursula in reply produces a little new-womanish morality about freedom in love, she is rebuked sternly for nihilism and sentimental canting. The lesson about the balance of opposites is reinforced by Birkin's cat, which proceeds to deal in an extremely male and lordly fashion with a fluffy little stray that has come into the garden. Ursula remains convinced that Birkin is trying to bully her with highfalutin nonsense, and at the end of the afternoon it is he who gives in, for the time, and admits, as an interim measure, that he loves her.

But nonsense or not, he goes on bullying her with it, till at one point she comes to hate him. They reach a stage where they both know that they are irrevocably bound together, but he would rather die than accept the kind of love she offers. It would be too long to follow the whole course of their feeling for each other; but the essentials concentrate themselves in two key chapters which especially demand attention.

The first is Chapter XIX, "Moony". It opens with the famous scene when Ursula, unobserved, watches Birkin in the wood by the side of Willey Water, furiously throwing stones at the reflection of the moon, breaking it into fragments and trying to drive it from the surface of the lake. It is a characteristic piece of Laurentian writing in that it is powerful in itself, purely descriptively; and in having as well a second layer of significance—Birkin's fury and Ursula's stunned bewilderment at it are absolutely appropriate expressions of their states of being at the time—which can be felt before it can be explained.

He stood staring at the water. Then he stooped and picked up a stone, which he threw sharply at the pond. Ursula was aware of the bright moon leaping and swaying, all distorted, in her eyes. It seemed to shoot out arms of fire like a cuttle-fish, like a luminous polyp, palpitating strongly before her.

And his shadow on the border of the pond, was watching for a few moments, then he stooped and groped on the ground. Then again there was a burst of sound, and a burst of brilliant light, the moon had exploded on the water, and was flying asunder in flakes of white and dangerous fire. Rapidly, like white birds, the fires all broken rose across the pond, fleeing in clamorous confusion, battling with the flock of dark waves that were forcing their way in. The furthest waves of light, fleeing out, seemed to be clamouring against the shore for escape, the waves of darkness came in heavily, running under towards the centre. But at the centre, the heart of all, was still a vivid, incandescent quivering of a white moon not quite destroyed, a white body of fire writhing and striving and not even now broken open, not yet violated. It seemed to be drawing itself together with strange, violent pangs, in blind effort. It was getting stronger, it was re-asserting itself, the inviolable moon. And the rays were hastening in in thin lines of light, to return to the strengthened moon, that shook upon the water in triumphant reassumption.

(XIX.)

Actually Birkin gives us the clue to this, for he hurls maledictions at the moon, calling her Cybele, the accursed Syria Dea; his mythology is a little rusty, but it is clear enough that the moon is the white goddess, the primal woman image, *das ewig weibliche*, by whom he is obviously haunted. He tries to drive her away, but of course she always comes back; as soon as he stops his stone-throwing the moon-image re-forms. At this moment Ursula appears; he gives up trying to drive the moon away, and they talk together—the same old impasse, she wants love and he wants something beyond it. They reach no solution, but the night ends in a mood of gentle tenderness. The next day Birkin thinks about a West African statuette, a female figure, that he has seen, in which he finds the expression of a purely mindless, purely sensual existence.

She knew what he himself did not know. She had thousands of years of purely sensual, purely unspiritual knowledge behind her. It must have been thousands of years since her race had died, mystically: that is, since the relation between the senses and the outspoken mind had broken, leaving the experience all in one sort, mystically sensual.

(XIX.)

This may well be anthropological nonsense, but it hardly matters; the point is that the African figure stands for that kind of experience to Birkin, and that he has more than once talked, up to now, as though it was precisely this that he wanted. He has often thought that the negation of consciousness, the reassertion of pure sensuality is the only escape from the hard-shelled separateness of modern civilisation. But in thinking of the African fetish, he is forced really to contemplate this process and he is repelled and frightened. Has our civilisation to go this way, too? True it would do it differently, since we are northerners, but the essential process would be the same—the destruction of the happy bond between mind and body, soul and sense, the destruction therefore of all specifically human creativity and the relapse into pure sensuality, hot and putrescent in the tropics, cold and icily destructive in the north. Birkin thinks of Gerald, and sees him as one of these dissociated creatures whose sensual life is cold and destructive and isolated. And suddenly he rejects all this.

There was another way, the way of freedom. There was the paradisal entry into pure, single being . . . a lovely state of free proud singleness, which accepted the obligation of the permanent connection with others . . . but never forfeits its proud individual singleness, even while it loves and yields.

(XIX.)

The language of all these passages is suggestive, evocative and obscure, and in thus stripping it of its overtones much of its quality is lost. But if Lawrence has the power of calling up a spontaneous assent in his readers, he is also apt to call up the demon of rejection; and because his darker and more vatic utterances contain statements that are literally nonsense, it has often been found easy to reject the whole as nonsense. The whole may very well be untrue, but it certainly makes a kind of sense; and to make this clear it is sometimes necessary to use a repellent crudeness of exposition. Crudely then, what is happening in Birkin's mind is this. He believes that the regeneration of society can only be accomplished by a new relation between individuals. Almost the only genuine relation that modern life offers is the "meeting and mingling", the cosy domesticities of ordinary married love. He has already violently rejected this as a denial, a reduction of freedom and necessary human pride. There are only two other possibilities—first, the complete abandonment of consciousness, art, living production, all the specifically human attributes, for endless progression in purely sensual knowledge. This is symbolised by the African fetish, and Gerald Crich represents a northern form of it. This also Birkin rejects. There remains then only one way—"the way of freedom"—a profound and permanent bond between a man and a woman which still leaves them separate and independent as persons; the achievement at the same time of freedom and relationship; freedom on the personal level, profound relationship at the deeper-than-personal roots of being. Birkin now knows what he must do, and elated by his discovery he goes off to propose marriage to Ursula.

But although Birkin knows what it is that they must do, the relation is still not achieved. Ursula has not yet shared Birkin's awareness, and the process of bringing her to the realisation is traced in the second of our two key chapters, Chapter XXIII, "Excurse". Exposition of this must be curtailed. Part of it is occupied with a violent quarrel in which Ursula abuses Birkin for his affair with Hermione Roddice, the cold, power-loving intellectual-spiritual woman who has dominated his life for years. Ursula's invective reaches an intensity that is remarkable even for Lawrence, though it was always part of his theory that integrity in human relationships is better achieved by violent quarrels than by not having things out. Birkin recognises the justice of much of what she says, and the quarrel ends, as even non-Laurentian lovers' quarrels often end, in a new access of tenderness. What happens afterwards I do not fully understand, and whatever it is I cannot convince myself that Lawrence has been successful in conveying it. He will persist in trying to be explicit about sensuous-emotional ecstasies that had better be left alone; and there are lapses into inflation and bathos. But the essential point is that suddenly Ursula, too, recognises this new relationship of unity and separateness—the profound connection between two beings who are nevertheless eternally different.

> She looked at him. He seemed still so separate. New eyes were opened in her soul. She saw a strange creature from another world, in him. It was as if she were enchanted, and everything were metamorphosed. She recalled again the old magic of the

Book of Genesis, where the sons of God saw the daughters of men, that they were fair. And he was one of these, one of these strange creatures from the beyond, looking down at her, and seeing she was fair.

(XXIII.)

She kneels on the hearthrug before him and embraces him, round what Lawrence is fond of calling the loins.

Unconsciously, with her sensitive finger-tips, she was tracing the back of his thighs, following some mysterious life-flow there. She had discovered something, something more than wonderful, more wonderful than life itself. It was the strange mystery of his life-motion, there, at the back of the thighs, down the flanks. It was a strange reality of his being, the very stuff of being, there in the straight downflow of the thighs. It was here she discovered him one of the sons of God such as were in the beginning of the world, not a man, something other, something more.

(XXIII.)

This is the kind of thing one wishes Lawrence would not do. The scene is possible enough, but when described it borders on the ridiculous. And it is only by a charitable effort of the imagination that one realises what is supposed to be happening—Ursula is doing homage to an essential transcendent maleness, *das ewig männliche*, if there is such a thing, which is more than Birkin's personal being, though it was in him that she was always destined to discover it. They spend the night together in the woods, all difficulties and antagonisms disappear, and their pilgrimage is at an end. The consummation is not entirely convincing—but in any attempt to get beyond the usual convention by which an achieved mutual love is regarded as an absolute, in any attempt to dig deeper into its mysteries, some failure of realisation is perhaps inevitable.

From then on the burden of the book falls on the relationship of Gudrun and Gerald, the pair who fail to achieve this mysterious polarity, and failing in that, fail in everything. From the point we have just indicated the relations of Birkin and Ursula are marked by an increasing mental sympathy, a growing gentleness, a sense of being really together. They marry and accept the responsibility of a permanent bond. It slowly becomes clear that Gudrun and Gerald are not going to do anything of the kind. Gerald agrees formally with all Birkin's criticism of stuffy and exclusive marriage—"the world all in couples, each couple in its own little house, watching its own little interests, and stewing in its own little privacy": but he has no alternative to offer, and ultimately would accept marriage as a mere convention.

> But he would not make any pure relationship with any other soul. He could not. Marriage was not the committing of himself into a relationship with Gudrun. It was a committing of himself in acceptance of the established order, he would accept the established order in which he did not livingly believe, and then he would retreat to the underworld for his life.

> (XXV.)

This throws light on the identification, at first sight very odd, between Gerald and that which is represented by the African carving. Successful as Gerald is at dealing with the conventional surface of the modern world, his real life goes on in an unintegrated sensuality not connected with the rest of his being. Lawrence expounds the process at length in *The Crown*, an important essay of this period. Similarly Gudrun, although she is described as a born mistress, cannot enter into any living relationship with another person. After she becomes Gerald's mistress, though he is perfectly satisfied, she remains too conscious, she will not give herself, her tenderness is something willed, not a real self-abandonment. And she, too, doesn't want marriage. The only image it evokes in her is a Royal Academy picture entitled 'Home'.

It seems to be Lawrence's intention to describe in Gerald and Gudrun two complementary types, different yet each equally wrong: Gerald conventionally successful, conventionally effective, yet divided from his own inner being, ultimately fighting and destroying himself; Gudrun a born free-lance, outside society, yet too assertive and self-conscious ever to find real rest, real self-forgetfulness. So that even the sensual bond between them is never complete, inevitably they are drawn into conflict. When, in the last section of the book they all go away together Gudrun realises that Gerald is naturally promiscuous, almost a professional lady-killer, and she resolves to combat him. The last three chapters of the book are a superb evocation of the combat. Taken by themselves, they are probably the finest part of *Women in Love*. The solitary snowed-in Alpine valley, the pressure of the four personalities on each other, the intervention of the Austrian sculptor Loerke—another nihilist like Gerald and another free-lance like Gudrun, and destined to have a fatally corrupting effect on both— all this is more concentrated, more powerful and more certain in its effect than anything that has gone before. But it is not an episode, it has its preordained place in the economy of the book as a whole. As the life of Ursula and Birkin flows more deeply and more steadily in its proper channel, so that of Gudrun and Gerald becomes more shattered and disrupted; and the violence and cruelty of the closing scenes is Lawrence's assurance that the forces we have been dealing with are not to be played with, that the success of Ursula and Birkin has not been an easy one, that the penalties for failure can be fury and destruction.

Outwardly the story is simple enough. In the relative isolation of an Alpine holiday, the antagonism between Gudrun and Gerald becomes more open. She resents his triumphant sexual success, and more and more openly resists him. She rejects the social world of money and industrialism to which he would bring her; and in token of this takes up with the sculptor Loerke. Like Gudrun, he is an artist and an outsider from Gerald's world; he is also a corrupt, disintegrated creature. This is very subtly conveyed—so is the fascination he holds for a woman of Gudrun's type. The two of them exploit their intimacy, as a weapon against Gerald and all that he represents. There is a scene of violent jealousy in which Gerald knocks Loerke down and nearly strangles Gudrun. And then Gerald goes off ski-ing by himself, climbs higher and higher into the cold, and is found dead of exposure.* I will not spoil these superb pages by attempting an exegesis—but Gerald's death is the climax of a process of disintegration that has been indicated all along. The self-destructiveness of Gerald's nature has been constantly if obscurely emphasised. For those who will not or cannot accept the responsibility of a real relationship, disintegration is the only end.

This is not the note on which the book closes. It closes with a conversation between Birkin and Ursula.

"Did you need Gerald?" she asked one evening.
"Yes," he said.
"Aren't I enough for you?" she asked.

* I do not think it has been noticed elsewhere that Gerald's end bears a re-markable similarity to that of Ibsen's John Gabriel Borkman.

"No," he said. "You are enough for me, as far as a woman is concerned. You are all women to me. But I wanted a man friend, as eternal as you and I are eternal."

"Why aren't I enough?" she said. "You are enough for me. I don't want anybody else but you. Why isn't it the same with you?"

"Having you, I can live all my life without anybody else, any other sheer intimacy. But to make it complete, really happy, I wanted eternal union with a man too: another kind of love," he said.

"I don't believe it," she said. "It's obstinacy, a theory, a perversity."

"Well——" he said.

"You can't have two kinds of love. Why should you?"

"It seems as if I can't," he said. "Yet I wanted it."

"You can't have it, because it's false, impossible," she said.

"I don't believe that," he answered.

(XXXI.)

This brings into unexpected prominence another theme that has been subordinate but recurrent throughout the book—the relationship between man and man. It has been troubling Birkin all along.

Suddenly he saw himself confronted with another problem—the problem of love and eternal conjunction between two men. Of course this was necessary—it had been a necessity inside himself all his life—to love a man purely and fully. Of course he had been loving Gerald all along, and all along denying it.

(XVI.)

He wants to swear a *Blutbrüderschaft* with Gerald, and in Chapter XX, where they both work off an obscure unease by wrestling violently with one another, we are to understand that some sacrament of this sort has been consummated. There is clearly a sexual element in all this which Lawrence was unwilling to acknowledge. It has already appeared in *The White Peacock*, and appeared occasionally in his life. But there is something else, too. It is as though Lawrence has all along an obscure realisation that it is not possible to found a whole way of life on the relation between man and woman, that a man must also play his part in the man's world. But we must postpone consideration of this for the present. This theme and its implications (never, as it seems to me, very clearly understood by Lawrence) plays a major part in his next three novels, and in placing it so prominently at the end of *Women in Love* he is giving, as he was wont to do, a clear lead into the next region of his work.

An outstanding character of the book of whom we have so far said little is Hermione. Individually she ranks as one of Lawrence's vividest creations, but she is not very closely integrated with the plot. She is notoriously a portrait from life, sketched in one of Lawrence's extreme revulsions of feeling, after an initial admiration; and many of her characteristics are the more or less accidental features of the original. But she soon turns into one of Lawrence's lasting and central symbols. Accidentally, she is a great lady, a patron of the intelligentsia, with something of a genius of her own for the æsthetic life, if not for æsthetic creation. Essentially, she is the type of possessive, intellectual-spiritual love, a love unwarmed by physical passion, desiring only to absorb and subjugate the mental being of its objects. We first see her in the opening scenes of the book, where we learn that she is tortured by uncertainties and insufficiencies, for all her social assurance; and that she is deeply in love with Birkin, who alone can help her towards wholeness. She fails, however, to form a real relationship with him, and can only continue to "pile up her own defences of æsthetic knowledge, and world visions, and disinterestedness."

Birkin treats her with consistent brutality. When she rather feebly echoes his own eulogy of spontaneity and instinctual knowledge, he replies:

> You are merely making words, knowledge means everything to you. Even your animalism, you want it in your head. You don't want to *be* an animal, you want to observe your own animal functions, to get a mental thrill out of them. It is all purely secondary—and more decadent than the most hide-bound intellectualism. What is it but the worst and last form of intellectualism, this love of yours for passion and the animal instincts. . . . It all takes place in your head, under that skull of yours. Only you won't be conscious of what *actually* is: you want the lie that will match the rest of your furniture.

(III.)

Yet the more decisively he rejects her, the more she tries to impose her will on him, to force him to become her confidant. "She laid as it were violent hands on him, to extract his secrets from him. She *must* know. It was a dreadful tyranny, an obsession with her, to know all he knew." For her passion is a purely mental one, driven by the will, working through the understanding. We may compare Lawrence's denunciations of Poe's lovers (in *Classic American Literature*), those "ghastly obscene *knowers*", with their crazed longing for the last degree of spiritual and mental intimacy, and no human warmth at all. To this Birkin opposes a steady self-possessed indifference, punctuated by open attacks on her whole ethos. No attempt is made to excuse Birkin's conduct, or even to explain it. If he hates Hermione and all her works, he has only to go away. But Lawrence's aim is less to create a plausible social situation than to show two ways of life in the most violent opposition—Birkin's desire for singleness and wholeness, Hermione's parasitic mental lust.

In the end the explosive forces latent in the situation break out. Hermione, maddened by Birkin's indifference, picks up a heavy stone paperweight and makes a spirited attempt to beat his head in. Then Birkin does go away. We are intended, it appears, to make the following deductions from the situation. First, and certainly, the destructive nature of Hermione's passion. If she cannot absorb Birkin mentally, then she must destroy him physically. Secondly, I suppose, that outraged physical nature will have its revenge. Hermione, who attempts to live entirely in the mind and the spirit, to frame a world of æsthetic and universal emotions, is betrayed into an act of vulgar physical violence. Thirdly, we are to suppose that she was right to act as she did. She herself concludes so: "She had only hit him, as any woman might do, because he tortured her. She was perfectly right. She knew that, spiritually, she was right." And on reflection Birkin agrees with her. "It was quite right of Hermione to want to kill him. What had he to do with her. Why should he pretend to have anything to do with human beings at all?" Hermione has come nearer to authenticity in trying to kill him than she ever did in trying to achieve a spiritual intimacy with him. Their relation has for a moment become real.

Yet all this does not prevent turning up again later at Birkin's house, arranging his furniture for him, and trying to give him a carpet that he doesn't want; delivering a lecture on the right use of the *will* in the meantime. We meet her only once again, this time in conjunction with Ursula. They meet in Birkin's rooms, the current mistress and the discarded one; and through the embarrassment of the situation have a moment of real contact in contemplating together the difficulties of Birkin's temperament. Then he comes in, and the tone of the encounter shifts abruptly to uncomfortable social comedy. Hermione plays on her old intimacy with Birkin, her real intellectual understanding and her superior social sophistication.

> Ursula felt she was an outsider. The very tea-cups and the old silver was a bond between her and Birkin. It seemed to belong to an old, past world which they had inhabited together, and in which Ursula was a foreigner. She was almost a parvenue in their old cultured milieu. Her convention was not their convention, their standards were not her standards. But theirs were established, they had the sanction and the grace of age. He and she together, Hermione and Birkin, were people of the same old tradition, the same withered deadening culture. And she, Ursula, was an intruder.
>
> (XXII.)

When Hermione starts to talk Italian to the cat it is too much, and Ursula retires discomfited.

These later scenes are on a lower level of intensity than the first, but they serve to complete the picture. It is a picture of some importance in Lawrence's collection of social types—that of a woman elaborately accoutred in a plate-armour of rank, culture, intelligence and personal distinction. All these attributes are perfectly genuine and rather formidable. Lawrence is not exposing a pretender, and he rarely makes the vulgar error of supposing that social differentiæ are unreal merely because he dislikes them. Yet within Hermione's armour there is only a will, an obsessive will, to impose itself on all who come within its orbit. Friendship and love from such a woman can only be a form of bullying. And the emotional and spiritual bullying must always continue, because the obsessed will can never be satisfied. Because it is never satisfied, there is always inner torment, inner unrest. And this uncertainty can only be palliated, or at least disguised, by presenting with ever more blatant assurance the hard accomplished social front. Hermione is one of Lawrence's most individual characters, and as such is never repeated; but the same spiritual elements, differently proportioned and combined, occur sufficiently often in later writings to be recognisable as one of the basic types which Lawrence used as keys to the understanding of his social world.

This outline of the main themes by no means exhausts the content of *Women in Love*. Indeed, it is only when one has tried to write some sort of a commentary on it that one begins to realise what a rich and crowded work it is. A great deal had happened to Lawrence since he began work on *The Sisters*, and much of this new experience goes into *Women in Love*, not, as one might expect, raw and undigested, but extremely maturely observed. In 1913 Lawrence and Frieda returned to England. They were now able to marry, Lawrence had the beginnings of a considerable literary reputation, and he thus began to enjoy, for the first time, some degree of social mobility. This was the period when the friendship with Middleton Murry and Katherine Mansfield began, and an introduction to Café Royal society and pre-war Bohemianism. Through David Garnett and Bertrand Russell, Lawrence met Keynes and some of the Cambridge-Blooms-bury circle. Through Lady Ottoline Morrell he met a variety of other distinguished people, both literary and political. Personally this did him very little good. The minor artistic society seems to have gener-ated a good deal of dreary *Schwärmerei*, which can be seen at its worst in Murry's memoirs of Lawrence: and the company of a number of people of some public importance seems to have encouraged Lawrence in the belief that he was a saviour charged with the mission of con-verting the English ruling class. From the point of view of his work, however, there were two effects of considerable importance. By associating with people accustomed to influence and the exercise of power, Lawrence comes very rapidly to see that ideas can have results, that what might be a very feeble spark in a provincial debating society might produce a considerable blaze if applied to a suitably central portion of the national scene. Round about 1915 in particular he is continually hoping, by contributing to little magazines, by lecturing on his philosophy, by associations with various other people, to change the face of English society, and this ambition is never wholly absent from him again. It is these years that see the début of Lawrence the prophet. The second effect of his new associations is the obvious one—an immense widening of his social experience. Up to now he had known working-class life in Eastwood, Nottingham University, the career of a school-teacher in a London suburb, a period of unor-ganised knocking about in Germany and Italy. Now, quite suddenly, he is introduced, on very favourable terms, to an extremely spacious and varied intellectual and social circle. He sees something of the effects of wealth, culture and position. It is often said that this made him snobbish, and it is true that he is often silly about these matters. In the circumstances it is surprising that he was not sillier, and from the novelist's point of view his new social orientation is almost pure gain. He had exiled himself from his own original social group; he was an interesting outsider in every other social group that he encountered, and this peculiar position gave him incomparable opportunities for observing the whole complex scene. Like many people who have changed their class position, Lawrence has a very acute sense of class differences, an infallible nose for the atmosphere of particular groups; and he is not tied to the standards of any one of them. An uncomfortable situation for anyone who wants a recognised niche in the hierarchy, but it is hard to imagine a better one for the novelist.

It is necessary to emphasise this because Lawrence is so often, and justly, seen as the painter of the interior landscape that we are apt to forget how penetrating an observer he is of the ordinary social scene. The evidence can be seen in *Women in Love*. The whole picture of the mining district, and the reactions to it of the two sisters who have partly escaped; the story of Gerald Crich's father who had created it all; Gerald's continuation of his work—there is a whole chapter of English social history in these passages. If we add to them the picture of Hermione and her world, the scenes in the Pompadour and the glimpses of Bohemian life that go with them, the society in the Tyrolean ski-ing resort—we can begin to see, perhaps more clearly than those who were nearer to Lawrence in time, that whatever else he has done he has contributed some unforgettable pages to the chronicle of an age.

VI. THE LOST GIRL; AARON'S ROD

After the completion of *The Rainbow* and *Women in Love* there seems to have been a temporary decline in the intensity of Lawrence's creation. *The Lost Girl* is in part a re-handling of a story begun in 1913, just after the completion of *Sons and Lovers*; but it was not finished till 1920, and the conclusion belongs to quite a different phase of his experience. The two parts do not hang together, and most of the book is the dullest and least characteristic Lawrence, the nearest thing to a pot-boiler that he ever wrote. *Aaron's Rod* is more of a genuine organism, but even this was hardly conceived as a whole. It was begun in England in 1918, then apparently abandoned; taken up again in Italy and finished in 1921. It, too, is heterogeneous in content and carelessly put together; but it remains a significant item in Lawrence's work, for it develops a theme already advertised for further exploration in *Women in Love*—the relation between man and man; and this was to remain important to him for some time to come. Both books reflect what has so far hardly appeared in his novels— the transition from the *Lehrjahre* to the *Wanderjahre*—the whole new outlook brought about by the passage from his native Midlands to a peripatetic life in Europe.

The Lost Girl does not demand very prolonged consideration. It seems to have originated in a far more superficial region of the mind than any of its predecessors except *The Trespasser*. At the time *Sons and Lovers* was being completed, in North Italy in 1912, Lawrence, who had no books with him and saw no contemporary English writing, was sent a copy of Arnold Bennett's *Anna of the Five Towns*. He did not like it; and reading Bennett, whose world was so near his own, brought him back to the industrial England from which he had just escaped.

> I hate England and its hopelessness. I hate Bennett's resignation. Tragedy ought really to be a great kick at misery. But *Anna of the Five Towns* seems like an acceptance.[37]

However, Bennett's resigned acceptance of industrial England had made him a best-seller; Lawrence was still unrecognised and extremely poor; and *The Lost Girl* seems fairly obviously an attempt to do Bennett's sort of thing—Midland naturalism, without any of the passionate psychological preoccupations that had lifted Lawrence's earlier books out of their setting.

"I hate Bennett's resignation," Lawrence writes, and he continues in the same letter with the passages quoted earlier, contrasting the dreary grubbiness of industrial England with the healthy, vigorous poverty of the Italians around him. But in the earlier chapters of *The Lost Girl* he seems to have forgotten about this irritated protest and to accept the world he writes about almost as wholly as Arnold Bennett does. The Woodhouse of *The Lost Girl* is Eastwood again— the setting is the same as that of *The White Peacock* and *Sons and Lovers*. But it looks different—simply because Lawrence himself is not there. The physical and social environment in *Sons and Lovers* is alive and actual because the perceiving consciousness is right in the midst of the scene. Eastwood is not a backdrop; it is in a state of constant interaction with a developing adolescent nature. *The Lost Girl* is without this principle of life. The first six chapters are excellent genre-painting, and make one realise what a competent social realist Lawrence could have been; but the story has not been lived through as *Sons and Lovers* was, it is merely presented. And any implied protest against the drabness of industrial England is in the rather contrived plot not in the texture of the writing.

There is a loss of physical immediacy. *Sons and Lovers* opens like this:

> "The Bottoms" succeeded to "Hell Row." Hell Row was a block of thatched, bulging cottages that stood by the brookside on Greenhill Lane. There lived the colliers who worked in the little gin-pits two fields away. The brook ran under the alder-trees, scarcely soiled by these small mines, whose coal was drawn to the surface by donkeys that plodded wearily in a circle round a gin. And all over the countryside were these same pits, some of which had been worked in the time of Charles II, the few colliers and the donkeys burrowing down like ants into the earth, making queer mounds and little black places among the corn-fields and the meadows.

Here is the corresponding passage from *The Lost Girl*:

> A well-established society in Woodhouse, full of fine shades, ranging from the dark of coal-dust to grit of stone-mason and sawdust of timber-merchant, through the lustre of lard and butter and meat, to the perfume of the chemist and the disinfectant of the doctor, on to the serene gold-tarnish of bank-managers, cashiers for the firm, clergymen and suchlike, as far as the automobile refulgence of the general-manager of all the collieries. Here the *ne plus ultra*. The general manager lives in the shrubberied seclusion of the so-called Manor. The genuine Hall, abandoned by the "County", has been taken over as offices by the firm.

Excellent writing, indeed; but at one remove from its material. The same contrast is found in the domestic dialogue; in *Sons and Lovers* every word seems to have been actually lived and uttered, so that the reader feels on his own nerves all the pressures of a Midland industrial home; in *The Lost Girl* he is aware simply of an able representation. The fact is that the world of *The Lost Girl* is still quite real to Lawrence, but it is no longer important to him. It is no longer contributing to his development; and all his most vital writing springs directly from a process of growth and change within himself.

What really interested Lawrence at this time, what was really making him live anew, was Italy and the fresh possibilities of life he had discovered there. The problem that faced him on taking up the novel again was to bring all this flood of new experience into relation to his piece of drab Midland naturalism. And this has to be done by what is obviously a very creaky piece of machinery. Alvina, the undeveloped daughter of the Woodhouse bourgeoisie, has to be delivered from her round of chapel-going and tea-drinking by the intervention of a troupe of strolling players. The Natcha-Kee-Tawaras, as Lawrence absurdly calls them, have a ridiculously invented air; they have no roots in experience, and are simply there to fulfil the exigencies of the plot. The only point of interest about them is that they are supposed to be Indians, and that we can find in them a slight premonitory fancy sketch of what Lawrence was later to find, or imagine he found, in the authentic Indians of the American south-west. Of course they are not really Indians, but assorted Europeans; and their purpose in the novel is to introduce Alvina to Cicio, the Italian who carries her off to his home in the mountains, and thus succeeds in approximating her experiences to those that really absorbed Lawrence at the time.

The figure of Cicio has been praised by Mr. Aldington, as an understanding picture of the Italian working class. This may well be; in the context of Lawrence's work, however, he figures as one of the long series of saturnine men of the people—gipsies, gamekeepers or what not—who carry off middle-class women and do them so much good. He is not individually very sympathetic or very convincing, but as soon as he and Alvina leave England his background becomes superb. Alvina's departure assumes to itself all the relief and all the melancholy, all the fears and all the hopes, of the Lawrences' departure for Italy in 1919, after their long war-time winter of discontent.

> Her heart died within her. Never had she felt so utterly strange and far-off. Cicio at her side was as nothing, as spell-bound she watched, away off, behind all the sunshine and the sea, the grey, snow-streaked substance of England slowly receding and sinking, submerging. She felt she could not believe it. It was like looking

at something else. What? It was like a long, ash-grey coffin, winter, slowly submerging in the sea. England?

(XIV.)

Cicio's home Pescocalascio is Picinisco in the province of Caserta, where the Lawrences spent a short time in the winter of 1919, and the vivid description of its icy and comfortless grandeurs in the closing chapters is virtually an expansion of a passage in the letters.

> It is a bit staggeringly primitive. You cross a great stony river-bed, then an icy river on a plank, then climb unfootable paths, while the ass struggles behind with your luggage. The house contains a·rather cave-like kitchen downstairs—the other rooms are a wine-press and a wine-storing place and a corn-bin: upstairs are three bedrooms, and a semi-barn for maize-cobs: beds and bare floor. There is one teaspoon—one saucer—two cups—one plate—two glasses—the whole supply of crockery. Everything must be cooked gipsy-fashion in the chimney over a wood fire. The chickens wander in, the ass is tied to the door-post and makes his droppings on the doorstep and brays his head off. . . . The village two miles away, a sheer scramble, no road whatever—the market at Atina, five miles away—perfectly wonderful to look at—costume and colour. . . . Withal, the sun shines hot and lovely, but the nights freeze; the mountains round are snowy and very beautiful. [38]

No, the last chapters are more than an expansion of this. They are, in fact, a striking example of how Lawrence can mix inspired reporting and creative imagination. Alvina's experiences are those of himself and Frieda; she sees what they saw. But Lawrence has contrived in the novel to put himself in the position of a girl who has burnt her boats and abandoned herself to this kind of life; and the lostness of the lost girl gives this account of the austerities of Pescocalascio a kind of visionary grandeur. Here as elsewhere Lawrence's imagination is fired by plunging one of his characters into the depths of a situation in which he himself had only dipped his toes. The Lawrences fled to Capri in a fortnight, Alvina is left in the mountains to work out her destiny.

I am aware that I have treated this last and best part of the book as travel-diary or autobiography, and that this is not consistent with recognising the artistic integrity of a novel. But we are constantly under this necessity with Lawrence, and increasingly so at this stage of his career. It is the same with *Aaron's Rod* and *Kangaroo*. The books of this period are either not fully integrated works of art, or their principle of integration is very different from that of the ordinary novel. On *The Lost Girl* the first judgment is evidently the right one; the splendid conclusion cannot make up for its inconsistency with what went before, and there is no concealed thread to bind the disparate elements together.

The fundamental defect of *The Lost Girl* is the lack of a significant human relationship. *Aaron's Rod* has the same sort of structural lapses, but it does try to work out some of the problems of human relationship, and its vitality and coherence is far greater in consequence. The relation between man and man is explored, if inconclusively, far more fully than in *Women in Love*; and, linked closely with this, there are failures and breakdowns in the relation between man and woman. The other elements of the book are miscellaneous. For a time the *Sons and Lovers* world is re-created, with most of the old force; the Bohemian-intellectual society of *Women in Love* reappears, not nearly so well done; there is a long section of not quite assimilated travel-diary; an abortive love-affair; and the hint of a new philosophy of power.

The chance of imposing unity on these heterogeneous materials seems slight. They could be successive episodes in a picaresque novel with Aaron as the central figure, and in a way they are. But Lawrence constantly suggests another kind of unity—a unity of purpose—and this is only fitfully maintained. The theme that seems to be announced in the opening pages is Aaron's attempt to find himself; or more broadly, the situation of the established man who finds that what he has achieved means nothing to him, and is irresistibly impelled to throw it all up and start again. Aaron is a particularly successful member of the mining community, with money in the bank, a 'good' home and a position of responsibility among his fellow-workers. The picture of Aaron's household has all the power and intimacy of *Sons and Lovers*, with a new recognition of the father's point of view, hitherto totally excluded. The undertone of sour disapproval from the good wife, the wrangling competitiveness of the well-brought-up children leave Aaron with only one domestic resource—his solitary flute-playing in the back-kitchen, and one outside distraction—the pub, with its atmosphere of masculine argument, presided over by the warm, sensual landlady. Aaron seems stoical, resigned, settled and fairly amiable; actually he is at the end of his tether. This is all presented, actualised, not discussed; and Aaron's sudden decision to leave his family becomes all the more convincing because its motives are not discussed. By the time we reach the end of this part of the book, Aaron's close, obstinate, rather inarticulate nature is firmly established.

The level drops abruptly when Aaron bumps into the Bricknells—a society of rich, rather tiresome post-war quasi-Bohemians. Lawrence is never secure and easy in the portraiture of the articulate upper middle classes that the English novel often does so well. Above a certain degree of intensity he manages something better than this rather commonplace achievement—an inspired penetration that is more than mere verisimilitude. He accomplished this in *Women in Love*, but he cannot repeat it here. This part of the book is weak, and it does not improve when Aaron meets the same circle again in London. We begin to be worried, too, by material and social improbabilities. Aaron is represented as an accomplished flute-player, therefore an artist; and this gives him both an *état civil* and an unusual degree of social mobility; but that he should be immediately employed in an operatic orchestra, immediately begin to move freely in moneyed, more or less artistic, circles rather strains our credulity. And Aarons who after all has just emerged from the mining village where he has spent all his life, suddenly becomes more articulate, more capable of conscious reflection than seems likely.

There is a still further decline when the interest shifts from Aaron altogether to Jim Bricknell and Lilly. The fact is that Lawrence has split his own consciousness between two characters in the story—Aaron and Lilly. Lilly is Lawrence the prophet, and Aaron is the escaped denizen of Eastwood. Here Lawrence the prophet, thinly disguised as Lilly, is seen preaching to the unregenerate English upper classes; but it is not until he is brought into relation with Aaron that the book regains imaginative integrity and again picks up its main threat.

It picks it up and intertwines it with a new one—a relationship between two men. Lawrence has just begun to realise that important as marriage is, it is not in itself a full-time occupation; that there are even emotional needs that it does not satisfy. Birkin had ended *Women in Love* by recognising that the completed Union with Ursula was not enough, that he needed "eternal union with a man, too; another kind of love". Lilly, the successor of Birkin, is now exploring this possibility in company with Aaron. However, the programme as advertised is not quite fulfilled. We are not witnessing the completion by another kind of love of a primary relationship with woman. Aaron has just broken his marriage and Lilly's is looking pretty uncertain. It seems far more as though they are trying to find in each other a substitute for an unsatisfactory relation with women. Lilly's attitude to Aaron is almost maternal, and they discuss marriage together with great bitterness. Lilly's solicitude for Aaron, his tending him in his sickness, his rubbing of his body with oil as a woman does a child—all this is strongly emphasised. But it is curiously connected with reflections about authority and power. In the very act of his womanly ministrations Lilly reflects:

> I wonder why I do it. . . . As soon as this man's really better he'll punch me in the wind, metaphorically if not actually, for having interfered with him. And Tanny would say he was quite right to do it. She says I want power over them. What if I do?
> . . . Why can't they submit to a bit of healthy individual authority.
>
> (IX.)

The burden of his complaint is that men are willing enough to submit to the authority of the mob or the state, but that they will not submit to the only real kind of authority, that of the individual person. And the mention of Tanny, his wife, is not accidental; for the bitterest complaint seems to be against women rather than men; they refuse to submit, and they use their children as a means of establishing their female dominance.

> Men have got to stand up to the fact that manhood is more than childhood—and then force women to admit it. . . . But the rotten whiners, they're all grovelling before a baby's napkin and a woman's petticoat.
>
> (IX.)

Lilly's proud spirit revolts against this situation, and recklessly thrusting aside the obstructing napkins and petticoats he proceeds to flourish the only weapon that occurs to him—a quasi-homosexual ganging up of the men against the whole female sex. But he feels little confidence in it.

That's why marriage wants readjusting—or extending—to get men on their own legs once more, and to give them the adventure again. But men won't stick together and fight for it. Because once a woman has climbed up with her children she'll find plenty of grovellers ready to support her and suffocate any defiant spirit. . . . And can you find two men to stick together without feeling criminal, and without cringing and without betraying one another? You can't.

(IX.)

Certainly Lilly and Aaron do not constitute such a pair. Aaron resists Lilly's influence; Lilly wants unfettered freedom of action, and decides to go off to Malta. The bond between them has not consolidated itself. Lilly returns to the idea of Birkin in *Women in Love*—that it is possible for a man to possess his own soul in separateness and for his wife to do so too.

"I don't care," said Lilly, "I'm learning to possess my soul in patience and in peace, and I know it. . . . And if Tanny possesses her own soul in patience and peace as well—and if in this we understand each other at last—then there we are, together and apart at the same time, and free of each other and eternally inseparable."

(X.)

But the hysterical tone of the preceding references to marriage and women do not inspire much confidence; and the queer semi-amorous wrangling between Aaron and Lilly that follows suggests that they are looking for a substitute for marriage rather than a solution of its problems.

A diversion follows. Herbertson, an army officer, comes in and recounts his war-experiences. In him we have a picture of a man who has gone through the whole ghastly war bravely, yet is now so obsessed by it that his capacity for life is destroyed. He leaves, and Lilly analyses his situation and his own reaction to the war— penetratingly, yet, one is bound to feel, presumptuously for one who has not been through it. Aaron is readier than Lilly to accept the necessities of power-politics—even the use of poison gas. They quarrel over this, and Lilly rejects Aaron absolutely; he refuses friendship unless he can have complete agreement on fundamentals. Aaron feels that Lilly has made a call on his soul; that he has refused it, and that Lilly has shut the door on him. Neither comes out well, and

Aaron dryly accepts the situation. The relation between man and man has proved no more satisfactory than that between man and woman.

If one had to interpret these Aaron-Lilly exchanges as a phase of Lawrence's own experience, it could only be as a dialogue of Lawrence with himself—a fairly honest if not a particularly edifying one. Lawrence hates the war, but, I am convinced, feels a deep inferiority for not having been in it. He feels both his position among men and his standing with women, his sexual authority, to be deeply impaired by his non-participation in the crucial experience of his time. The sense of failure with women is so strong that he is almost in a mood to reject them altogether. He wishes therefore to transfer some of his emotional energy into a relation with a man; but he is clear-sighted enough to see that this is unlikely to work, that men do not respond easily to such emotional demands. The real solution to all such inter-personal dilemmas is the singleness-in-relation that he has described so often. But this is something merely hoped for rather than securely possessed.

However, this interior dialogue is very successfully dramatised. Lilly and Aaron behave as subsistent personalities. The natural bond between them, their tentative yet abortive attempts at friend-ship, are admirably shown. These conversations also mark a significant stage in Aaron's progress. Lilly has begun to make him aware of himself. He has made him see his flute ('Aaron's rod') as a symbol of his creative life and as the means by which he can live freely and independently. And he leaves Aaron—one feels that he has not yet finished with him—with the ideal of independence, non-attachment.

The next chapter, the eleventh, turns back in order to clinch these lessons. Aaron goes back to his home and meets his wife again. She meets him first with bitter reproaches and then with a sexual and emotional appeal; but immediately the old question of dominance comes up. He has left and she wants him back, but he must submit to her before she will have him, he must admit how wrong and cruel he has been. As of course he has. But neither will give in.

> She was defeated. But she too would never yield. . . . Come life, come death, she too would never yield. And she realised now that he would never yield. . . . He too would never yield. The illusion of love was gone for ever. Love was a battle in which

each party strove for the mastery of the other's soul. So far, man had yielded the mastery to woman. Now he was fighting for it back again. And too late, for the woman would never yield.

(XI.)

So Aaron goes away again for good, and determined henceforth on single life, not double—"sheer, finished singleness".

The next seven chapters pursue the thread of Aaron's single life. They are, in fact, almost pure travel-diary, one of Lawrence's best. Aaron is endowed with all the experiences of Lawrence travelling down Italy in 1919. An intermittent effort is made to keep up the character, but for long periods it is forgotten. These things could have happened to Aaron; but Aaron, as he has been up to now, could never have seen them with this clear and critical eye; and Lawrence knows it and admits the imposture.

> In his own powerful but subconscious fashion Aaron realised this. . . . Don't grumble at me then, gentle reader, and swear at me that this damned fellow wasn't half clever enough to think all these smart things, and realise all these fine-drawn-out subtleties. You are quite right, he wasn't, yet it all resolved itself in him as I say, and it is for you to prove that it didn't.

(XIII.)

The dramatisation was complete in the Aaron-Lilly passages; now it breaks down, and about a third of the book consists of this incompletely assimilated episode. But how brilliant it is in itself. The account of the household of Sir William Franks, the sketches of Florentine society, are among Lawrence's most sparkling pieces of social comedy. And blowing through it all is the cold and windy exhilaration of being free of Europe again after the war. On the actual journey Lawrence was temporarily on his own, while Frieda was visiting relations in Germany; and this unaccustomed bachelordom seems to have contributed something towards the characterisation of Aaron—the contrast between curiosity, exploration, freedom and the constraint of the marriage that had been abandoned. In the main, however, observation is directed to the outward scene. Aaron exists, if we are to grant that he exists in these chapters at all, only as a spectator. He records, but does not change or enter into any real relation with anyone. His history as a developing and suffering being is resumed in Florence.

The chapter in which Aaron finally leaves his wife ends as follows:

> As for future unions, too soon to think about it. Let there be clean and pure division first, perfected singleness. That is the only way to final, living unison: through sheer, finished singleness.
>
> (XI.)

Singleness is not seen as an end, only as a means towards fuller relationship. And like most people who talk about the need for solitude, Aaron shows a remarkable facility for getting tied up with others. In Florence he meets an American woman married to an Italian Marchese. She has been a singer, but now suffers from some inhibition that has deprived her of her singing voice. Aaron's flute-playing releases her, and she is able to sing again to his accompaniment. He is attracted to her sexually and she to him, and they become lovers, in a strangely half-hearted fashion.

> "You don't want emotions? You don't want me to say things, do you?" he said.
> A faint ironic smile came on her face.
> "I know what all that is worth," she said, with a curious, calm equanimity. "No, I want none of that."
>
> (XVIII.)

At first this looks like a parody of Laurentian sexual theory, an assertion of the value of the 'dark' forces, divorced from all other emotions and sympathies. In fact, this episode is an excellent example of the way Lawrence can supply the corrective to his own eccentricities; for the relationship begun in this bleak, disengaged fashion comes to nothing. Aaron soon realises that the Marchesa is not for him: he is drawn to her, but only superficially; though he has left his wife Lottie for ever, he still feels married to her and to her alone. In fact, Aaron realises what anyone could have told him, that his marriage, however unsuccessful, simply because it has at one time involved his whole emotional nature, is more valid and living even in its decay than an attempt in Lilly's fashion at relationship without entanglement, sex without emotional surrender. So Aaron meets his second failure with a woman, and again goes away feeling at heart only resentment and dislike.

During this latter half of the book Aaron's flute has been assuming greater and greater importance, both material and symbolical. It is in the first place his means of livelihood. It is by his talents as a performer that Aaron earns his living and is free to wander round Italy, so that the flute is not only the symbol but the very instrument of his liberation. It was Lilly who pointed out its possibilities to him, told him that he could live by it—at worst he could put on a big black hat and play outside the cafés. It was Lilly who had called the flute Aaron's rod, and associated it with what he called his charm— that is to say, with Aaron's personal vital force. And sure enough, it was the flute that had enabled him to live, it was the flute that had gained him the interest and sympathy of the people he had met on his travels, it was the flute that had released the frost-bound Marchesa. So far it had led him progressively forward on his new life of adventure. But can it continue to do so, and where is it leading him?

After the breakdown of the affair with the Marchesa, Aaron feels stunned and withered. Lilly has turned up in Florence, but has not yet had much to say for himself. Now Aaron finds himself at a café with Lilly and two others. While they are there a bomb is thrown, there is a violent explosion, and in the resultant confusion Aaron's flute is irretrievably smashed. Aaron's rod, the budding symbol of his new life, is broken.

> "Throw it in the river, Aaron," said Lilly. "It's an end."
> Aaron nervelessly dropped the flute into the stream. . . . He was quite dumbfounded by the night's event: the loss of his flute. Here was a blow he had not expected. And the loss was for him symbolistic. It chimed with something in his soul: the bomb, the smashed flute, the end.
>
> (XX.)

When Aaron asks what he is to do now, Lilly replies dryly that he will have to live without a rod in the meantime. There are times when the creative, progressive force of life lapses. Then there is nothing to do but to endure.

At this point Lilly makes a decisive reappearance. Although he is the prophet of the book, he does not represent achieved and certain wisdom. His own way is unsettled, his marriage is uncertain. Yet he possesses and represents a certain force, a spring of vitality that is always flowing, that cannot be quenched. In the last chapter, rather deprecatingly called "Words", he transmits this *mana* to Aaron. This fact is more significant than what he says, though what he says is striking enough. He says that there are two life-modes, love and power. Aaron, like modern Western man in general, has tried to live by the love-mode alone, and he has exhausted its possibilities. Christendom has tried to live by the love-mode, and it has come to the end of it. No further progress is possible in that direction, we have reached breakdown and failure. If life is to continue, a shift must be made to the power-mode, the fact and the necessity of power must be accepted. A man must find his own power, and to find it he must first learn to submit to superior power when he meets it.

"And whom shall I submit to?" Aaron said.
"Your soul will tell you," replied the other.

With these words the book ends. It is a sketch—no, less than a sketch, a mere hint of a new philosophy, not yet an exposition of it. Lawrence is doing what he so often does, ending a book with the foretaste of what is to come. This emphasises the essential character of *Aaron's Rod*, which is that of an interim report. And because the question of power and its implications are only touched on here, we are absolved from discussing it further at the moment. Its fuller exposition is in the contemporaneous *Fantasia of the Unconscious*. When we come to consider it we shall have to recall, not only that Nietzsche had said something of the same sort before; that Yeats was saying it at about the same time as Lawrence; but that all the Fascists of Europe were to build on this philosophy a few years later. Our next task is to pursue the themes of power and leadership as they appear in the novels immediately succeeding *Aaron's Rod*.

VII. KANGAROO

Kangaroo, to a superficial glance, is even more desultory in plan and mixed in content than *Aaron's Rod*; so much so that recollection of it is likely to be of incoherence and artistic failure. On re-reading, the brilliance of much of the writing and the vitality of the separate elements almost overcomes all other impressions. And further reading shows an underlying unity of a kind not immediately obvious.

It was the most rapidly written of Lawrence's books and the most rapidly conceived. The Lawrences were little more than two months in Australia, between May and August 1922, and the novel was almost completed in five weeks of that time. So that much of the book is the swift, immediate travel-sketch in which Lawrence excels, with himself and Frieda firmly in the middle of the picture. But Lawrence's travels are guided by ideas as well as circumstances; and the movement of thought in *Kangaroo* continues and develops that which has been going on since *Women in Love*. *Cœlum non animum mutant*—and Lawrence is simply carrying to Australia questions that had long been fermenting in his mind. Marriage, that for a time had seemed a settled and established thing, now reveals unsuspected problems; and there is accordingly a good deal of straight autobiography about himself and Frieda. The marriage question is closely connected, as in *Aaron's Rod*, with the relation between man and man, a relation which takes on a decisively political complexion for the first time in Lawrence's work. This leads to a further development of the ideas about love and power outlined by Lilly at the end of *Aaron's Rod*. And this new concern with political ideas is embodied in a fable—a streak of pure fiction, with characters and incidents wholly invented, running through a book whose substance is mainly of another kind. In the middle a chapter called "The Nightmare" is introduced, autobiographical and almost wholly irrelevant to the progress of the narrative, describing Lawrence's experiences in war-time England.

An outline of the plot will be helpful. Richard Lovat Somers, a writer, and his wife Harriet come to visit Australia where they know no one. They make a casual neighbourly friendship with a typical Australian couple, Jack and Victoria Callcott. Jack wishes the friendship with Somers to be deeper and more binding, and Somers is inclined to resent and resist these demands. Jack is deeply concerned about the political future of Australia, and belongs to a quasi-fascist organisation of returned soldiers called the Diggers, who hope at some time of crisis to seize power. Jack is impressed with Somers' ideas and wants him to join them. He introduces him to their leader, a Sydney lawyer, Ben Cooley, who goes by the name of Kangaroo. Somers finds him fascinating and strangely compelling, but in spite of his sympathy he is unwilling to surrender his freedom to a movement or himself to Kangaroo. Harriet meanwhile is bitterly contemptuous of the whole business, and what Somers thinks of as playing a man's part in the world she thinks of as schoolboy nonsense. The struggle in Somers' mind whether to engage in political action or to preserve his independence continues. A further highly emotional appeal by Kangaroo to Somers is resisted; and having rejected Kangaroo, Somers begins to fear him. This reminds him of his old fear of being conscripted and dragged into the war, and he recalls the whole story. The break with Kangaroo is decisive, and when Jack meets Somers afterwards he accuses him bitterly of being a spy. Somers has also interested himself in the Labour point of view, and he goes to a meeting in Sydney at which Struthers the workers' leader makes a long socialist speech. The Diggers provoke a riot, and there is a violent scene, in which Kangaroo is shot. Later Somers sees Kangaroo on his deathbed, and Kangaroo appeals for Somers' love. Somers refuses and Kangaroo dies. All is over, and Somers and Harriet leave Australia.

Interwoven with the plot are sketches of Australian scenery and manners; long analyses of Somers' and Harriet's matrimonial state, of Somers' need to extend his life into the world of men and affairs; reflections on authority, revolution, politics generally. The themes are not dealt with separately—they are constantly interwoven, and directly autobiographical passages are mingled with pure fiction. The political events, for instance, correspond to no Australian actuality. On the face of it the material is even more heterogeneous than that of *Aaron's Rod*; as a narrative it is even more disjointed and interrupted. But the major structural faults of *Aaron's Rod* have in fact disappeared. Lawrence has realised the mistake, in a book of this kind, of crudely splitting the perceiving consciousness between two people, as he did between Lilly and Aaron; and of giving the central rôle to a relatively unselfconscious person. *Kangaroo* is plainly a record of Somers' experience; all is seen through his eyes; that Somers is Lawrence is not very important; that he is living his way through a complex of experiences, related because they are factors in his development, is everything. *Aaron's Rod* should have been organised on this plan, but the temptations of irrelevant social portraiture were too strong; Lilly is seen on his own, apart from Aaron's perception of him; and Aaron in other places sees more than, given his character, he could. *Kangaroo* avoids these faults by becoming more frankly a part of Lawrence's spiritual autobiography; not circumstantial biography, though there is some of that, but a faithful reflection of the actual development of his mind at this time. We begin to see what some of Lawrence's fulminations about form in the novel mean; form for him was just this—the following out of an authentic process of living growth. Let us look at the apparently scattered themes of *Kangaroo* from this point of view.

The political theme is decisively announced in the first chapter. Somers arrives in Australia because he thinks that Europe is finished. But he immediately begins to feel homesick. The shapeless, unfinished uniformity of Australian life makes him long for the lovely richness and variety of the old world. Yet he finds much to admire in Australia, and he begins to speculate on the difference. He finds it in the negation of authority in Australia, the real sense of democracy.

> Of course he was bound to admit that they ran their city very well, as far as he could see. Everything was very easy, and there was no fuss. Amazing how little fuss and bother there was—on the whole. Nobody seemed to bother, there seemed to be no policemen and no authority, the whole thing went by itself, loose and easy, without any bossing. No real authority—no superior classes—hardly even any boss. And everything rolling along as easily as a full river, to all appearances.
> That's where it was. Like a full river of life, made up of drops of water all alike. Europe is really established upon the aristocratic principle. Remove the sense of class distinction, of higher and lower, and you have anarchy in Europe. Only nihilists aim at the removal of all class distinction, in Europe.
> But in Australia, it seemed to Somers, the distinction was already gone. There was really no class distinction. There was a difference of money and of "smartness". But nobody felt *better* than anybody else, or higher; only better-off. And there is all the difference in the world between feeling *better* than your fellow-man, and merely feeling *better-off*.
>
> (I.)

And Somers hates it—"though he had no antecedents whatsoever, yet he felt himself to be one of the *responsible* members of society". For himself, as an Englishman, this distinction is radical.

> You may be the most liberal Liberal Englishman, and yet you cannot fail to see the categorical difference between the responsible and the irresponsible classes. You cannot fail to admit the necessity for *rule*. Either you admit yourself an anarchist, or you admit the necessity for *rule*—in England. The working classes in England feel just the same about it as do the upper classes. Any working man who sincerely feels himself a responsible member of society feels it his duty to exercise authority in some way or other. And

the irresponsible working man likes to feel there is a strong boss at the head, if only so that he can grumble at him satisfactorily. Europe is established on the instinct of authority: "Thou shalt." The only alternative is anarchy.

(I.)

A sure instinct impels Lawrence to announce this theme at the start, for all the diverse topics of what appears to be a casually constructed book are linked with these initial reflections. The question of dominance in marriage; the acknowledgment of innate superiority between man and man; the nature of this acknowledgment (is it a submission to love or to power?); the rights of the individual against authority; the Nightmare chapter—all spring from the same root. Even the enchanting descriptions of the Australian natural scene—in part an acknowledgment of the charms of a virgin country—is in part a recognition that it is not until the land has submitted to man's domination that it becomes spiritually assimilable.

The admirable second chapter, "Neighbours", places these half-formed speculations in the setting of daily living, feels them in the form of the everyday tensions between people. At the high tea, for example, where the Somers entertain their new-found neighbours the Callcotts, Somers feels that he is returning to the frontierless, relaxed intimacy of his working-class boyhood, and he resents it, for he has since learnt a more reserved, more self-contained manner of life which really suits him better. Jack Callcott, for his part, is a little resentful of Somers' distinction and wants to pry out its secret. But Victoria is wholly fascinated.

> Somers knew the attitude, and was not going to be drawn. He talked freely and pleasantly enough—but never as Jack wanted. He knew well enough what Jack wanted: which was that they should talk together as man to man—as pals, you know, with a little difference. But Somers would never be pals with any man. It wasn't in his nature. He talked pleasantly and familiarly —fascinating to Victoria, who sat with her brown eyes watching him, while she clung to Jack's arm on the sofa.

(II.)

The various shades of difference—social, national, intellectual and sexual—and the varying stresses they set up are excellently discriminated.

Somers soon discovers something else about Jack Callcott—his political earnestness. Beneath the Australian indifference is a real concern for the state of his country. When Jack demands his friend-ship and his help, Somers feels a challenge to that activity in the world of men which the isolated domesticity of a much-married writer has entirely denied him. It is in this context that the marriage question first makes its appearance. Harriet revolts against the talks with Callcott—"all this intimacy and neighbouring". To which Somers replies: "I've got to struggle with men and the world of men for a time yet. . . . As a man among men I just have no place." The subject crops up again continually throughout the book; it is probably the personal psychological root of most of the conflicts with which *Kangaroo* deals. It is brought most plainly into the foreground in Chapter IX, "Harriet and Lovat at sea in marriage". Here Somers shows himself possessed by the idea that perfect equal love is not an enduring condition, that sooner or later the question of dominance comes up. He believes, like many men, that a healthy marital relation depends on the acknowledgment of male dominance. Harriet, like many women, refuses to recognise this. She will not acknowledge Somers in this way. Lawrence does not sufficiently reflect that the male dominance that has to be asserted so explicitly is not worth very much; but he puts his finger on one significant point in the prob-lem (Somers' and, biographically speaking, his own) when he writes:

> How could one believe in such a man! If he had been naturally a master of men, general of an army, or manager of some great steel works, with thousands of men under him—then, yes, she could have acknowledged the master part of the bargain, if not the lord. . . . Whereas . . . he had absolutely nothing but her.
>
> (IX.)

Lawrence is discovering the Nemesis of his earlier preoccupation with marriage: by making marriage all-important you not only leave out a great deal of necessary experience, you endanger the security of marriage itself. Like most married people in moods of irritation, Somers and Harriet are over-dramatising their difficulties. Somers need not go so far as being a general; what he needs is a job that will take him out of the house from nine to five every day; no man can be a hero to a woman if he is perpetually under her feet. And Harriet might be less preoccupied with the deficiencies of her husband if her marriage had any biological significance, if she had, or were likely to have, any children to look after. These passages are an honest bit of discursive autobiography—and very fair, for Harriet's point of view gets as good a show as Lovat's; but they are something less than profound, and they present a private and professional rather than a universal dilemma.

It is characteristic of Lawrence that he refuses to suggest a solution in commonplace social terms, though in a marriage as fundamentally successful as Somers' and Harriet's (or Lawrence's and Frieda's) it was perhaps mainly some lesser adjustment of that kind that was required. To admit this, however, would enslave Somers-Lawrence, the artist, the free-lance, to the ordinary exigencies of society. For Lawrence the acknowledgment of mastership must be the result of a profound change within himself, of some ultimate, divinely inspired metanoia, not of any vulgar adaptation to the world of men. Somers unwillingly recognises this.

> He did not yet submit to the fact which he *half* knew: that before mankind would accept any man for a king, and before Harriet would ever accept him, Richard Lovat, as a lord and master, he, this self-same Richard who was so strong on king-ship, must open the doors of his soul and let in a dark Lord and Master for himself, the dark god he had sensed outside the door. Let him once truly submit to the dark majesty, break open his doors to this fearful god who is master, and enters us from below, the lower doors; let himself once admit a Master, the unspeakable god: and the rest would happen.
>
> (IX.)

So Somers in the end refuses all invitations to political or social action, and although the dark god is mentioned not infrequently in this book, we do not yet learn who he is or how he is invoked.

The practical problem, of course, is not the one that Lawrence is interested in solving. The domestic question of who wears the trousers is faintly absurd, as he acknowledges by his ruefully comic treatment of it. But Lawrence's concern with the question of leadership, of sacred priority, of innate differences of function and quality between individuals is wholly serious. It involves doubts not only about the equal-companionship theory of marriage, but doubts about the whole democratic idea. Somers does not want democracy, he wants some other kind of relationship.

But what? He did not know. Perhaps the thing that the dark races know: that one can still feel in India: the mystery of lordship. That which white men have struggled so long against, and which is the clue to the life of the Hindu. The mystery of lordship. The mystery of innate, natural, sacred priority. The other mystic relationship between men, which democracy and equality try to deny and obliterate. Not any arbitrary caste or birth aristocracy. But the mystic recognition of difference and innate priority, the joy of obedience and the sacred responsibility of authority.

(VI.)

A minor character, William James, quite early warns the Somers about Australian democracy, that it will drag them down. And when Jack tells Somers of the Diggers' clubs, with their fascist organisation and their overt acknowledgment of the principle of authority, Somers is fascinated apparently on those grounds alone. It never becomes clear what the Diggers would do with their power if they got it; the interest is simply in power and the sources of power. What does become clear is that power for Lawrence is something that embodies itself in individuals, in unequal degrees, and that its source is outside them, a dark god unacknowledged in the modern world. The problem is to find out where the dark god has incarnated himself. It is also the problem of much of Carlyle's political writing; and much of this book, like much of Carlyle, is occupied with saying, Not here, not here.

The authority of the Diggers is concentrated in their leader Kangaroo, and for a time it seems that he is an authentic source of power. When Somers meets him he is captivated by his conversation and his personal magnetism. We unfortunately are not, and the book begins to get into difficulties. Somers and Harriet are activated from within, from intimate inside knowledge; Jack and Victoria are lively character-drawings from the outside. Kangaroo is conceived in another way, and in spite of the considerable effort that is expended on describing his physical presence, he remains an unassimilated and only partly realised symbolical figure. But symbolical of what? Lawrence has something on his mind, but he does not succeed in communicating it clearly. Kangaroo is credited with "a wonderful Jehovah-like kindness", besides the subtlety that gives him his political strength. He wishes to rule, but to rule through love. He proposes a kind of authoritarian government, but it is that of "a quiet gentle father, who uses his authority in the name of living life, and who is absolutely stern against anti-life". He offers himself in this father rôle, and Somers is almost willing to accept him, for he likes the authority and is won by the charm; but to the reader Kangaroo remains strangely ambiguous, and there is a strong element of that curious homosexual feeling that Lawrence never seems to have recognised as such, which we have already noticed between Gerald and Birkin, Aaron and Lilly. Like Lilly, Kangaroo sometimes suggests a mother rather than a father figure:

> But he had such an innocent charm, an extraordinary winsomeness. . . . His presence was so warm. You felt you were cuddled cosily, like a child, on his breast, in the soft glow of his heart, and that your feet were nestling on his ample, beautiful "tummy".
>
> (VI.)

No doubt this is so mawkishly silly because Lawrence dare not contemplate the nature of the feeling he wants to convey; and no doubt the same lack of penetration accounts for the numerous false notes in Kangaroo's discourse.

In his first big speech he offers to fight the ant-hill of modern civilisation with the fire of his own love.

> I fight them with the warm heart. Deep calls to deep, and fire calls out fire. And for warmth, for the fire of sympathy, to burn out the ant-heap with the heat of fiery, living hearts: that is what I stand for.
>
> (VI.)

Later he makes another big speech about love.

> "Is there any other inspirational force than the force of love?" continued Kangaroo. "There is no other. Love makes the trees flower and shed their seed, love makes the animals mate and birds put on their best feathers and sing their best songs. And all that man has ever created on the face of the earth, or ever will create— if you will allow me the use of the word create, with regard to man's highest productive activities."
>
> (VII.)

It is all strongly reminiscent of Elmer Gantry, and it is not in the least surprising that Somers rejects such novelettish clap-trap. All that is surprising is that he (and Lawrence) should make such heavy weather of it, that on the evidence presented Kangaroo should be thought worth taking so seriously. Somers diffidently proposes his own dark god as the true source of power in the universe; Kangaroo, oozing love at every pore, rejects the forces of darkness; there is a struggle, and Somers remains unconvinced.

Lawrence is attempting something that does not come off; and to explain it we have to abandon his terms of reference and step outside the book altogether. Surely what Kangaroo represents is Christianity —not doctrinal or institutional Christianity, but the whole religious outlook that sees love as the motive power of the Universe. He is almost a symbol of the Saviour. The love that he recommends in his cheap journalese is a parody of *l'amor che move il sole e l'altre stelle*, and it is nothing less than this that Somers (and Lawrence) rejects. Kangaroo's faith is secularised and divorced from the normal symbolism of Christianity because Lawrence is not concerned to attack the Church or the doctrine of the Incarnation. Indeed, incarnation is a concept that is entirely consonant with Lawrence's cast of mind; but it is a different kind of god that he wishes to see taking man's nature upon him. Lawrence has to face two difficulties of presentation. The first is that he has no real alternative to propose. Dostoevsky's Grand Inquisitor turns to Satan from the impossibilities of Christ: Somers does not know where to turn from the demands of Kangaroo; his dark god is a *deus absconditus*. The second difficulty is that Lawrence has no adequate symbolism to hand, and in the atmosphere of rather easy-going everyday realism in which most of this book moves, it is practically impossible for him to devise one. Some of the conversations between Somers and Kangaroo are vaguely reminiscent of the Grand Inquisitor dialogue, which had always exercised a negative fascination on Lawrence, but the grotesque figure of Kangaroo himself is more like Chesterton's Man who was Thursday, to whom, I cannot help feeling, this part of Kangaroo owes something. The fact that Lawrence can fall back on these grotesque *espiègleries* shows that his imagination has not risen to the level of his task.

When Kangaroo pursues Somers with his love, the result within the naturalist framework of the book is an absurdity. But Kangaroo is supposed to be a sort of Hound of Heaven; and in the bizarre love-scene between him and Somers in Chapter XII Somers is making the great refusal—rejecting finally the love which his culture had for two thousand years regarded as the highest good. This explains the fantastically overstrained nature of the scene, regarded as an encounter between men; and even more clearly, it explains why Kangaroo, once rejected, becomes terrible, an object of fear. There is nothing in Kangaroo or his circumstances as a man to inspire this terror. But Somers has, in effect, just rejected what his whole civilisation has told him was the living God; and he is afraid because he may fall into his hands after all. But he withstands his fear and escapes. The refusal of the dying Kangaroo's appeal for love is an equally explicit rejection of the other appeal of Christianity—the pathos of the dying Saviour. Somers has already rejected love offered; he now refuses love asked for: he escapes to be with himself and a dark god whose nature he does not yet know.

Inadequate to their theme as these passages are, they still have great force. If we can abstract the essential situation from the unfortunate circumstantial detail with which it is surrounded, this force can more easily be felt. But many questions arise. Does Lawrence know what he is doing? Does he think that Kangaroo's inflated and sentimental cant is all that is to be said for Christian love? I think that Lawrence does know what he is doing, and that the obscure power that seems to emanate from Kangaroo, in spite of the inadequacy of its presentation, is a sign that Lawrence was well aware of the magnitude of what he was rejecting. Kangaroo is a token, a shorthand notation for a complex of ideas, by now wholly a familiar to Lawrence, clustering round the concept of love as the central power in the universe. He fails to make this token valid for his readers largely because of his habit of shoving his ideas into any local setting that happens to interest him at the moment, regardless of its congruence with what he wants to convey. Kangaroo as a colonial politician can just be believed; Kangaroo as an ideological focus for Somers' opposition can be understood: but he hardly manages to be both at once, and still less can he be an adequate mouthpiece of ideas as massive and as profound as those which he is supposed to stand for. The setting and circumstances are too local and peculiar to carry the weight that Lawrence wants to put on them. They would remain so even if Lawrence had what he has not—the Dostoevskian power of feeling the adversary's case as strongly as his own.

In the light of these scenes the rest of the book explains itself. If this love is to be rejected, the Australian matiness of Callcott and his friends is to be rejected too, in spite of its democratic charm—

because it denies the essential separateness and individuality of the human spirit. If Kangaroo's hierarchical and authoritarian love is to be rejected as a political force, with even stronger reason we must reject the snarling egalitarianism of Struthers the Labour leader, in spite of the justice of many of his complaints. And submission must be made to—what? To the sacredness of power, unequally distributed among men according to the degree in which the dark god dwells in them.

It is easy to regard Lawrence's dark god as a piece of portentous flummery: it is quite true that he is continually using, in key places, an idea that he himself does not understand; and those who are unwilling to accept his work as a genuine exploration must, I suppose, reject such vague concepts. The defence of Lawrence is that, indefinite as the concept may be, he is in process of defining it; and as a first step he distinguishes the kind of power he is disposed to worship from the wrong kind of power—mere mass bullying. This is the relevance of the Nightmare chapter, startlingly irrelevant as it seems.

It is ingeniously if awkwardly introduced. After Somers has rejected the alliance with Kangaroo and rejected his love, Kangaroo suddenly becomes horrible and fearful to him. "He stood up in a kind of horror, in front of the great, close-eyed horrible thing that was now Kangaroo. Yes, a thing, not a whole man. A great thing, a horror." He feels fear, and this casts his mind back to the other times he has felt fear: panic terror in Sicily, and more powerfully a fear of the mass spirit in England during the war. "But in England, during the later years of the war, a true and deadly fear of the criminal *living* spirit which arose in all the stay-at-home bullies who governed the country during those years. From 1916 to 1919 a wave of criminal lust rose and possessed England, there was a reign of terror, under a set of indecent bullies. . . ." What follows, in Somers' name, is an account of Lawrence's own war-time experiences. He was called up under conscription for various medical examinations and was suspected, foolishly enough, as a spy, because he insisted on living in a cottage on the Cornish coast and talking and acting with considerable indiscretion at a time when invasion was expected. There are people who admire this piece of writing. I can see no grounds for regarding it with admiration or even with respect. The horrors of war cannot be indicted by hysterical sulking and screaming. There is no moral basis for Somers' indignation. His objection is to the upsetting of his domestic privacy. He is not a pacifist or a conscientious objector—he simply wants to be medically rejected and to run home to his own wife and cottage. He will not make his protest on any grounds that are fit to be stated or fit to be heard, as Russell and the other objectors did. The Somers who insists on the virtues of authority and obedience is horrified at the mildest regimentations of barrack life, and pathologically horrified by medical examination.

> Yes, they were running him to earth. They had exposed all his nakedness to gibes. And they were pining, almost whimpering, to give the last grab at him, and haul him to earth, a victim. Finished!
>
> But not yet! Oh no, not yet. Not yet, not now, nor ever. Not while life was life, should they lay hold of him. Never again. Never would he be touched again. And because they had handled his private parts, and looked into them, their eyes should burst and their hands should wither and their hearts should rot. So he cursed them in his blood, with an unremitting curse, as he waited.
>
> (XII.)

The most curious feature of all this is that it is partly an intensified literary re-creation. Lawrence's actual letters of the war-time period are far less hysterical, far less full of egotistical self-pity, far more sane and balanced. The explanation, I think, is provided in *Kangaroo* itself. When Somers is present at the riot in the Labour meeting, he feels an impulse to join in the violence.

> He wanted to go back into the town, into the mêlée. . . . Why not die? Why stay outside the row? He had always been outside the world's affairs.
>
> (XVI.)

Lawrence is finding by now that he hates his own rôle in the war-time business. Objectively this was quite unnecessary, since he was far too ill ever to have been called up for military service. But he feels deeply shamed by his own non-participation, by the fact that he had neither joined in the sufferings of his fellows nor made an audible protest against them. This becomes clearer to him after it is all over; the hatred and disgust that fills the Nightmare chapter is self-hatred and self-disgust. Lawrence possessed many kinds of integrity, but the kind that would have enabled him to make his testimony against war he did not possess. His protest fails because it is impure.

This is a bad place in *Kangaroo*, otherwise one of the most genial and
least hate-ridden of Lawrence's books. But it does serve a purpose,
other than that of private psychological relief. The dark god who is
so darkly hailed as an alternative to Kangaroo's love could easily be
conceived as a god of mere force and cruelty. The Nightmare chapter
forbids us to do this. God is not love, but he is not tyranny either.
The god of power may be terrible, but he must also be a god of healing
and life-giving power. Lawrence is sometimes so near to nihilism and
devil-worship that his repudiation of it takes the form of a wild,
horrified revulsion in which all control is lost. But this is better than
no revulsion at all. The false dark god is repudiated, the true dark
god remains hidden; and we have still to wait for a further revelation
of his nature.

I have dwelt rather long on these sulphurous politico-theological
speculations, but by themselves they give a false impression of the
book. Large tracts of it are pitched in a much more comfortable key.
There are tolerant, appreciative sketches of Australian life and manner,
and of the Somers, easy-going old travellers, fitting themselves into
the picture. New scenes, new contacts, a sense of vagabond irresponsibility, always bring out Lawrence's most amiable qualities. Here he
was faced with a new continent, and, something he had never seen
before, a country largely untouched by man. He half fell in love with
it.

> By the stream the mimosa was all gold, great gold bushes full
> of spring fire rising over your head, and the scent of the Australian,
> spring, and the most ethereal of all golden bloom, the plumy,
> many-balled wattle, and the utter loneliness, the manlessness,
> the untouched blue sky overhead, the gaunt, lightless gum-trees
> rearing a little way off, and sound of strange birds, vivid ones of
> strange, brilliant birds that flit round. Save for that, and for some
> weird frog-like sound, indescribable, the age-unbroken silence of
> the Australian bush.
> But it is wonderful, out of the sombreness of gum-trees, that
> seem the same, hoary for ever, and that are said to begin to wither
> from the centre the moment they are mature—out of the hollow
> bush of gum-trees and silent heaths, all at once, in spring, the most
> delicate feathery yellow of plumes and plumes and plumes and
> trees and bushes of wattle, as if angels had flown right down out
> of the softest gold regions of heaven to settle here, in the Austra-
> lian bush. And the perfume in all the air that might be heaven,
> and the unutterable stillness, save for strange bright birds and

flocks of parrots, and the motionlessness, save for a stream and
butterflies and some small brown bees. Yet a stillness, and a
manlessness, and an elation, the bush flowering at the gates of
heaven.

(XVIII.)

At the end, Somers and Harriet forget the human entanglements
and, enchanted by this virgin beauty, almost want to stay. The
radiant, quivering sense of the life of nature, enfolding and flowing
through the life of man, pervades *Kangaroo* as it has not done any of
the novels since *The White Peacock.*

* * * * *

The only other major fruit of the Lawrences' Australian sojourn
is *The Boy in the Bush*; but as this is a re-writing of a novel by Martin
Skinner, it hardly belongs in the Lawrence canon. It is, however, an
admirable novel of action—the career of a young settler in West
Australia in the early part of the century. Lawrence is provided here
with a theme of vigorous physical adventure that lay quite outside
his own experience. He seems to find it thoroughly congenial, and
makes Jack, the boy in the bush, into an authentic Laurentian hero—
a more convincing one, indeed, than many of the others whose pursuit
of the instinctual forces is limited to marrying and talking. Lawrence's
gospel would often have been more acceptable if the range of physical
effort open to him had been greater. It is remarkable evidence, too,
of his sheer executive competence that he is able to put so much dash
and conviction into re-writing someone's else's story.

VIII. THE PLUMED SERPENT; THE WOMAN WHO RODE AWAY

It would be easy to make the mistake of referring the development
of Lawrence's ideas to his geographical migrations—to describe
Kangaroo as inspired by Australia, *The Plumed Serpent* by Mexico
and so forth. The fact is that it often works the other way. Lawrence
moves to a new country because he is developing new ideas, and needs
a landscape and a society to match them. Australia was only a temporary halting-place on the way to America, and *Kangaroo* is an
interim report, as *Aaron's Rod* had been. The American south-west,
where he was now bound, was a real destination. Lawrence went
there to find something; perhaps he even found it. It was at all events

only illness and the American immigration laws that drove him away again after three years.

The Lawrences left Australia, arrived in the United States in September 1922, and went straight to Taos, New Mexico. The total time spent there was not very long. Though Lawrence did not leave Taos finally till September 1925, his stay was broken by a return of nearly a year to Europe and several journeys to Old Mexico. The trip to Europe was a failure and was not important; the travel in Mexico was very important indeed. It was Mexico, Old and New, that dominated his imagination for the whole of these three years. It was a prolific three years, for it produced *The Plumed Serpent, St. Mawr, The Princess* and *The Woman Who Rode Away*, besides the travel book *Mornings in Mexico* and a few similar essays reprinted in *Phœnix*. Our present concern is with *The Plumed Serpent*; but it is not an easy book, and some of the best commentary on it is provided by the essays and travel sketches in which Lawrence records his American impressions directly. For a long time Lawrence had cherished the notion that the aboriginal inhabitants of America possessed some esoteric life-secret. A slight foretaste of this idea is found in the Natcha-Kee-Tawaras of *The Lost Girl*; and Lilly in *Aaron's Rod*, amid a good deal of ethnographical nonsense, looks to the Aztecs as exemplars.

> I would have loved the Aztecs and the Red Indians, I know they had the element of life that I am looking for. They had living pride. The American races—and the South Sea Islanders—the Marquesans, the Maori blood. That was the true blood. It wasn't frightened.
>
> (IX.)

The preliminary correspondence with Mabel Dodge Luhan, his New Mexican hostess, shows that Lawrence undertook the journey almost in the expectation of a revelation. One of the *Phœnix* essays, "America Look to Your Own", exhorts the Americans to return to what he regards as their own spiritual resources—meaning the continent itself, the Indians, the Aztecs, the Mayas, the Incas—instead of bowing down before the obsolete idols of Europe. The obvious pragmatic answer to this (and it was duly made) is that there is no continuity between American aboriginal culture and that of a nation of mixed European immigrants. Most of the early American culture has long been dead, and the culture of the United States, historically speaking, is simply a powerful offshoot of that of Europe. Of course Lawrence knows this as well as anyone, and he is not speaking historically.

> That which was abhorrent to the Pilgrim Fathers and to the Spaniards, that which was called the Devil, the black Demon of savage America, this great aboriginal spirit the Americans must recognise again, recognise and embrace. [39]

The Indians were devil-worshippers to the Pilgrim Fathers; but the Devil is simply all that the European cultural ideal represses and refuses to recognise. Lawrence, like Jung, now begins to believe that psychic health can only be restored by reincorporating into our life all this repressed and unrecognised experience. His advice to America is "turn to the unresolved, the rejected". Historically, the ancient cultures can be destroyed, and almost have been; psychically, that which they represent is a part of the universal human heritage, and is indestructible. The modern white inhabitant of the United States, as far as his conscious life is concerned, is farther away from his primeval roots than his European counterpart; but still, he lives in America, the vast lonely continent, still fundamentally untamed; and he can see in the Indian life of his own south-west a faint survival of the primitive spark. Above all, he can turn away, if he wants to, from the two thousand years of history that the European inevitably feels pressing around him. Lawrence finds himself in the paradoxical position of asserting that the white North American is farther from salvation than the European; but just because he is more bound by the conscious will, more tense, more brittle—he is potentially nearer to psychic revolution.

However, his first reaction to what he saw of American primitivism was largely negative. He is forced to laugh at the musical-comedy aspect of New Mexico—the artists, the writers, the rich intellectuals, the seedy intellectuals, all busy patronising the Indians and playing a self-conscious Wild West act. His first contact with the Aztec art of Old Mexico revealed only its hideousness and cruelty, and he took a poor view of Quetzalcoatl, later to become his culture-hero.

> These old civilisations down here, they never got any higher than Quetzalcoatl. And he's just a sort of feathered snake, who needed the smoke of a little heart's blood now and then, even he. [40]

Neither the old gods of Mexico nor the modern seekers after the primitive had much to say to Lawrence; what was a complete revelation to him was Indian religion and Indian tribal ritual.

> I think New Mexico was the greatest experience from the outside world that I have ever had. It certainly changed me for ever. Curious as it may sound, it was New Mexico that liberated me from the present era of civilisation, the great era of material and mechanical development.[41]

He describes the proud beauty of the landscape, so much more satisfying to him than any he had seen before. This was the first revelation. The second was that for the first time Lawrence experienced what to him was fundamental religion.

> And that was the second revelation out there. I had looked over all the world for something that would strike *me* as religious. The simple piety of some English people, the semi-pagan mystery of some Catholics in southern Italy, the intensity of some Bavarian peasants, the semi-ecstasy of Buddhists or Brahmins: all this had seemed religious all right, as far as the parties concerned were involved, but it didn't involve me. . . . I had no permanent feeling of religion till I came to New Mexico and penetrated into the old human race-experience there. It is curious that it should be in America, of all places, that a European should really experience religion, after touching the old Mediterranean and the East. It is curious that one should get a sense of living religion from the Red Indians, having failed to get it from Hindus or Sicilian Catholics or Cingalese.[42]

Lawrence makes all the necessary reservations—insists that he does not praise the modern Red Indian as he reveals himself in contact with white civilisation, insists that the modern man cannot go back; but it is still in the surviving Indian rituals that the core of religious experience, the bare recognition of the numinous, is revealed to him. The passage in which he recognises this is a particularly fine one. He is listening to an old Indian ceremonially reciting some piece of tribal lore.

> The voice out of the far-off time was not for my ears. Its language was unknown to me. And I did not wish to know. It was enough to hear the sound issuing plangent from the bristling darkness of the far past, to see the bronze mask of the face lifted, the white, small close-packed teeth showing all the time. It was not for me, and I knew it. Nor had I any curiosity to understand. The soul is as old as the oldest day, and has its own hushed

echoes, its own far-off tribal understandings sunk and incorporated. We do not need to live the past over again. Our darkest tissues are twisted in this old tribal experience, our warmest blood came out of the old tribal fire. And they vibrate still in answer, our blood, our tissue. But me, the conscious me, I have gone a long road since then. And as I look back, like memory terrible as bloodshed, the dark faces round the fire in the night, and one blood beating in me and them. But I don't want to go back to them, ah, never. I never want to deny them or break with them. But there is no going back. Always onward, still further. The great devious onward-flowing stream of conscious human blood. From them to me, and from me on.

I don't want to live again the tribal mysteries my blood has lived long since. I don't want to know as I have known, in the tribal exclusiveness. But every drop of me trembles still alive to the old sound, every thread in my body quivers to the frenzy of the old mystery. I know my derivation. I was born of no virgin, of no Holy Ghost. Ah, no, these old men telling the tribal tale were my fathers. I have a dark-faced, bronze-voiced father far back in the resinous ages. My mother was no virgin. She lay in her hour with this dusky-lipped tribe-father. And I have not forgotten him. But he, like many an old father with a changeling son, he would like to deny me. But I stand on the far edge of their firelight, and am neither denied nor accepted. My way is my own, old red father; I can't cluster at the drum any more.[43]

There is not much callow primitivism here, and Lawrence seems in no danger of a mere return to the tribe. But it is just because he is aware of this danger that he subjects the religious intuition actually received in Taos to a complete transmutation in *The Plumed Serpent*. New Mexico was too cluttered up with personal *Schwärmerei* and the wrong kind of sensation-seeking. Ample confirmation of this can be found in Mabel Dodge Luhan's *Lorenzo in Taos*. So Lawrence transfers the whole experience that had moved him so profoundly to Old Mexico, where in fact he had periodically been obliged to flee, for a rest and to be alone. And at bottom he always knew that the pueblo Indians were merely the efficient cause of an experience in himself that is not essentially tied to any particular place or culture. He lost a good deal by the transference. The beautiful immediacy of the New Mexico sketches is gone. He has to place his actual religious experience in a partly excogitated setting, to present it as a revival of a defunct Aztec religion whose pantheon is not particularly sympathetic to him and whose ritual he has to invent. But this is necessary. He is trying to deal with what was perhaps the central revelation of his life, and in the first place he has to remove it from unpropitious surroundings. Even more pressing is the need to match the intensity of the impression received by an imaginative intensity of his own that will lift the whole thing above the level of mere playboy anthropology.

In *The Plumed Serpent* the relaxed structure of *Kangaroo* is considerably tightened up. Like all Lawrence's later books, it moves on two different levels, but the transition from reporting to prophecy, whatever the quality of the prophecy, is no longer an uneasy switch—it is a real progress, accountable and accounted for within the narrative framework. It is no longer necessary to look for explanations outside the book itself, in Lawrence's immediate biography or the development of his ideas; and all that has just been said about his reactions to primitive America is a useful preliminary, but no more. He does not want his new religion to be a regression to witch-doctoring, and the quality he wants in it is not primitive in the straightforward anthropological sense. He wants to re-animate the wisdom, not of ancient barbarism but of ancient civilisation, a wisdom that he believed really to have existed and to have almost vanished from the world. Later he was to believe that he had found it among the Etruscans. At this time he places it among the Aztecs—partly because they were the vanished civilisation that was nearest to hand, and partly because they were a vanished *civilisation*, not an awkwardly present and partly corrupted primitive society.

The Plumed Serpent, then, is a return to full-scale creation after the rather diffuse and desultory writing of *Aaron's Rod* and *Kangaroo*. It does, in fact, take up the story of the Lawrences' travels where *Kangaroo* left them, but Lawrence himself has disappeared. The central character is a woman, Kate, who bears a considerable resemblance to Frieda; and fragments of Lawrence are distributed between the two men Ramon and Cipriano. But he has now got away from the unsatisfactory habit of placing a slab of only partly digested autobiography in the centre of the picture. He is now planning and creating, and is less inclined merely to record what happens to be going on at the moment. In other ways the book takes up the theme of *Kangaroo*. The power of Kangaroo the man was ultimately the gift of the dark god, and half-way through the book Lawrence began to realise that his quest was not a social or political but a religious one.

The Plumed Serpent is an attempt to realise more fully the nature of the religion that he is looking for.

Of course he has already made tentative attempts at the same thing. There is a sketch of a "religion of the flesh" in the foreword to *Sons and Lovers*. This has now been lost sight of, or abandoned, I believe for two reasons. First, it provides no social bond except that between man and wife; and secondly, Lawrence has realised that marriage is not everything—a man must have a place in the world of men. He is moving away from his more obviously personal problems and has now a much completer experience to express. The abandonment of Christianity and the rejection of love as an all-sufficing motive in *Women in Love* and *Kangaroo* also look like attempts at defining a religious position. It is now time to make a new attempt at positive construction.

The opening chapters of *The Plumed Serpent* are excellent travel sketches in the familiar manner. Kate, a widow in early middle age, is in Mexico City as a tourist with two young Americans. (These two fairy-like creatures are a good companion-piece to the two young Englishmen of similar complexion in *Aaron's Rod*.) They all go to a bull-fight, and Kate hates it—both the squalid cruelty of the event and the squalid sadism of the spectators who enjoy it. She makes her way out, and is caught in a violent rainstorm at the gateway of the enclosure. She is rescued from the storm and the crowd by an unknown Mexican officer who has excellent manners and turns out to have been educated in England. He is General Viedma, known as Don Cipriano. This chapter, besides being a brilliant piece of reporting, has two purposes —first to show the corrupt degradation of modern Mexico City, and then to establish the character of Kate. She is rich, human and generous, in contrast to the two washed-out American *voyeurs*; she is sane, kindly and normal, in a familiar English sense (Lawrence can't bear actually to make her English, so he makes her an Irish-woman) ; she is not an amateur of blood, violence and darkness.

> She was more afraid of the repulsiveness than of anything. She had been in many cities of the world, but Mexico had an under-lying ugliness, a sort of squalid evil, which made Naples seem debonair in comparison. She was afraid, she dreaded that anything might really touch her in this town, and give her the contagion of its crawling sort of evil.

(I.)

A tea-party in one of the suburbs follows. Here the documentary interest gets a little out of hand, but the chapter does serve to establish more firmly the Mexican scene and modern American attitudes towards it. (Throughout *The Plumed Serpent* modern America stands for the civilisation of money and mechanism.) At this tea-party Kate meets Don Cipriano again, with his friend Don Ramón. A dinner-party later gives her more opportunity of observing them—Cipriano small, dapper and Indian; Don Ramón large, handsome and Spanish. She is impressed by a sort of sombre vitality in them. She reads in a newspaper of a reported return of the ancient gods of Mexico in Sayula, a lakeside village in Jalisco. She hears that Don Ramón has an estate near by, and when her American companions have to leave she determines to go there.

So far her reaction to Mexico has been chiefly one of repulsion, mixed with fascination, it is true; and the fascination is increased by her interest in Cipriano and Ramón. She goes up to the lake—the journey is beautifully described—and as she goes by boat from the rail-head to Sayula a man bathing in the river announces himself as one of Quetzalcoatl's men, and demands her tribute to the ancient gods. She is enchanted by the beauty of the country, but horrified by the stories of cruelty; of hideous and brutal murders that have been committed near by. The narrative transitions here are handled far more skilfully than in *Aaron's Rod* or *Kangaroo*. The men of Quetzalcoatl, the mystic leitmotiv of the book, appear natural in their setting, and the passage from modern Mexico City, with its trams, tourists and hotels, to the mysterious hinterland is effected without incongruity or disconcerting change of level. Kate's oscillations between acceptance and rejection of Mexico set the pattern for the whole book. She hates the horrors and the darkness, but she hates what she calls the "mechanical cog-wheel people" of the civilised Western world, too.

> Give me the mystery and let the world live again for me! Kate cried to her own soul. And deliver me from man's automatism.
>
> (VI.)

It is characteristic that the mystery is unapprehended, and that Kate is driven back and forth between two repulsions rather than drawn by contrary attractions.

Don Ramón, it appears, is the hierophant of the revived Quetzalcoatl mysteries, and Cipriano is his devoted disciple. Kate finds a
small house in Sayula, and as soon as she arrives she has her first
sight of the new-old religion in action. (In this brief tracing of the
central thread of the book I am omitting much splendid and easy
description of places and people, as rich and full here as anywhere in
Lawrence.) She goes to the plaza with her maid Juana and sees first
the local elegance—youths in white flannel trousers, girls in organdie
frocks. But gradually they give way before the swelling crowd of
peons. The modern dance music stops and the sound of a drum is
heard. Kate joins the crowd of men round the drummer. They hand
her a sort of broadsheet from which they are singing a hymn. It is a
hymn in which Quetzalcoatl announces that Jesus is going home,
that he is going to take the place of Jesus in Mexico. Kate is profoundly affected by the ceremony and the music.

> There was no recognisable rhythm, no recognisable emotion,
> it was hardly music. Rather a far-off, perfect crying in the night.
> But it went straight through to the soul, the most ancient and
> everlasting soul of all men, where alone can the human family
> assemble in immediate contact.
> Kate knew it at once, like a sort of fate. It was no good resisting.
> There was neither urge nor effort, nor any speciality. The sound
> sounded in the far-off innermost place of the human core, the ever-
> present, where there is neither hope nor emotion, but passion sits
> with folded wings on the nest, and faith is a tree of shadow.
>
> (VII.)

Kate meets Doña Carlota, Don Ramón's wife, and learns that she
is a Catholic, *exaltée*, and immersed in charitable works. She worships
her husband, and loves Don Cipriano too, but is horrified at their
wrongness, at their insane and wicked attempt to restore the old gods.
Doña Carlota is a person in her own right; she is skilfully and not
unsympathetically drawn; but her main function in the economy of
the book is to define Don Ramón's faith by showing it in contrast with
Christianity. She is a less grotesque embodiment of the Christian
spirit than Kangaroo; and quite appropriately she attributes Ramón's
perversity to pride.

> He says he wants to make a new connection between the people
> and God. He says himself, God is always God. But man loses his
> connection with God. And then he can never recover it again,

unless some new Saviour comes to give him his new connection.
And every new connection is different from the last, though God
is always God. And now, Ramón says, the people have lost God.
And the Saviour cannot lead them to Him any more. There must
be a new Saviour with a new vision. But ah, Señora, that is not
true for me. God is love, and if Ramón would only submit to love,
he would know that he had found God. But he is perverse. Ah,
if we could be together, quietly loving and enjoying the beautiful
world, and *waiting in the love of God.*

(X.)

There was a gap of nearly eighteen months after the composition of
this part of the book. The next movement begins with Chapter XI,
and the next three chapters, largely devoted to more Quetzalcoatl
ritual and yoga, are virtually the beginning of a new plot. We should
at this point be learning more about the new religion, but it must be
admitted that illumination eludes us. A sort of physico-mystical
brotherhood and a dim chthonic piety are all that emerge from the
account of these religious exercises. All, that is to say, except an
uncomfortable feeling of inflation and pretence. It is notable that here
we desert Kate's consciousness for the first time, and observe the
actions of Ramón and his companions directly, without her mediation.
It is here that the sense of dissatisfaction begins. Everything seen
through the eyes of Kate is adequate and realised. It is seen through
a sympathetic but critical consciousness whose kind of vision we have
already been brought to understand. Ramón's ritual junketings attain
reality just so far as they are a part of Kate's experience. Presented on
their own they inspire neither acceptance nor revulsion; they merely fail
to suspend our disbelief. The charge of inflation and pretence is made by
Kate herself: "Everything is a sort of game, a put-up job, to you Mexicans. You don't really believe in anything." Yet in all the conversations
between her and Cipriano, between her and Ramón, belief and vitality
return. Between Kate, with her common-sense scepticism on the one
hand, her discontent with the empty husks of Western civilisation
on the other; Ramón with his hope that a new reality can be created
by acting as though it were there; and Cipriano with his profound
instinct for discipleship—between these three there really does emerge
the sense of struggle for a new apprehension of life. Lawrence may
be attempting prophecy rather than novel-writing, but he remains
a better novelist than prophet. It is only as it is embodied in the clash

of wills and temperaments that the new outlines of the new apprehension become clear.

Kate is partly attracted and partly repelled by this extraordinary movement in which she has become involved. Cipriano wants to marry her, but although she is drawn to him she feels his foreignness, the lack of ordinary human contact between them. Her friendship with Ramón deepens, and she even enters into a sort of alliance with him. The Quetzalcoatl movement grows; and so, in the meantime, does the opposition to it. Ramón has to contend with the hostility of the Church, and at home with the deepening hostility of Doña Carlota and his two sons. Ramón's relation to his message remains ambiguous. "Quetzalcoatl is just a living word to these people, no more," he says. "All I want them to do is to find the beginnings of the way to their own manhood, their own womanhood." Yet his ritual personifies Quetzalcoatl as a living, outward power. He and Cipriano go to see the bishop in Mexico City, and the bishop talks to them of the Catholic Church. To which Ramón replies:

"Then why not let it be really catholic? Why call it catholic, when it is only not just one among many churches, but is even hostile to all the rest of the churches? Father, why not let the Catholic Church become really the universal Church?"

"It is the Universal Church of Christ, my son."

"Why not let it be the Universal Church of Mohammet as well; since ultimately, God is One God, but the peoples speak varying languages, and each needs its own prophet to speak with its own tongue. The Universal Church of Christ, and Mohammet, and Buddha, and Quetzalcoatl, and all the others—*that* would be a Catholic Church, Father."

"You speak of things beyond me," said the Bishop, turning his ring.

"Not beyond any man," said Don Ramón. "A Catholic Church is a church for all the religious, a home on earth for all the prophets and the Christs. A big tree under which every man who acknowledges the greater life of the soul can sit and be refreshed. Isn't *that* the Catholic Church, Father?"

"Alas, my son, I know the Apostolic Church of Christ in Rome, of which I am a humble servant. I do not understand these clever things you are saying to me."

"I am asking you for peace, Father. I am not one who hates the Church of Christ, the *Roman* Catholic Church. But in Mexico I think it has no place."

(XVII.)

And he announces that he is going to remove the holy images from the church at Sayula and with reverence burn them upon the lake. Then he will set about building the church of Quetzalcoatl in Mexico.

A poignant little conversation between Don Ramón and his sons does rather more to clear up the nature of this religious eclecticism.

"They say also that you pretend to be the Aztec god Quetzalcoatl."

"Not at all. I only pretend that the Atzec god Quetzalcoatl is coming back to the Mexicans."

"But, papa, it is not true."

"How do you know?"

"Because it is impossible."

"Why?"

"There never was any Quetzalcoatl, except idols."

"Is there any Jesus, except images?"

"Yes, papa."

"Where?"

"In heaven."

"Then in heaven there is also Quetzalcoatl. And what is in heaven is capable of coming back to earth."

(XVIII.)

All the gods, in fact, are in heaven, and each in his due time may reign on earth. Quetzalcoatl, whose return is now due, stands among other things for the restoration of sensuality to its place in the divine. As Ramón says to Kate, slipping into the old Laurentian dialect: "I am a man who yearns for the sensual fulfilment of my soul. I am a man who has no belief in abnegation of the blood desires." All the accounts of Quetzalcoatl rituals up to now have emphasised the impression of intense, controlled physical vitality. The reign of Jesus, which is now coming to an end, was an attempted reign of spirituality which has failed. It comes to an end in Sayula when Don Ramón carries out his threat to the bishop, and the holy images are ceremonially carried out of the church, and the farewell hymn of Jesus to the people is sung.

Jesus, the Son of God, bids you farewell.
Mary, the Mother of God, bids you farewell.
For the last time they bless you, as they leave you.
Answer *Adios*!
Say *Adios*! my children.

(XVIII.)

The images—the dead Christ, the Scourged Christ, the Sacred Heart, Jesus of Nazareth with outstretched hands, the Blessed Virgin with blue mantle and lace and a golden crown, Saint Anthony of Padua, Saint Francis, Saint Joaquin and the rest—are placed on a large black *canoa*, rowed slowly out to an island in the lake, and then, amid a mixture of fear, agony and longing, are solemnly burnt. "Sayula was empty of God, and, at heart, they were glad."

The Plumed Serpent is a book that has no one centre; its movement is an alternate backward and forward one, and it clusters round a number of nodal points. This scene (the chapter is called "Auto da Fé") is one of them. Imaginatively it is one of the most powerful. The impulse behind the book is to ritualise, to express in outward form and action what so far has been largely expressed in argument by characters like Birkin, Lilly and Somers. When this fails, as it does in most of the Quetzalcoatl rituals, the effect is of windy bathos. Here there is considerable success. Ramón is committing what is, on the one hand, an act of deliberate sacrilege, on the other hand, and in his eyes, an act of liberation. The inevitable accompaniments are pathos, agony and terror. Iconoclasm is a solemn matter when the icons typify something real. In *The Plumed Serpent* they do. To Ramón, Quetzalcoatl and Jesus are realities of the same kind, they are both real principles, and the conflict between them is a real conflict.

An attack on Don Ramón's house follows the *auto da fé*. It is an attempt by the Church party to murder Ramón; and Kate is involved in it and saves Ramón's life. The whole episode is presented with vivid and brutal realism. Its effects are ambiguous. In a sense it binds Kate more closely to Ramón; but it also produces a revulsion in her against all this violent physical horror.

From then on the book goes to pieces, with a partial recovery towards the end. Or rather, it does not go to pieces as far as the outward narrative structure is concerned—it preserves a mere narrative integrity, but fails in imaginative conviction. More and more we desert Kate's vision and see the activities of Ramón and Cipriano on their own. The novelist's method is abandoned for that of the amateur mystagogue, and the result is the windy emptiness of the Quetzalcoatl hymns and the dressed-up absurdity of what even the protagonists know to be a kind of charade. This excogitated ceremonial diverges farther and farther from congruity with the Mexican setting that has already been so brilliantly established, and from anything that Kate could reasonably be expected to participate in. Yet she does participate ; in spite of continual movements of revolt she becomes more and more involved in the Aztec revival, even to the point of assuming a place in its pantheon. It is here that the cohesion of the work is destroyed. Kate as an interested observer of the Quetzalcoatl movement is probable and consistent. Kate as an active participant is simply not the same figure as we have learnt to know in the earlier part of the book. Yet all is not lost. What remains consistent is her developing relation with Cipriano and Ramón ; she often revolts against it, yet it continually strengthens. And in the end, though there has been a breakdown in the means by which we are brought to our destination, we are brought to it, and we can see that some dumb, inexpressible, more-than-personal bond has been established between Ramón and his wife, Cipriano and Kate, that makes her unwilling to leave.

The narrative continues as follows. After the attack on the homestead Kate is numbed and bewildered. She learns that Ramón is the living representative of Quetzalcoatl, and that Cipriano is to become the living representative of Huitzilopochtli, god of death and destruction. Cipriano assumes, rather than asks, that Kate will become his bride. With a strange passivity she submits, and Ramón conducts a mystic marriage ceremony between them, described with a good deal of sartorial and cosmetic detail. Ramón's allocution on the occasion harks back to the old religion of marriage outlined by Birkin in *Women in Love*. Yet Kate and Cipriano are married "in the world of Quetzalcoatl" only ; they are not yet man and wife in the ordinary sense.

It is now time that the empty church shall be filled with the new gods, and Ramón formally enacts the coming of Quetzalcoatl. In the midst of the ceremony, Carlota interrupts, in an ecstasy of horror, and prays that the blasphemies shall be stopped and that Ramón may die while it is still possible to save his soul. The intention of this, I think, is clear. It is to indicate the scale of Ramón's revolution by confronting him directly with his opposite, Carlota, the representative of Christian love. It might indeed, with better writing, have succeeded in turning dressing-up and play-acting into genuine blasphemy—something significant if only negatively. In fact, the result is bathos.

Ramón looked back at Carlota, across a changeless distance. Not a muscle of his face moved. And Kate could see that his heart had died in its connection with Carlota, his heart was quite, quite dead in him; out of the deathly vacancy he watched his wife. Only his brows frowned a little from his smooth, male forehead. His old connections were broken. She could hear him say: *There is no star between me and Carlota.*—And how terribly true it was!

(XXI.)

But it is Carlota who dies, and at this point the old sexual obsessions return. What is being defeated in Carlota is partly indeed Christianity, but partly the "white" woman who has given to her husband charity and devotion, but never herself.

The next chapter prepares for a similar theophany of Huitzilopochtli. Cipriano appears as a commanding officer, a sort of *petit caporal*, going round sternly yet genially among his troops. He has reached the not very original conclusion that "discipline is what Mexico needs, and what the whole world needs". He now wants Kate to assume a formal place in the Mexican pantheon, to become the goddess Malintzi, wife of Huitzilopochtli. But she is disgusted, and in one of those blinding moments of common sense in which Lawrence intermittently criticises his own conceptions, she says so.

"Oh!" she cried to herself, stifling. "For heaven's sake let me get out of this, and back to simple human people. I loathe the very sound of Quetzalcoatl and Huitzilopochtli. I would die rather than be mixed up in it any more. Horrible, really, both Ramón and Cipriano. And they want to put it over me, with their high-flown bunk, and their Malintzi. Malintzi! I am Kate Forrester, really. . . . I was born Kate Forrester, and I shall die Kate Forrester. I want to go home."

(XXII.)

The ceremony to celebrate the coming of Huitzilopochtli is followed by the execution of the "traitors" who had led the attack on Ramón. Two of them are strangled and three are stabbed by Cipriano publicly, in the presence of the army and the people, and of Kate herself. The word used in the text is execution; but the spirit of the scene is that of ritual human sacrifice. The accompanying Huitzilopochtli hymns celebrate his ruthless destructive power. Lawrence, having rejected love, is evidently anxious to make his Aztec revival whole-hearted, and to accept the horrors as well as the exaltations of the old religion.

But there is a lurking and horrible impurity in these scenes. No doubt the leader of a Mexican pronunciamento may be expected to shed blood without much compunction; and no doubt if he sees himself as the representative of a revived Aztec god he may be expected to ritualise it. What we feel here is the covert complicity of the author— a cold enjoyment of what has been coldly done. Cipriano concludes the ceremony with these words:

> The dead are on their way. Quetzalcoatl helps them on the longest journey.—But the grey dogs sleep within the quick-lime, in the slow corpse-fire.—It is finished.
>
> (XXIII.)

The solemn banality of the language asks us to celebrate the virtues of the, hangman and the concentration-camp guard. The penalty is paid by the degradation of the character of Kate—evident, inconsistent, yet unrecognised by Lawrence as a degradation. Kate, who was disgusted, horrified to the roots of her being by the bull-fight, is merely made "gloomy and uneasy", "shocked and depressed" by the killings she has witnessed. She begins to see them as part of the will of God.

> The Will of God! She began to understand that once fearsome phrase. At the centre of all things, a dark, momentous Will sending out its terrific rays and vibrations, like some vast octopus. And at the other end of the vibration, men, created men, erect in the dark potency, answering Will with will, like gods or demons.
>
> (XXIV.)

She begins to see herself as the complement to this quality in Cipriano, and when he asks her to come to the church with him and become Malintzi, she does so. She goes to the church, puts on the ceremonial robes, sits in the throne of the goddess; and Cipriano possesses her, presumably on the church floor. Afterwards she reflects on the situation.

> So when she thought of him and his soldiers, tales of swift cruelty she had heard of him: when she remembered his stabbing the three helpless peons, she thought: Why should I judge him? He is of the gods. . . . What do I care if he kills people? His flame is young and clean. He is Huitzilopochtli, and I am Malintzi. What do I care, what Cipriano Viedma does or doesn't do? Or even what Kate Leslie does or doesn't do!
>
> (XXIV.)

This is the nadir of the book; and it might well end there—with the unintended confession that the new religion leads only to death and to a sadistic sexuality without human contact or a human setting. But this is not really what Lawrence set out to say, or not all that he set out to say. So this long interlude of mumbo-jumbo and perversion and cruelty is followed by a return to the original plot, concerned with Mexico, with relations between people, conceived in the novelist's terms. A couple of months later Ramón surprises Kate by marrying again. The bride is Teresa, a young Spanish woman of good family, who has been oppressed and insulted by two brutish brothers. She worships Ramón, because he has restored her self-respect, her belief in herself as a woman. At first Kate, all her submission to Huitzilopochtli forgotten (forgotten by Lawrence, I mean), is inclined to be contemptuous of her submissive adoration. She takes the expected line of the independent Western woman, and the continuity of her character, hopelessly disintegrated during the preceding Aztec episodes, is resumed. Next, however, she notices the reserves of power in Teresa. Ramón is harassed and exhausted by his public concerns, and Teresa thinks only of serving him. Kate accuses her of sacrificing herself to Ramón.

"Oh, no!" replied Teresa quickly, and a little flush burned in her cheek, and her dark eyes flashed. "I am not sacrificing myself to Ramón. If I can give him—sleep—when he needs it—that is not sacrifice. It is——" She did not finish, but her eyes flashed and the flush burned darker.

"It is love, I know," said Kate. "But it exhausts you too."

"It is not simply love," flashed Teresa proudly. "I might have loved more than one man: many men are lovable. But Ramón!— My soul is with Ramón."—The tears rose to her eyes. "I do not want to talk about it," she said, rising. "But you must not touch me there, and judge me."

She hurried out of the room, leaving Kate somewhat dismayed. Kate sighed, thinking of going home.

(XXV.)

Kate tries to persuade Teresa of the doctrine of "living her own life", but Teresa rejects it.

"No, thank God! I have not got a life of my own! I have been able to give it to a man who is more than a man, as they say in their Quetzalcoatl language. And now it needn't die inside me, like a bird in a cage.—Oh, yes, Señora! If he goes to Sinaloa and the west coast, my soul goes with him and takes part in it all. It does not let him go alone. And he does not forget that he has my soul with him. I know it.—No, Señora! You must not criticise me or pity me."

(XXV.)

And Kate, who is accustomed to looking on other women as her inferiors, wonders whether Teresa is not a greater woman than she. Both her Western self-assertion and her aristocratic pride are insulted. She feels that all the time Mexico is making the assertion— "Blood is one blood. We are all of one blood-stream. In the blood you and I are undifferentiated." And she wants to escape to Europe, to the land of self-possessed individualism. And yet when Cipriano again asks her to marry him in civil marriage, she consents, and goes to live with him in Sayula. With a half-unwilling mind, she finds a curious passivity and rest.

> The strange, heavy, *positive* passivity. For the first time in her life she felt absolutely at rest. And talk, and thought, had become trivial, superficial to her: as the ripples on the surface of the lake are as nothing, to the creatures that live away below in the unwavering deeps. . . .
> The universe had opened out to her new and vast, and she had sunk to the deep bed of pure rest. She had become almost like Teresa in sureness.

(XXVI.)

She even ceases to care for sexual satisfaction, she forgoes the orgasm in their love-making. She feels absolutely bound to Cipriano, yet in a sense she hardly knows him.

> There was hardly anything to say to him. And there was no personal intimacy. He kept his privacy round him like a cloak, and left her immune within her own privacy.

(XXVI.)

Yet she still wants to go away, to go back to Europe, at least for a time. Ramón says they need her, that she belongs with them.

> It was as if she had two selves: one, a new one, which belonged to Cipriano and to Ramón, and which was her sensitive, desirous self: the other hard and finished, accomplished, belonging to her mother, her children, England, her whole past. This old accomplished self was curiously invulnerable and insentient, curiously hard and "free". In it, she was an individual and her own mistress. The other self was vulnerable, and organically connected with

Cipriano, even with Ramón and Teresa, and so was not "free"
at all.   (XXVII.)

She sees the poinsettias, which in Mexico are Christmas flowers,
and longs to see the mistletoe among the oranges in a fruiterer's
shop in Hampstead, buses rolling on the mud in Piccadilly on Christmas
Eve. The immediacy and truth of this passage is striking after the
cruel inflated falsities of Huitzilopochtli in Sayula church. And just
as Kate has returned to the character we knew in the earlier part of
the book, so Cipriano has become himself again, sensitive, alive,
enigmatic, having nothing in common with a bogus Aztec death-god.
Kate sits with Ramón, Teresa and Cipriano, looking at the rich earthy
beauty of the Mexican scene, but still thinking of England. Then she
thinks of the empty lives, the withered grimalkin quality of the
independent middle-aged women she knows at home; and thinks her
ego and her individuality not worth the price of becoming like them.

> "Why should I go away!" said Kate. "Why should I see the
> 'buses on the mud of Piccadilly, on Christmas Eve, and the crowds
> of people on the wet pavements, under the big shops like great
> caves of light? I may as well stay here, where my soul is less
> dreary. . . ."
> Already she could see the yellow and reddish, tower-like upper
> story of Jamiltepec, and the rich, deep fall of magenta bougain-
> villea, from the high wall, with the pale spraying of plumbago
> flowers, and many loose creamy-coloured roses.

(XXVII.)

Cipriano is tender and protective. (He too has resumed continuity
with his earlier character, disastrously interrupted by the Huitzilpochtli
passages.) Indeed, an elegiac tenderness, a sense of not unhappy
uncertainty, yet of fulfilment—fulfilment for the time, which is the
best that human existence can offer—pervades this final scene. Kate
knows that her heart is not entirely in this Mexican life, that in part
she is acting—the most satisfactory rôle she has ever had to play, but
still a rôle that does not quite coincide with her whole being. Yet at
the end, when Cipriano says that he wants her, she knows that she
has decided to stay.

"You won't let me go!" she said to him.

*   *   *   *   *

The Plumed Serpent is a curiously mixed work. Its moral keynote
is ambiguity; Kate with her all-but-last words opens a loophole of

escape from that to which she is about to commit herself. And the dual movement is expressed in the narrative structure. For there are two plots. The first is Kate's *Bildungsroman*, or a section of it—yet the section implies the whole—the opening out of her life from the modern Western woman's mode of separateness, self-assertion, the life of the ego, to another mode, of profound and inarticulate communion of which the separate activity of the ego is only an incidental part. The other figures in this plot, Ramón, Cipriano, Carlota and Teresa, exist only to further this movement, though, to be sure, they have a sufficient, independent life of their own. The Mexican scene itself, which carries so much of the weight of the book, is a pervading influence in the same direction. This plot is admirably rich in incident and scene, with Lawrence's sensibility to the immediate at its most delicate and powerful; and it is firmly directed to one end—Kate's progress from one mode of life to another. The progress is not uniform—the movement is one of oscillation, and the needle has not ceased to tremble at the end. But the direction of the force and the change in Kate's disposition that it effects are not in doubt; there is no failure of realisation. Nowhere else has Lawrence so successfully integrated the spirit of place and the development of character, or organised his scenes so completely to contribute to a general theme. And, although its elements are instinctual and unconscious movements largely foreign to the classical novel, this plot is conceived in normal novelistic terms.

Beside this first plot and interwoven with it is another one—the whole story of the Quetzalcoatl movement. It is interwoven with Kate's story because her interest in Ramón and Cipriano is first aroused by their activities in reviving the ancient gods, and because it is an important part of their fascination for her that they have a mission in the world outside their personal being. More fundamentally, the Quetzalcoatl revival is intended to provide an explanation of the changes that are going on in Kate's nature, the way her sympathy flows and recoils. It is the religion which, whether she knows it or not, is giving its meaning to her new way of life. Nearly all of it is implicit in the first plot. We would be just as fully possessed of all we need to know about Kate's progress without any details of the Quetzalcoatl ritual. But Lawrence cannot leave it implicit. He forgets his own warnings against the "indecent desire to have everything in the head"; and insists on furnishing his religious intuitions with a ceremonial, almost with a theology. The method here is not a normal novelistic one. The special vehicle of the second plot is the Quetzalcoatl hymns with their accompanying ceremonies. There is no place here for Lawrence's special gifts—the sensibility to landscape, the power of recording deep, unconscious movements of personality; instead there is only ritual and symbolic exposition.

The Quetzalcoatl ritual is Lawrence's attempt to translate into English words what he feels to have been expressed in the ritual chanting of the old Indian so beautifully described in the passage quoted earlier. There, however, he had an actual experience in the outer world as a point of departure; and there is no attempt to represent the *content* of the Indian's chant. Here all is to be done from within, and all is to be made explicit. And the failure is almost complete. The hymns are formally abominable; the prose virtues of intelligence are in abeyance, and the loose rhythm is never strong enough to turn them into poetry. The imagery is false: it is meant to suggest the embodiment of deep inarticulate instincts in symbolic form; what actually happens is the reverse—the deliberate translation of a few quite conscious ideas about sex and power into superficial and carelessly chosen images. We can spare ourselves the burden of detailed illustration—this section is already long, and the evidence is sufficiently obvious to speak for itself. With this formal disintegration goes a moral disintegration. When Kate is concerned in this second plot her character is subject not to the credible and natural oscillations that make up the better part of the book, but to violent breaches of continuity. Ramón and Cipriano become posturing dummies. And, as always when imaginative integration fails, there are violent intrusions of the author in the raw; in this case intrusions of sexual anger, quasi-Fascist deifications of discipline and a relish for cruelty.

Yet this failure does not become complete all at once. At the point where the two plots intersect, where Kate first meets the men o Quetzalcoatl in their natural setting, it looks as though the second plot is going to arise naturally out of the first, and with it become part of a greater whole. Where the new religion is seen in relation to Christianity, this does happen, more than once. Christianity we know; since the new religion is the antagonist to Christianity, we can in some measure know it by contrast. But as soon as it is necessary for the faith of Quetzalcoatl to stand alone, it is seen as a parasite; it can exist only in opposition. For the novel this could have been enough; its theme could have been the conflict; and over-explicitness about the nature of the rival faith could have been avoided. It should have been enough for Lawrence; that is, he should have refused to go outside his own genuine imaginative experience. Mabel Luhan describes his reaction to her discovery of Jungian psychology. "More attempts to know and to understand! More systems and more consciousness! All he wanted was the flow, and not the knowing about it!" But he falls into just the sort of conscious systematising that he condemns. This is one of the cases where something that is not yet clear and articulate, perhaps could never be, is forced to explicitness by Lawrence, regardless of the cost. As it turns out, the cost is not merely a certain amount of matter that can be pruned away or omitted in reading. For *The Plumed Serpent* demands to be seen as a whole—it has sufficient structural unity for that; an extensive and vital passage out of tone is as disastrous as it would be in a painting. As it is, we can only guess at what the book might have been if Lawrence had avoided the temptation to illicit god-making.

It is not surprising, then, that there should be varied opinions of *The Plumed Serpent*—that some should find it Lawrence's greatest visionary achievement, while others turn from it with disgust. The only surprising thing is that either view should exist unmixed—for both are justified.

At this point we must enlist the aid of *The Woman Who Rode Away*. Formally, of course, it is in a different kind—not a novel but a *Novelle* in the German sense, with a different sort of unity. And I had hoped to keep the genres separate. But *The Woman Who Rode Away* is an inseparable part of the experience that gave rise to *The Plumed Serpent*; and it succeeds in telling more of the truth about that experience because it is formally and imaginatively more complete. There is therefore much to be gained by discussing it now. I do not want to anticipate what is to be said about Lawrence's shorter pieces; but it is obvious enough that a story of this scope (about forty pages) cannot have the diversity of scene and incident of a long novel, or establish character by showing it in a variety of situations. What I have called the first plot of *The Plumed Serpent* does this, and *The Woman Who Rode Away* does not attempt to rival it.

What it does is to provide an imaginative equivalent for the abortive second plot. Where the actual tendency of the Quetzalcoatl mysteries is left uncertain, *The Woman Who Rode Away* is clear. On the other hand, where *The Plumed Serpent* is over-explicit—in all the pinchbeck contrived detail of ritual and hymns—*The Woman Who Rode Away* is content to suggest. The imaginative integrity thus achieved enables Lawrence to face his concept of Mexican religion, not so much with less ambiguity (ambiguity is an essential element of both stories), but with less evasion. And to see it for what it is, as he does here, is an important step towards turning away from it.

The Woman Who Rode Away was written in the summer of 1924, in the interval between the first and the second parts of *The Plumed Serpent*. It therefore represents Lawrence's first thoughts about Mexican religion, and the latter part of *The Plumed Serpent* the second thoughts. As often with Lawrence, the first thoughts are the best. It is not quite a matter of chronology: it is rather the spontaneous reaction to a new scene or a new complex of feelings against a doctored revised version, heavy with rationalisation. We have already noticed Lawrence's first reaction to Quetzalcoatl: a fuller and equally spontaneous reaction to the whole Aztec pantheon is recorded in *Mornings in Mexico*.

> The Aztec gods and goddesses are, as far as we have known anything about them, an unlovely and unlovable lot. In their myths there is no grace or charm, no poetry. Only this perpetual grudge, grudging, one god grudging another, the gods grudging men their existence, and men grudging the animals. The goddess of love is goddess of dirt and prostitution, a dirt-eater, a horror, without a touch of tenderness. If the god wants to make love to her, she has to sprawl down in front of him, blatant and accessible.
>
> And then, after all, when she conceives and brings forth, what is it she produces? What is the infant-god she tenderly bears? Guess, all ye people, joyful and triumphant!
>
> You never could.
>
> It is a stone knife.
>
> It is a razor-edged knife of blackish-green flint, the knife of all knives, the veritable Paraclete of knives. It is the sacrificial knife with which the priest makes a gash in his victim's breast, before he tears out the heart, to hold it smoking to the sun. And the Sun, the Sun behind the sun, is supposed to suck the smoking heart greedily with insatiable appetite.
>
> This, then, is a pretty Christmas Eve. Lo, the goddess is gone

to bed, to bring forth her child. Lo! ye people, await the birth of the Saviour, the wife of a god is about to become a mother.

Tarumm-tarah! Tarumm-tarah! blow the trumpets. The child is born. Unto us a son is given. Bring him forth, lay him on a tender cushion. Show him, then, to all the people. See! See! See him upon the cushion, tenderly new-born and reposing! Ah, *qué bonito!* Oh, what a nice, blackish, smooth, keen stone knife!

And to this day, most of the Mexican Indian women seem to bring forth stone knives.[44]

It is the death-worship, the total negation of all humanity and tenderness, that first strikes Lawrence about Aztec religion, as it must everyone who looks at Aztec art. He saw the same qualities in the Mexican people around him; and he was partly fascinated but even more repelled by them. But a little earlier, in New Mexico, the present-day religion of the Indians there had called from him a deep and wholly positive response. Now for some reason he wishes to identify the two. What historical justification there is for regarding the religion of the present-day pueblo Indians as a legitimate descendant of that of the Aztecs I do not know. Anyway, it is irrelevant; it is hardly necessary to say that we are not discussing the actualities of Mexican religion: we are discussing Lawrence's religion projected into the Mexican scene. With whatever reason, he had always seen the Aztecs and the Indians as one. "I would have loved the Aztecs and the Red Indians," Lilly remarks in *Aaron's Rod.* And in *The Woman Who Rode Away* the Chilchui tribe are supposed to have among them the descendants of the old Aztec kings, and old priests who still keep up the ancient rites and offer human sacrifice. So the revelation of life received in New Mexico and the revelation of death in Old Mexico are to be the same. How is this to be accomplished?

Of course by a quite traditional religious transformation. Death is to be a sacrifice, bringing new power and new life. Lawrence, as Richard Aldington puts it, was "at once horror-stricken and fascinated by the old Mexican belief that power could be acquired by cutting out the heart from a living victim to hold up, still palpitating, to the blood-red sun".[45] This is the myth on which *The Woman Who Rode Away* is based.

Lawrence is successful here, as he so rarely is in the long novels, in finding a mode midway between realism and symbolism that allows him to transform the actual, the given, without any breach of unity.

Psychological insight is not contradicted by visionary theorising, but becomes its complete expression; a profound sensibility to places and scenes ceases to be exercised for itself and becomes a powerful element in a highly organised whole. The story has a clear and simple outline. A woman, tired of an empty life on a silver mine in Mexico, becomes fascinated by tales of an Indian tribe in the hills who preserve the ritual of the old gods. She rides off to find them, through a lonely and terrifying landscape. She meets three members of the tribe, who take her off to their village. There she is kept in an honoured imprisonment. A young Indian tells her that the white men have captured the sun, and that she is to be an emissary to tell him to come back to the Indians. Gradually it becomes apparent to her that she is intended as a sacrifice. In a scene of great and horrible power, she is led out in the presence of the tribe and placed on an altar. The book ends just as the knife is about to descend on her heart.

Lawrence does not fall into the mistake of making the woman a self-conscious, competent cosmopolitan like Kate of *The Plumed Serpent*, or of giving her a circumstantial and literal social setting. She is an American woman, confident and hardened in the life of the ego; but her conscious development has stopped with her marriage. Her husband, the indomitably energetic little tin-miner, keeps her in a kind of moral subjection: mechanically she performs the duties of her station, teaches her children and supervises the house. But we do not see her doing any of these things; and we do not become so aware of her as a social being that her later adventures become incredible. Her surroundings are already so squalidly dead that we can well believe that she would choose another kind of death.

> The dead, thrice-dead little Spanish town forgotten among the mountains. The great, sun-dried dead church, the dead portales, the hopeless covered market-place, where, the first time she went, she saw a dead dog lying between the meat stalls and the vegetable array, stretched out as if for ever, nobody troubling to throw it away. Deadness within deadness.
>
> (I.)

Death is the keynote of this tale. The woman's life has reached a dead end. Her husband is a boss and a manager, lives purely the life of the will. The little Spanish town is dead, for it represents an alien civilisation, unable to keep alive among the blank ferocious hills.

The Church is dead because it represents a rootless and alien faith. The whole scene exists powerfully in its own right; but it is also a grim symbol of modern Western civilisation withering amid the terrifying powers of nature with which it has no living connection.

It is a visitor's chance remark that quickens her interest in the Indians and their ancient religion. At once, with the briefest of transitions, she makes her crazy plan to go and see them. Anything to get away. And during an absence of her husband, she simply rides off. The journey is one of Lawrence's most potent pieces of description, and the more potent because it is not mere landscape description, but the flight of a human soul into the unknown. The first night, camping alone, she thinks she hears "a great crash at the centre of herself, which was the crash of her own death. Or else it was a crash at the centre of the earth, and meant something big and mysterious". It is already becoming hard to distinguish what is happening to the woman herself and what is happening to the world at large. As she nears her destination she meets three Indians: in response to their questions she says she wants to visit the Chilchui, to see their houses and to know their gods. They catch hold of her horse's bridle, and half lead her, half take her captive. She resents their silent power, but it is no use. They are quite oblivious of her as a person and as a woman. She is angry, but faintly exhilarated; and then suddenly she knows that she has ceased to exist as a person, that she is already dead.

Her mere riding away has been the sacrifice of her old way of life— a kind of psychic death; what is to follow is simply the physical elaboration of what has already taken place in her soul: When she arrives at the village, she repeats that she is tired of the white man's god and has come to look for the god of the Chilchui. When the aged chief of the tribe asks if she brings her heart to the god of the Chilchui, she answers yes. She is stripped before the old chief and the men, who regard her quite sexlessly; and she is given a drugged drink. From this time on her separate human consciousness is increasingly in retreat, and the effect of the drink is to make her supernaturally conscious of the movements of the physical world.

> She felt as if all her senses were diffused on the air, that she could distinguish the sound of evening flowers unfolding, and the actual crystal sound of the heavens, as the vast belts of the world-

atmosphere slid past one another, and as if the moisture ascending and the moisture descending in the air resounded like some harp in the cosmos.

(II.)

They had brought a little female dog to share her captivity, and once in this trance of the senses she felt she heard the little dog conceive, in her tiny womb. The days and the weeks go by, in a sort of vague contentment. At length this drugged state becomes the only state of consciousness that she really recognises.

Then she could actually hear the great stars in heaven, which she saw through her door, speaking from their motion and brightness, saying things perfectly to the cosmos, as they trod in perfect ripples, like bells on the floor of heaven, passing one another and grouping in the timeless dance, with the spaces of dark between. And she could hear the snow on a cold, cloudy day twittering and faintly whistling in the sky, like birds that flock and fly away in autumn, suddenly calling farewell to the invisible moon, and slipping out of the plains of the air, releasing peaceful warmth. She herself would call to the arrested snow to fall from the upper air. She would call to the unseen moon to cease to be angry, to make peace again with the unseen sun like a woman who ceases to be angry in her house. And she would smell the sweetness of the moon relaxing to the sun in the wintry heaven, when the snow fell in a faint, cold-perfumed relaxation, as the peace of the sun mingled again in a sort of unison with the peace of the moon.

(III.)

She sees a ceremonial dance, and feels in it her own obliteration, her own death. "Her kind of womanhood, intensely personal, was to be obliterated," she felt; and in a conversation with a young Indian she begins to suspect, with a pang of fear, that she is actually destined to be a sacrifice.

"White people," he said, "they know nothing. They are like children, always with toys. We know the sun and we know the moon. And we say, when a white woman sacrifice herself to our gods, then our gods will begin to make the world again, and the white man's gods will fall to pieces."

(II.)

When the young Indian again tells her that the Indians have lost their power over the sun and are trying to get it back, she says: "I hope you will get it back." That is to say, she accepts her fate. And she sets the formal seal on this when she makes the sign of peace and

143

farewell in the prescribed manner to the old chief. The young Indian
explains to her that the white woman has got to die and go to the
sun, and "tell him that we are the people on the world again".

"The white women don't let the moon come down out of the
blue corral. The moon used to come down among the Indian
women, like a white goat among the flowers. And the sun want
to come down to the Indian men, like an eagle to the pine-trees.
The sun, he is shut out behind the white man, and the moon she
is shut out behind the white woman, and they can't get away.
They are angry, everything in the world gets angrier."

(III.)

Personally, she realises, the young Indian likes her and pities her;
but behind that is a pure impersonal hate. The tale has been marked
by a gradual extinction of all personality and personal relations, as
the woman passes from normal to drugged consciousness. And when
the day of the sacrifice at last comes, all personal emotions have
disappeared, and she only thinks: "I am dead already. What difference
does it make, the transition from the dead I am to the dead I shall be,
very soon?" The terror of this final scene is not minimised, but it is a
vast impersonal terror, in which the priests and the watching Indians
seem to share as much as she. The sacrifice is to take place away from
the village, on a bleak wintry day. The long procession files out to a
cave among the hills. There the woman is placed upon an altar. The
mouth of the cave is overhung with a great column of ice. When the
red setting sun sends its ray through the pendent icicle, the old chief
is to "strike, and strike home, accomplish the sacrifice and achieve
the power. The mastery that man must hold and that passes from
race to race."

These are the last words of the tale. A mystery of death and re-
birth, certainly; but not one of the joyful mysteries in which the
victim itself is to be reborn. What is reborn is an impersonal power,
mana, and the victim is simply there to accomplish its transfer from
one people and one mode of consciousness to another. The white
woman's ego–consciousness is to be killed and killed for good; another
kind of consciousness and another kind of power are to supersede it;
and its living representatives are to be a different race. The death is
extremely horrible, and the fact that it is half accepted, the gradual
abandonment of normal will and normal consciousness before the
event, is hardly less so. It is essential that it should be as it is. A

different and weaker ending would be that the woman should live with the Chilchui, learn to know their gods, but remain herself—and then return to the world, or at least keep open a loophole for return to the world. This is what Kate does in *The Plumed Serpent*. But here Lawrence knows quite clearly that the sacrifice of the autonomy of the ego, its submergence by the flood of the unconscious, is a terrible thing, and that no compromise is possible. The fatal weakness of *The Plumed Serpent* is an unresolved contradiction between the two plots. Kate remains Kate, yet also becomes the goddess Malintzi; she is sickened by a bull-fight, yet witnesses human sacrifice with no more than a qualm of uneasiness; she feels compelled to remain in the narcotic orbit of Ramón and his new religion, yet knows well enough that she is keeping an escape route open to the buses and the crowds of Piccadilly. Kate would like to die provisionally, so there is no sacrifice and nothing is reborn.

Her story is very much that of Lawrence himself in his relations with Mexico—the story of one who wants to swim without getting wet. And so far beautifully portrayed; the hesitations, the revulsions, the partial committals, the alternate fascination and fear, all the constituents of the first plot are deeply realised. Yet Lawrence wants to convince himself of something else—that this tentative conversion can produce all the effects of a total change of heart. He wants a genuine rebirth with only a mock sacrifice. But still he can only be true to his deepest imaginative intuition. He knows in his heart when he has been guilty of falsification; and all the obstinate persistence with which the second plot of *The Plumed Serpent* is hammered out, the laboured evocation of the new-old religion, is in vain, and the book regains conviction only at the end, when vacillation and ambiguity are admitted again to the central place that rightly belongs to them.

It is probable that in a long novel, with characters fully developed as social and personal beings, Lawrence could never have gone farther than this. But he can do it in a fable. And *The Woman Who Rode Away* is perceptibly nearer to a fable than to a realistic novel. The woman is never very fully realised as an individual; and half-way through the story her personal consciousness is superseded by the sort of cosmic, impersonal awareness that she achieves under the influence of the drugged drink. She is just sufficiently a person for the sacrifice to be terrible and real; yet she is unindividual enough to become a symbol of the whole 'white' consciousness, the ego-life of Western civilisation, sick of itself, dying on its feet, and almost willing to perish that a new kind of life may come to birth in the world, even a new kind of life in which it can bear no part. This is the dedicated self-destructiveness of a life that has reached the end of its tether; the end of an order, and its supersession by another which negates all existing values so thoroughly that the change can be symbolised only by a willed and horrible death. Yeats in later life saw something of the same vision. A primary dispensation that is "dogmatic, levelling, unifying, feminine, humane" is to give way before an antithetical dispensation that is "expressive, hierarchical, multiple, masculine, harsh, surgical".

> And what rough beast, his hour come round at last,
> Slouches towards Bethlehem to be born?

The political acting out of this myth can be seen plainly enough in the history of the last forty years, and the performance is probably not finished yet. Lawrence does not here attempt anything like political vision. He gives his myth a local actuality by placing it in the setting and landscape where the revelation had in fact come to him. The particular setting is an important element in its strength; but in a sense, Mexico and the Indians are only an accident, and the vividness with which they are realised does not obscure the real foundation of the story, which goes far below the local and circumstantial. Lawrence has done larger and more complex things in the pure tradition of the novel: I should say for myself that *The Woman Who Rode Away* is his completest artistic achievement. It is also his profoundest comment on the world of his time.

Of course a value judgment is implied, if not an absolutely clear one. For Lawrence "the life that arises from the blood" is generally the supreme value, and he would always prefer to welcome a destructive blaze than fan a dying flame. With this judgment we may disagree; if civilisation as we have known it is to continue, we must. Even Lawrence has his doubts. There is a profound ambiguity in the story between exhilaration and horror. But the weight of the book does not lie in the value judgment—it lies in its presentation of a process, a process that can be seen at work in a number of different fields. In the individual life the sacrifice of the ego to the flood of unconscious and instinctual forces; in social and political life the sacrifice of liberal individualism to the collectivity; in religion the sacrifice of a personal and transcendent God to an obscure, undifferentiated *mana*. Lawrence takes his glimpse into this abyss in his Mexican writing—then draws back, baffled and appalled. Whether the sacrifice of the white woman proved acceptable in the eyes of the Lord, whether it really brought back the sun to the Indians, we do not know. Lawrence does not know, and so cannot symbolise the process. It is significant that the story stops short just before the final blow is struck.

Students of Jung will recognise this phase of Lawrence's experience as an incomplete example of what this psychologist (a good deal later than the period of which we are writing) was to call integration. This is a process which involves displacing the centre of the personality from the ego-consciousness to a new centre whose circumambient circle includes the whole unconscious. It should result in a new harmony of conscious and unconscious life. But in the middle stages of the process there is a real danger that the consciousness will be swamped by the upsurge of uncontrollable unconscious contents. And this prospect is rightly felt as terrifying. Jung never tires of insisting on the dangers of the road to integration, the "perils of the soul". Kate trembles on the brink of these perils; the woman who rode away is swept down on the flood. Neither of them comes safely through the trial to the integration that lies beyond. Neither did Lawrence. And as always he insisted on making the journey alone. Hence the almost insane quality of his behaviour at certain periods of his Mexican sojourn, and the natural incomprehension of those who were with him at the time. Lawrence actually heard a good deal about Jung's psychology just before writing the second half of *The Plumed Serpent*, for Mabel Luhan continually tried to force it upon him in letters. But he was impatient and rather irritated by it all. I suspect some influence all the same. It is perhaps a pity that it was not more openly recognised; though if Lawrence at the crises in his life had been more capable of receiving external guidance and support, he would have been a different person. As it is, his solitary and almost maniacal adventure involved an expense of spirit that his weakened health could ill afford.

He had his glimpse into the abyss, hesitated on the brink, and in the end turned back appalled. But the mere glimpse was enough to effect a permanent alteration; as Frieda remarked, Taos changed him. But he was not destined to stay there. Immediately after the completion of *The Plumed Serpent* he fell desperately ill in south Mexico, and was very near to death. The revulsion against the whole environment is gently and movingly expressed in the fragment called *The Flying Fish*, written during his illness, and printed only posthumously in *Phœnix*. It is the story of a man lying ill in Mexico and summoned back to his ancestral home in Derbyshire. This home has its own legend and its own faith. The 'greater day' that is enshrined in the legend is a gentler version of the 'greater day' that has been glimpsed in the Mexican landscape. Lawrence is reaching out towards the possibility of a less fearful and inhuman kind of illumination; and he is turning back towards Europe again—even towards his own countryside.

IX. LADY CHATTERLEY'S LOVER

It is not necessary to record much more of Lawrence's personal history. He left America for the last time in 1925. The return to England was a failure; Lawrence could not bear it, and left after a few weeks. He came back again only once, in 1926; and for the last years of his life he was mostly in Italy, and increasingly ill. He died in the south of France in 1930. The quarrels with Murry and the failure in picking up his old relationships at home have been more than sufficiently described. They are of little literary importance, and will not be discussed here. Lawrence was by now a confirmed expatriate; yet during these last years, his own country and its troubles exercised a renewed spell over his imagination. *The Virgin and the Gipsy*, *Lady Chatterley's Lover* and many of the late short stories are on English themes. The note of almost wistful tenderness towards home in *The Flying Fish* fragment was not sustained by the actual homecoming, but there is no return to the exoticism of the Mexican stories. It is as though Lawrence had begun to realise that merely to move on, to be continually getting away from it all, is no solution to anything; and *Lady Chatterley* represents a fresh attempt at least to confront the problem of living out a life, of coping with a determined set of conditions, instead of running off to another continent to find new ones.

This change of emphasis coincides with another change. Lawrence now gives up the worry about leadership, mastery over men, that had occupied him intermittently ever since *Aaron's Rod*. Three years after *The Plumed Serpent*, while he was composing *Lady Chatterley's Lover*, he wrote to Witter Bynner:

> The leader of men is a back number. After all, at the back of the hero is the militant ideal; and the militant ideal, or the ideal militant seems to me also a cold egg . . . the leader-cum-follower relationship is a bore. And the new relationship will be some sort of tenderness, sensitive, between men and men and between men and women, and not the one up one down, lead on I follow, ich dien sort of business.[46]

Tenderness is a sentiment that is conspicuously lacking in *The Plumed Serpent*, and a good many of the book's false notes are due to Ramón's strained efforts to become a politico-religious culture-hero, and Cipriano's to be a Fascist condottiere. We need not, perhaps, take "the new relationship" too seriously. Whatever Lawrence happens to be feeling at the moment is apt to appear to him as a new phase in the history of the world; what is certainly heralded here is a new phase of Lawrence's development. At one time he thought of calling *Lady Chatterley* "Tenderness", and the word is conspicuous in his comments on the book in letters. And the tenderness is to be a private and sexual thing, without any of the political overtones we have become accustomed to in the recent novels.

> I always labour at the same thing—to make the sex-relation valid and precious, instead of shameful. . . . Beautiful and tender and frail as the naked self is. . . .[47]

> It is a nice and tender phallic novel—not a sex novel in the ordinary sense of the word. . . . I sincerely believe in restoring the other, the phallic consciousness: because it is the source of all real beauty and all real gentleness. And those are the two things tenderness and beauty, which will save us from horrors. . . .[48]

There is a good deal more, too, about "phallic consciousness" against "sex consciousness", by which Lawrence means to assert the primacy of the deepest instinctual forces over the more superficial and personal kinds of attraction more commonly recognised in the civilised world. There is of course little that is particularly new in this. It is almost a return to the attitude of *Women in Love*, and we hear echoes of Birkin's demand for something other than love and more than it in his relations with Ursula. How far Lawrence advances on this position in these latest works, we must now inquire.

All the business of private printing, newspaper attacks and the subsequent *succés de scandale* of *Lady Chatterley* do not concern us here. Indeed, one would be glad to put all this entirely out of mind in order to see the book as it is in itself and in its continuity with Lawrence's previous work. Nor need we deal in detail with the stages in its growth. Indeed, the evidence is not fully available, and since the story is not closely involved with Lawrence's biography the steps in its composition do not represent a real development, as do those of *Sons and Lovers*. *The Virgin and the Gipsy* looks like an abortive first attempt at *Lady Chatterley*, and *Lady Chatterley* itself was written three times. The earliest version (published in 1944 as *The First Lady Chatterley*) seems only an incomplete realisation of the intentions of the final one. The character of the gamekeeper is not very firmly established, and the difference between him and the men of Lady Chatterley's world is shown too much as a mere matter of social class. The second version has not been published, but it has been described, and it seems to be a further step towards the final form. There is of course an expurgated version of which I shall say a word later on. In effect, however, the only edition of *Lady Chatterley* that matters is that privately printed in Florence in 1928.

Though the book has circulated less widely than any other of Lawrence's, the outline of its plot is probably the best known of all. The motive of a woman of higher class who gives herself to a man of the people and is made happy by his superior vitality and tenderness has appeared often enough in Lawrence's work. It is often said that this is a projection of his own biography, but there are hints of it, without the happy consummation, even in *The White Peacock*, long before his marriage. Mr. Eliot has remarked that Lawrence has a particularly acute sense of class differences; and this is true. The implication which I think I detect here—that this is only an accident of Lawrence's own social origins, or a chance talent for a particular kind of social portraiture, is not. Lawrence had always been impressed by the difference between the quality of personal reticence and separateness of upper-class life and the working-class capacity for fusion and mingling. His own attitude towards it was ambiguous. No one could be quicker to resent unwarranted matiness or intrusion, as we see in *Kanagroo*. Yet his deepest detestation was always reserved for the "hard-shelled, separate people" of whom he found so many among the English and American upper classes. In the achievement of separateness all capacity for tenderness and warm human relationship was lost. This is particularly true in the physical and sexual sphere, and it is the women who suffer most. It is on this long-standing conviction of Lawrence's that *Lady Chatterley* is built; and so far we have nothing new.

The plot is a particularly clear and simple one. By the normal structural canons of the novel (and I have not up to now seen much reason to depart from them, in spite of Lawrence's protests), it is better built than any of his works since *Sons and Lovers*, and, though less rich, has a closer unity even than that. In its simplest outline, the story is as follows. Constance Chatterley's husband, Sir Clifford Chatterley, is left crippled and impotent by a war wound. He makes the best of his situation, and becomes a writer of some distinction. They are rich, and have an intelligent and not disagreeable circle of friends. Constance devotes herself loyally to looking after her husband, but nevertheless becomes gradually oppressed by the aridity and emptiness of her life. She meets Mellors, her husband's gamekeeper, a bitter, lonely man who has also been unhappily married. They fall violently in love, she finds a sexual fulfilment that she has never known, and after many misgivings decides to leave her husband. There are difficulties in the way, and the book closes with Constance and Mellors apart, but preparing, not to flee to Mexico or Italy, but to begin a new life together on a farm in England. Stated so, the plot seems almost vulgarly conventional. On this there are two things to be said. One is that the convention has been established by Lawrence himself. Until his days, novels were commonly about the approaches to marriage. To-day, as a reviewer has recently remarked, they are commonly about marriage, and every marriage in the novel is a problematic one. The shift of emphasis is largely the result of Lawrence's work. The second remark is that the peculiar quality of the book depends less on the bare situation than on the fullness, fidelity and scrupulousness with which the situation is worked out. In spite of a general belief that *Lady Chatterley* was written *pour épater* and in spite of some real and strident false notes, I should state my conviction at the start that it is one of the most careful, consistent and solidly based of Lawrence's fictions. This we must now proceed to illustrate.

In doing so we shall find ourselves returning to many of the themes and motives of *The Rainbow* and *Women in Love*. There is the profound and bitter concern with English society, yet this time with an occasional tenderness for his own country foreshadowed in *The Flying Fish* fragment. There is the belief in sheer sensuality as a purifying force, and the conviction that somehow it can become the regenerating force for society as a whole. There are admirable pictures of both the industrial and the rural scene. There is the incidental (and distasteful) cruelty; but here it is not something willed and external, as in the Mexican books—it is the cruelty that is perhaps an inevitable part of life. And of course the attempt—far more successful than in the earlier books—to present as fully as possible the sexual process and the sexual act.

The rapid, assured exposition of Connie's background and situation in the early chapters is one of Lawrence's most accomplished pieces of pure straightforward narrative. It is noticeable throughout *Lady Chatterley*, apart from certain special passages to be discussed later, that the writing is exceptionally natural and sure of itself, with no straining after half-realised or unattainable effects. We are at once possessed of Connie's earlier history—of emancipated, pre-war, mildly Bohemian young womanhood. There are the experimental love-affairs which never really went deep, the mixing with the young Cambridge group:

> the group that stood for "freedom" and flannel trousers, and flannel shirts open at the neck, and a well-bred sort of emotional anarchy, and a whispering, murmuring sort of voice, and an ultra-sensitive sort of manner.
>
> (I.)

Clifford comes from another world—an old family, rather isolated and reserved, cut off from the industrial Midlands from which their modern fortune is derived. Connie and he seem to fulfil a need in each other. She gives him a glimpse of a wider life than he has known, and he gives her a companionship that goes beyond sex, where sex indeed seems almost irrelevant. The Chatterleys live utterly apart from the pits and the miners that crowd up to their park gates. The old bond between the classes has gone. Lawrence comments further on this in a valuable essay, "A Propos of *Lady Chatterley's Lover*":

This, again, is the tragedy of social life to-day. In the old England, the curious blood-connection held the classes together. The squires might be arrogant, violent, bullying and unjust, yet in some ways they were at one with the people, part of the same blood-stream. We feel it in Defoe or Fielding. And then, in the mean Jane Austen, it is gone. . . . So, in *Lady Chatterley's Lover* we have a man, Sir Clifford, who is purely a personality, having lost entirely all connection with his fellow-men and women, except those of usage. All warmth is gone entirely, the hearth is cold, the heart does not humanly exist. He is a pure product of our civilisation, but he is the death the great humanity of the world.[49]

It is an essential part of Lawrence's creed that the social pattern is a reflection of the private sexual pattern. Clifford's isolation from the miners on whom his wealth depends has its root in his isolation from his wife. He wants to say something to Connie about the kind of life that his disability forces upon her, but he cannot bring himself to do it—"he was at once too intimate with her and not intimate enough. He was so very much at one with her, in his mind and hers, but bodily they were non-existent to one another, and neither could bear to drag in the *corpus delicti*." It is tacitly left that he does not mind what steps she takes to remedy the deficiency, as long as he does not positively know about it.

It must inevitably seem here that Lawrence's case is in a fair way to being spoilt by Clifford's physical paralysis. What should be an essential defect of his nature is the result of gross accident, not a part of himself. Lawrence deals with the point in "A Propos of *Lady Chatterley's Lover*":

I have been asked many times if I intentionally made Clifford paralysed, if it is symbolic. And literary friends say, it would have been better to have left him whole and potent, and to have made the woman leave him, nevertheless.

As to whether the 'symbolism' is intentional—I don't know. Certainly not in the beginning, when Clifford was created. When I created Clifford and Connie, I had no idea what they were or why they were. They just came, pretty much as they are. But the novel was written, from start to finish, three times. And when I read the first version, I recognised that the lameness of Clifford was symbolic of the paralysis, the deeper emotional or passional paralysis, of most men of his sort or class to-day. I realised that it was perhaps taking an unfair advantage of Connie to paralyse him technically. It made it so much more vulgar of her to leave him.

Yet the story came as it did, by itself, so I left it alone. Whether we call it symbolism or not, it is, in the sense of its happening, inevitable.[50]

The real answer is that Lawrence as a novelist, partly by his own fault in using so much of his fiction as the vehicle of doctrine, is often saddled with doctrinaire purposes beyond the actuality. He is not concerned to blame Clifford. As far as the book is doctrinaire its purpose is not to approve one type of character or class against another —it is to show the inevitability of certain profound rhythms of human life. That Clifford cannot help himself, that Connie is a loyal and kind woman, and that there is every moral and humane reason against her doing as she does, makes Lawrence's position all the stronger. And outside the novel, are we not accustomed to consider painful situations, which are no one's fault, and from which no outcome could be happy, as among the most powerful materials of literature?

The slow degeneration of Connie's existence continues.

> Time went on. Whatever happened, nothing happened, because she was so beautifully out of contact. She and Clifford lived in their ideas and his books. She entertained . . . there were always people in the house. Time went on as the clock does, half-past eight instead of half-past seven.
>
> (II.)

She embarks on a love-affair with one of Clifford's acquaintances, Michaelis, a dramatist. But there is nothing in it, she is as unsatisfied by it as by the utter nothingness before. Clifford's friends are intelligent, in a superficial way, and are even capable of great insight into their situation, though without power to do anything about it. One of them, Tommy Dukes, almost becomes Lawrence's mouthpiece.

> "I wasn't talking about knowledge . . . I was talking about the mental life. Real knowledge comes out of the whole corpus of the consciousness; out of your belly and your penis as much as out of your brain and mind. The mind can only analyse and rationalise. . . . And if you've got nothing in your life but the mental life then you yourself are a plucked apple . . . you've fallen off the tree. And then it is a logical necessity to be spiteful, just as it's a natural necessity for a plucked apple to go bad."
>
> (IV.)

And Tommy Dukes does not possess the capacities that he sees to be so essential.

"I'm not really intelligent, I'm only a mental-lifer. It would be wonderful to be intelligent: then one would be alive in all the parts, mentionable and unmentionable. The penis rouses his head and says: How do you do? to any really intelligent person. Renoir said he painted his pictures with his penis . . . he did too, lovely pictures! I wish I did something with mine. God! when one can only talk!"

(IV).

Meanwhile Connie meets the gamekeeper Mellors. Clifford has been entertaining the possibility of her having a son by another man, to provide an heir for Wragby. They are out in the woods one day, Clifford in his chair, and Mellors helps to push it up the hill. Connie is struck by him—quiet, aloof and positive. He is the son of a collier; went to India and became an officer in the war; his wife left him while he was away and now he lives alone as a gamekeeper—a deracinated, solitary man. He seems a poor example of the warmth and intimacy he might be supposed to represent, and we have here a good illustration of how Lawrence can forget doctrine, become possessed by the genius of fiction—entirely to the advantage of his work. Mellors is an extremely living and upstanding character, existing in his own right—but he is by no means the obvious embodiment of what the ideological drift of the book seems to have been up to now. Indeed, in these opening stages of Connie's acquaintance with Mellors, all doctrine seems to have been forgotten, and we have simply the intimate, closely observed record of the secret growth of a relationship between two people separated by the barriers of class and condition. Dukes in part prepares the way for this by maintaining to Connie that mental intimacy and proper sex relationship are incompatible. She rebels against the idea, but inwardly she knows he is right. Her next encounters with Mellors are mostly disagreeable. He slips into speaking dialect to her, and his manner is coarse and sneering. She goes to deliver a message at his cottage, accidentally sees him washing in the yard, and rather to her annoyance is deeply moved by the sight of his naked torso. This time his manner is perfectly natural and easy; he is "almost a gentleman", and for a while things remain in this somewhat enigmatic condition.

There is a fairly long interlude which serves further to develop Clifford's nature.

Poor Clifford, he was not to blame. His was the greater mis-fortune. . . . Yet was he not in a way to blame? This lack of warmth, this lack of the simple, warm, physical contact, was he not to blame for that? He was never really warm, nor even kind, only thoughtful, considerate in a well-bred, cold sort of way! But never warm as a man can be warm to a woman, as even Connie's father could be warm to her. . . . Clifford was not like that. His whole race was not like that. They were all inwardly hard and separate. . . . What was the good of her sacrifice, her devoting her life to Clifford? What was she serving, after all? A cold spirit of vanity, that had no warm human contacts.

(VII.)

There are more conversations, in which some of Clifford's friends look forward to a future from which all the bother of physical life has been eliminated. Duke alone stands out, hoping for a resurrection of the body as the only regenerator of a sick civilisation. Connie becomes ill, and it is necessary to relieve her of some of the task of tending Clifford. Mrs. Bolton, a nurse from the village, is called in, and Connie begins to breathe more freely.

A good deal is made of Mrs. Bolton. She is one of the vividest minor characters in Lawrence, with a Dickensian sort of vividness that he rarely attempts. Her account of her own life, and her talk about Tevershall, the colliery village, are admirable mimetic writing. Even in the dialogue of *Sons and Lovers* Lawrence does little to imitate the actual speech peculiarities of his characters, but Mrs. Bolton is set before us with less intervention of the author than any other of his personages. When her life is described in *oratio obliqua* it is heavily tinged with her own turns of expression, and when she "talks Tever-shall" directly, we have a brilliant piece of sheer mimicry. Imitation of this kind is impossible without a measure of sympathy, and Mrs. Bolton is portrayed with sympathy. She is a vulgar woman, and her part in the plot is an ambiguous one, yet the account of her married life and her husband's death (quoted in part in the Introduction) is one of the few simply moving passages in Lawrence. The sympathy is part of an unwilling tenderness for the country of his boyhood that wells up occasionally in *Lady Chatterley*; but it has another bear-ing as well. Commonplace, rather commonly power-seeking as she is, by mere virtue of her class Mrs. Bolton avoids the etiolation of the Chatterleys. Her love for her husband has been something real, and her interest in her neighbours, for all its gossipy viciousness, is a kind of human contact. To warmth and humanity on this very low level—so low that he can safely patronise it—Clifford can respond; and he slips more and more under her dominance. The part she plays in the economy of the book, therefore, is to be a counterpoise to Mellors. In a perverse and cross-grained fashion she provides for Sir Clifford some shadow of what the gamekeeper does for Connie. This gives an added symmetry to the plot, which Lawrence is not likely to have cared much about, and, more important, it lessens the burden on Connie when she ultimately decides to leave.

We come now to the heart of the book. Connie becomes increasingly unhappy and dissociated from the life around her. Clifford, on the other hand, finds a new lease of life in managing the mines. It was Mrs. Bolton's suggestion that he should turn his attention to reviving the failing pits, and this cements the alliance between them. Connie goes frequently to a hut in the woods which Mellors uses for breeding pheasants. At first he resents her presence and does his best to rebuff her. The place is cool and solitary, and the spring flowers suggest new life, the possibility of which has long been denied to Connie. The sight of the new-born pheasant chicks brings this home to her even more acutely.

> Then, one day, a lovely sunny day with great tufts of primroses under the hazels, and many violets dotting the paths, she came in the afternoon to the coops and there was one tiny, tiny perky chicken tinily prancing round in front of a coop, and the mother hen clucking in terror. The slim little chick was greyish-brown with dark markings, and it was the most alive little spark of a creature in seven kingdoms at that moment. Connie crouched to watch in a sort of ecstasy. Life, life! Pure, sparky, fearless new life! New Life! So tiny and so utterly without fear! Even when it scampered a little scramblingly into the coop again, and disappeared under the hen's feathers in answer to the mother hen's wild alarm-cries, it was not really frightened, it took it as a game, the game of living. For in a moment a tiny sharp head was poking through the gold-brown feathers of the hen, and eyeing the Cosmos.
>
> Connie was fascinated. And at the same time, never had she felt so acutely the agony of her own female forlornness. It was becoming unbearable.

(X.)

Mellors appears, and he shows her how to take the chick in her hands. Suddenly she finds she is crying. He comforts her and takes her up into the hut. And then—the commentator finds himself against the very barrier that Lawrence is trying to break through in the rest of the book. How are we to describe what happens? He makes love to her, he sleeps with her, they become lovers? The hopeless inadequacy of all the standard phrases reveals the difficulty that Lawrence is trying to meet. There is no adequate language in which the sexual encounter can be even referred to, still less described; and the new literary problem presented by *Lady Chatterley* is the attempt to find ways of overcoming this inadequacy.

The first method is simply to describe in detail, and with more candour than has ever been used before in English letters (or so far as I know in any other except avowed *erotica*) the immediate sensations of the lovers:

> Then with a quiver of exquisite pleasure he touched the warm soft body, and touched her navel for a moment in a kiss. And he had to come in to her at once, to enter the peace on earth of her soft, quiescent body. It was the moment of pure peace for him, the entry into the body of the woman.
> She lay still, in a kind of sleep, always in a kind of sleep. The activity, the orgasm was his, all his; she could strive for herself no more. Even the tightness of his arms round her, even the intense movement of his body, and the springing of his seed in her, was a kind of sleep, from which she did not begin to rouse till he had finished and lay softly panting against her breast.
>
> (X.)

Their first encounter is thus briefly described. The kind of frantic obscurity in similar attempts in *The Rainbow* is quite absent, the sensations are simply and explicitly presented. So far as this goes, here and in similar succeeding passages, a new range of possibilities is opened for the novel. But the experiment is juridical and social rather than literary. Lawrence is simply describing, in perfectly familiar terms, something that everyone knows but that fiction does not commonly describe. He is replacing the novel's conventional row of asterisks with the words that they conceal. But there is no new development of language, nor even much of sensibility. All that is needed is the determination to break a taboo. How far is this worth doing, and how far does it succeed? To answer this question we must trace the relations of Connie and Mellors farther.

In this first meeting she is just passive and finds no positive enjoyment. Yet it brings her great peace. She is happy afterwards, but he is troubled by foreboding, by the thought of all the complications to follow. We could know all this just as clearly, be just as well aware of what had happened, if we had had the row of asterisks instead of the paragraph of description. But from now on the whole development of the relation of Connie and Mellors depends on the depth and quality of their sexual experience of each other. In many kinds of novel, describing many kinds of relationship, this would be irrelevant; but it is the essence of this particular situation. Therefore if Lawrence is to realise his conception at all fully and openly he must present what is going on as explicitly as possible, must discriminate as fully between different kinds and degrees of sexual fulfilment as the ordinary novelist does between different kinds of sentimental encounter. To put it in the baldest expository terms—Connie gradually comes to experience more direct pleasure in their love-making. There are some failures, more periods of fulfilment, and in the end the experience of complete and abandoned sensual enjoyment, simply for its own sake. Mellors also describes in detail to Connie his earlier married life, and explains to her exactly why he has found happiness with her that he never found in the unsensual loves of his boyhood or with his brutish wife.

Similar material is part of the experience of most men and women. It is obvious that the nature and quality of sexual experience has a powerful influence on character and development. We cannot therefore deny that Lawrence has opened up a wide new territory to the novel by presenting openly what everybody knows in private and what everybody knows to be important. However, other questions remain. How has fiction got on at all in the past, if such a large part of life has been kept behind the curtain? Of course by presenting the subsequent emotional effects of sexual activity, its consequences in character and action, without attempting to present the sexual activity itself. It may well be that this is the right procedure. Not only are intimate sexual experiences not commonly talked about in the novel, they are not commonly talked about at all. No one ordinarily puts such experiences into words. So Lawrence is certainly breaking more than a mere taboo of the printing-house. The instinct for sexual reticence—shame, if one likes to use the pejorative word—though it takes various forms, seems to be deeply ingrained in nearly all cultures. The crucial question, therefore, is whether what is ordinarily never put into words at all can be put into words without altering and deforming the experience. It is a purely empirical question, and I think the unprejudiced answer must be that it can; in the passages I have discussed Lawrence succeeds. The experience of reading this part of the book is less of shock than of recognition. We can say of it what Dr. Johnson said of wit—it is at once natural and new; it is not obvious but on its first production it is acknowledged to be just. Another, and a largely social, question is whether it is necessary or useful to break such a deeply ingrained prohibition. The answer I think is that Lawrence's purpose could not be achieved without it, and that his purpose—to show what he believes to be the place of sensuality in life—is a perfectly legitimate one. But, it must be added, the gain for the novel in general is probably less than might be supposed, and less than has often been claimed. For Lawrence's particular ends it is necessary to describe sexuality in greater detail than has been customary. But his ends are highly individual, the consequence of a quite peculiar development. The freedom to present any aspect of experience is always a gain; but for the purposes of most novelists the traditional method of allowing the detail of sexual life to be inferred from its overt consequences in feeling and action will probably always be more useful.

The question of censorship and all that goes with it does not concern us here. It actually concerned Lawrence very much, since he suffered by it. No one's reactions are purified by this kind of persecution, and the effect on Lawrence was to produce a good deal of blind anger, and a good deal of vapouring about frankness and freedom and bringing sex out into the open and so forth. It looked good in its day, and its effects in weakening the sillier kinds of prudery have been excellent. Lawrence was partly wrong, all the same. There are arcana in nature as well as in religion, and nothing that affects the emotional life as intimately and individually as sex can or ought ever to be fully "in the open". The passages we have just discussed, describing the sexual act more fully than has ever been done before, can be justified by the whole intention of the book: but when we come

to the obscene words and Lawrence's campaign for their revival, I
think we encounter an excessive reaction to censorship and prudery.
Lawrence uses in *Lady Chatterley* five four-letter words not commonly
seen in print, and uses them probably not more than a hundred times
in all (I have not counted) in the course of a longish novel. So in
any case they cannot make much difference. They are all put into
Mellors' mouth, and are meant to show his frank carnality and its
vivifying power. So far they are an integral part of Lawrence's
purpose. But still more, one suspects, they are part of the extra-
curricular activity of bringing "sex out into the open", and like all
such secondary purposes in a work of fiction they are so far an irrelevance. Of course it is quite true, we have no proper vocabulary to
discuss sex. There is the scientific, which sterilises it by depriving it
of all emotional content, and the obscene. Lawrence's remedy is to
use the obscene words familiarly and seriously, so that the tabooed
acts and parts of the body can be talked about in natural and native
words. An admirable intention, no doubt, but doing no great credit
to his literary sense. Writers are masters of language, but they can
only become so by respecting its nature. No writer can alter the connotations of a whole section of the vocabulary by mere fiat; and the
fact remains that the connotations of the obscene physical words are
either facetious or vulgar. And very useful they are in these contexts.
But in any context where dignity, tenderness, respect for one's own
person or that of another is concerned, they are impossible. The effect
of putting them into Mellors' mouth as they are is either to create
the impression that he is, as one of Lawrence's acquaintance described
him, a crude sexual moron, or that whole passages of his discourse
are disastrously out of character.

There are a few other lapses, all, I believe, dictated by the extrane-
ous passion against the spirit of censorship. They can be briefly
dismissed. Connie's dancing in the rain, and her subsequent decoration
of Mellors' person with forget-me-nots are bits of self-conscious
nudism that fall heavily into the ridiculous. And there is a disastrous,
impossibly vulgar conversation between Mellors and Connie's father
which simply shows Lawrence hopelessly at sea, and failing un-
pleasantly in inventing a tone for a dialogue that he has not really
felt. But these passages are relatively short, and so inessential that
unless one chooses to dwell on them they do little to affect the book

as a whole. Indeed, to my mind, even the expurgated edition, where most of the specific sexual detail is cut out, and there is therefore considerable loss, suffers less by the omissions than has often been alleged. It is better that it should have appeared than that the whole book should have remained inaccessible; for its fundamental merits are simply those of any novel in which the relations between men and women are patiently and truthfully explored.

To return to the plot. Connie's progress in sensual satisfaction has already been outlined. It is not an isolated experience; it is accompanied by the experience of warmth, humanity and tenderness as she has never known it before. This expansion of Connie's nature is paralleled by Clifford's development as an industrialist. He makes himself an expert on modern mining methods and soon becomes a considerable power in the colliery world. Connie hates these new interests and the side of Clifford's nature that they bring out. By all ordinary standards this new activity of Clifford's would seem to be an excellent thing; within the context of the book there is a sharp opposition between the expansion of Connie's nature by the warmth of sensual love and the narrowing of Clifford's by the cold lust for power. The hostility between industrial civilisation and sensual tenderness that Ursula had perceived in *The Rainbow* reappears here in all its old force, and the almost agonised concern with what England had become.

> The car ploughed uphill through the long squalid straggle of Tevershall, the blackened brick dwellings, the black slate roofs glistening their sharp edges, the mud black with coal-dust, the pavements wet and black. It was as if dismalness had soaked through and through everything. The utter negation of natural beauty, the utter negation of the gladness of life, the utter absence of the instinct for shapely beauty which every bird and beast has, the utter death of the human intuitive faculty was appalling. The stacks of soap in the grocers' shops, the rhubarb and lemons in the greengrocers! the awful hats in the milliners! all went by ugly, ugly, ugly, followed by the plaster-and-gilt horror of the cinema with its wet picture announcements, "A Woman's Love!", and the new big Primitive chapel, primitive enough in its stark brick and big panes of greenish and raspberry glass in the windows. The Wesleyan chapel, higher up, was of blackened brick and stood behind iron railings and blackened shrubs. The Congregational chapel, which thought itself superior,

was built of rusticated sandstone and had a steeple, but not a very high one. Just beyond were the new school buildings, expensive pink brick, and gravelled playground inside iron railings, all very imposing, and mixing the suggestion of a chapel and a prison. Standard Five girls were having a singing lesson, just finishing the la-me-doh-la exercises and beginning a "sweet children's song". Anything more unlike song, spontaneous song, would be impossible to imagine: a strange bawling yell that followed the outlines of a tune. It was not like savages: savages have subtle rhythms. It was not like animals: animals *mean* something when they yell. It was like nothing on earth, and it was called singing. Connie sat and listened with her heart in her boots, as Field was filling petrol. What could possibly become of such a people, a people in whom the living intuitive faculty was dead as nails, and only queer mechanical yells and uncanny will-power remained?

(XI.)

The description of Tevershall that begins thus continues for the next five pages, and modulates into a hopeless lament, seeing only endlessly increasing vistas of squalor stretching into the future.

England my England! But which is *my* England? The stately homes of England make good photographs, and create the illusion of a connection with the Elizabethans. The handsome old halls are there, from the days of Good Queen Anne and Tom Jones. But smuts fall and blacken on the drab stucco, that has long ceased to be golden. And one by one, like the stately homes, they are abandoned. Now they are being pulled down. As for the cottages of England—there they are—great plasterings of brick dwellings on the hopeless countryside.

. . . . .

What would come after? Connie could not imagine. She could only see the new brick streets spreading into the fields, the new erections rising at the collieries, the new girls in their silk stockings, the new collier lads lounging into the Pally or the Welfare. . . . What next?
Connie always felt there was no next. She wanted to hide her head in the sand: or at least, in the bosom of a living man.

(XI.)

What she sees around her are not living men; but they are all that industrial England has left of humanity.

So she thought as she was going home, and saw the colliers trailing from the pits, grey-black, distorted, one shoulder higher than the other, slurring their heavy ironshod boots. Underground grey faces, whites of eyes rolling, necks cringing from the pit roof, shoulders out of shape. Men! Men! Alas, in some ways patient and good men. In other ways, non-existent. Something that men *should* have was bred and killed out of them. . . . Supposing the dead in them ever rose up!

(XI.)

The common gibe at Lawrence was that he believed in the regeneration of England by sex. We can begin now to understand what he meant. No society that had preserved a living sense of the full human reality could ever have allowed this degradation to happen. There is no evident cure. One can only hope—a hope not unmingled with fear—that the living sense of human reality may some time rise from the dead. Connie makes her protest against the all-pervading hideousness to Clifford, and is answered, quite rightly from his own premises, with the standard arguments for industrialism and the managerial society. When she complains of the hopelessness of the workers' lives and of their own, he replies that this is just a relic of "swooning and die-away romanticism". And she wonders angrily why Clifford is so wrong, yet she can never tell him where he is wrong. Of course he is quite right, by all the assumptions on which modern society is based; and Connie only dimly knows that if people were rightly related to each other as individuals such a society would be impossible.

There is not much more to relate of the personal story of Connie and Mellors. The situation becomes more and more impossible. It is decided that Connie shall go away for a holiday to think things over, and she goes off to Venice with her father and her sister—but not before her sister has been made aware of the love-affair with Mellors. All the detail of this development is presented with a fullness and a leisurely power that we should hardly expect. Lawrence has quite grown away from his earlier habit of neglecting the ordinary and the circumstantial to concentrate only on moments of unnaturally heightened sensibility. The sketch of Connie's sister, the holiday glimpses of Paris and Venice, no less than the earlier ones of Mrs. Bolton and Tevershall are done with a strength and confidence that mark a summit in Lawrence's fiction. When Connie returns she decides that she cannot go back to Wragby. In the meantime Mellors' wife has turned up and is making trouble. Besides the cruelty and the pain of telling Clifford of the decision, there are many frustrating difficulties of circumstance. There is no pretence that society does not exist: Connie and Mellors bump up against it with a vengeance. They have to separate for a time, with only the hope of coming together again later. Yet a sense of peace, of a measure of fulfilment achieved, of decisions taken, pervades the close of the book.

Lawrence has often been criticised for the implied cruelty of the attitude to Clifford, and for building so much on a relationship that has been an exclusively physical one. I formerly shared this view, but have now come to believe, within the given context, that it is wrong. Connie's actions towards him are not excused, for they are never discussed, in ordinary moral terms. To do so is not part of the subject of the book. Its subject is the working out of deep natural laws of human life, which any real morality, according to Lawrence, must take into account. We can then proceed to criticise Lawrence's whole moral scheme (in the end we must do so); but it is not legitimate to introduce ordinary social morality piecemeal into the consideration of an individual work. The relevant questions are whether the work is self-consistent, and whether its premises are sufficiently consistent with experience to be worth considering. These have been answered implicitly in all that has been said up to now. The cruelty in the book is the cruelty of life rather than that of the author or even of his characters. Lawrence has weighted the scales against himself by making Clifford an object of pity as well as of legitimate dislike; but no one could maintain that the development from the given circumstances is not probable in itself or not consistent with the nature of things. It is true that the relation of Connie and Mellors is an extremely limited one; they have hardly even held a normal conversation together. But Lawrence does not suggest or attempt to foresee what their life together in the future will be like. Still less does he imply that they married and lived happily ever after. Among the comments on the book that he quotes in "A Propos of *Lady Chatterley*" is the following: "Well, one of them was a brainy vamp, and the other was a sexual moron, so I'm afraid Connie had a poor choice—as usual!" I do not think that this is quoted quite without the concurrence of the author. He is remarkably dispassionate towards his characters. It is the forces working through them that arouse him most strongly, rather than their personal being; certainly not the tendency of their actions to move towards a conventional happy ending.

A more valid criticism is that the relation of Connie and Mellors is so unlike a normal love relation. Both are deeply injured and un-happy people: what they find in each other is the almost desperate satisfaction of desires that have long been cramped and distorted. And that is not at all like the simple flowering of natural passion and tenderness which Lawrence wishes to recommend. Perhaps this is merely to say that the book is more successful as a novel—for the novel is always about particular people in a particular situation—than as the sexual tract that it is often taken to be. But it remains true that there is an inconsistency between what the book actually does and what Lawrence in some of its discursive passages and in the comments in his letters suggests that it does.

It is also true that here, for the first time, there is no real advance in thought upon earlier work. Up to now, Lawrence's career as a novelist has been a continual exploration of new territory. There has been much repetition, but always combined with an advance. Now for the first time we find him returning upon himself. The message of *Lady Chatterley* is hardly different from that of *The Rainbow* and *Women in Love*; nor is there any further indication of how it could be applied to existing society. There is the same belief in a tenderness and passion between individuals transcending the conscious and personal; the same deep sense that the right kind of tenderness and passion between individuals must totally negate the spirit of industrial civilisation. But we know no more than Ursula in her vision of the rainbow how the one is to overcome the other. The same message, however, is expressed (apart from the well-defined and separable false notes that we have indicated) with far greater ease, confidence and maturity of style. *Lady Chatterley* is Lawrence's last major work, and speculation about what would have happened if he had lived longer is an idle business. The evidence, however, seems to suggest that his spiritual *Wanderjahre* were over, at least for the time. If he had had a longer period of health and relative stability, it would probably have been devoted to clarifying and consolidating the insights already gained. We should probably have had nothing completely new, but a saner and less frenetic statement of much that is already present in the novels. The Etruscan essays and the little newspaper articles of his last years all point in this direction. As it is, if after *Lady Chatterley* we are to look for one word more, it is to be found in *The Man Who Died* and in *Last Poems*.

Chapter III

THE TALES

So far, by confining ourselves to Lawrence's major novels we have been able to trace a fairly continuous and consistent course of development. This continuity is found in the major fiction alone. If we take as our text the shorter stories and tales, and study them chronologically as we did the novels, the sense of reading a series, of watching the gradual unfolding of a personality is absent. By themselves the stories present no consistent pattern; though they are full of illuminating parallels and cross-references to the novels, the links among the tales themselves are fewer. And the tales themselves include a wide diversity of types. They vary in length, for instance, from the merest sketches or anecdotes, such as "Smile" or "Things", to what are in effect short novels, with a full development and a wide range of character and incident, like "St. Mawr" or "The Captain's Doll". And in between is the normal long-short story which Lawrence utilised with success at all stages of his career. It does not look as if he ever gave much conscious thought to these varying scales on which fiction can be practised. "The Fox" is almost a classical *novelle*, with its central symbol, its small group of characters, its restricted and unified plot. "The Captain's Doll", on the other hand, is a miracle of compression; it contains matter enough for a far longer story than it is. And it seems to be only by accident that "St. Mawr" does not expand to the length of a full-scale novel. The range and comprehensiveness of the plots, and the length at which they are treated seems, in fact, to be mainly decided by the amount of time, material and energy Lawrence has to spare from his longer fictions. The importance he attached to the stories and the degree of achievement is equally variable. He believed "The Ladybird" to have "more the quick of a new thing than the other two stories" in the same volume. But to the unprejudiced reader it is surely far surpassed by the others—"The Fox" and "The Captain's Doll". "The Woman Who Rode Away" is in an obvious sense the by-product of *The*

167

Plumed Serpent; yet it is far superior in æsthetic organisation. Such stories as "Smile" or "Rawdon's Roof" are trivial or ill-tempered *jeux d'esprit*; while "The Woman Who Rode Away" and "The Man Who Died" are the vehicles of Lawrence's deepest intuitions. The two last are also sharply distinguished from all the others by making little attempt at realism. In them we are approaching the realm of myth and fable; in "The Fox" and "Odour of Chrysanthemums" we are firmly planted on common earth.

With all this diversity there is perhaps only one thing the tales have in common—and that is something negative; they are *not* the growing points of Lawrence's fiction. Perhaps this is in the end the only way of distinguishing between what are conventionally called his short stories and what are conventionally called his novels. It is never, I think, in the short stories that a new phase of Lawrence's development opens. His new ideas are hammered out in the long novels (that is why a consistent development can be seen through them); and the short stories are related to these arduous voyages of exploration in a variety of ways. Sometimes they are simply surplus material—as many of the early stories seem to be left over from *The White Peacock* and *Sons and Lovers*. Sometimes they are more compact and fully realised versions of what a novel was trying to do, like "The Woman Who Rode Away". Sometimes they are quite independent creations, in the mode of whatever long novel he was engaged on at the time. Precisely because it is not in these shorter tales that the original exploration is done, they are often superior in artistic organisation to the long exploratory novels. In a restricted form, preaching and repetition are bound to be kept to a minimum; and those who say, as many do, that Lawrence's best work is in his shorter pieces have much reason on their side. In sustained realisation, in formal completeness there is certainly nothing to better the best of his shorter tales. But simply to prefer them probably implies some reduction in the importance of Lawrence as a whole; by the student of Lawrence the stories can best be seen in relation to the solid range of his longer works.

As far as date is concerned, the relation can be briefly outlined. There is an early group of stories (they mostly appear in the *Prussian Officer* volume, some in a posthumous collection called *A Modern Lover*) very closely connected with *The White Peacock* and *Sons and*

Lovers, both in themes and treatment. There is a second group, collected under the title of *England My England*, all written during the war, showing a similar but less intimate connection with *The Rainbow* and *Women in Love*. A third group is formed by the three long stories, "The Ladybird", "The Fox" and "The Captain's Doll", written about the time of *Aaron's Rod*. Mexico gives us a fourth series—"St. Mawr", "The Princess" and "The Woman Who Rode Away"; and the last years in Europe a miscellaneous collection—some satiric and rather trivial, in the vein of the more acid *Pansies*; a good long story "The Virgin and the Gipsy"; and the unique "Man Who Died"; the one a foretaste and the other a supplement to *Lady Chatterley*.

The early stories are very unequal in sheer technical competence. "A Fragment of Stained Glass" is a feeble juvenility, with its laborious but pointless indirect narration and its absurd attempt at historical evocation. There are two stories directly concerned with the Miriam relationship: "A Modern Lover" and, rather more developed, "The Shades of Spring". In both a Midland young man, now half-sophisticated by a spell of metropolitan life, comes back to see the girl he has left. In both stories she has found another man, but the endings are different. In "A Modern Lover", the less real of the two, the girl returns to the hero; in "The Shades of Spring" she reproaches him for his futility, and reveals that on the day of his marriage she has given herself to her new gamekeeper lover. The constant re-handling of this theme reveals an unsolved personal problem, and neither story makes any advance towards a solution. This sounds irrelevant, but it is not quite; the integrity of Lawrence's writing on this theme depends on progress in self-knowledge. Here we have a mere compulsive circling round. Both stories are nearer to *The White Peacock* than to *Sons and Lovers*, and the uneasy element of half-deprecatory preening in the presentation of the hero is even more apparent. "Second Best" presents a similar situation from the girl's point of view, and is the better for the hero's absence.

A far stronger group of tales is the one that takes up the firm, objective manner of the early part of *Sons and Lovers*, and fixes itself upon the portrayal of working-class life in a mining district. "The White Stocking" and "Odour of Chrysanthemums" are the best of these. Both are admirable. They show little trace of the characteristic

Laurentian promise, but they are complete achievements. In them, as in all the less intimately personal parts of *Sons and Lovers*, we see what Lawrence might easily have become (what in passing, perhaps, he did become)—the classic novelist of the English workers. "The White Stocking" tells the story of a young miner and his skittish little wife, of her fascination by a flashy rival and their ultimate return to each other. It is absolutely uncontrived, in detail authentic at every point, and formally complete. "Odour of Chrysanthemums" is on the tragically familiar theme of the miner brought home dead after a pit accident. He has been a drinker and a bad husband, and it is from this ironic standpoint that the tragedy is seen. Depth and complexity are added in the final scene by showing it through the eyes of two women, his wife and his mother, with radically different attitudes. If we do not require Lawrence's peculiar kind of insight, with all its possibilities and all its perils, these stories are as perfect achievements, on their own scale, as anything he wrote.

"Daughters of the Vicar" is a more ambitious tale, in length, elaborateness of pattern and social range. It broaches some of the familiar Laurentian themes—the emotional etiolation of the well-bred, the lady who allies herself with a man of the people. And they appear in this story without tendentiousness, as a natural outcome of the social circumstances. An impoverished country parson has two daughters, one cool, proud and withdrawn, the other buxom and out-going. The first marries, against all natural inclination, a sickly, pedantic and repellent little cleric who can, however, give her social status and economic security. The other in the course of her parochial duties is thrown in with a young collier. They are strongly attracted to each other, and she resolves to end the course of withered genteel poverty by marrying him. The elder sister and her husband owe something to Dorothea and Casaubon in *Middlemarch*, and the patient objectivity of the treatment shows, I think, the influence of George Eliot in general. This story also marks the beginning of Lawrence's criticism of English class-relations: though without the verve of some of his later efforts in the same direction, it is remarkable for its moderation and for the refusal of the picture to step outside the frame.

Two stories in this period are of quite a different kind—"The Prussian Officer" and "The Thorn in the Flesh". They are both studies of German militarism and its impact on simple lives; and the outside stimulus to them can only have been provided by a brief contact with German military authorities in the few weeks after Lawrence first left England. They mark a decisive step in the development of his literary imagination. Up to now he has always written of a world that was familiar to him and on themes very close to his own experience. Here he is making a leap into a world of which he can only have had the merest glimpse; yet there is not the slightest failure of imaginative realisation. "The Prussian Officer" is a repulsively powerful story of a sadistic, quasi-homosexual relation between the officer and his peasant orderly. The focus is on the psychology of the individuals, but the implied picture of the society in which all this could occur is equally compelling. Nothing of the sort had ever been part of Lawrence's experience, and this is perhaps the place to remark on a prevailing characteristic of the short stories. Whatever depth of personal experience lies behind them, they are far more objective and self-contained than the long novels. The novels constantly spill over into Lawrence's personal life, and can hardly be explained without reference to it. The outer world is used as the vehicle of an expanded metaphor for a process going on in the depths of his own psyche. The short stories, with two notable exceptions, are more the result of what we might call the normal novelist's imagination—the result, that is to say, of observation, intuitively deepened and expanded, but still observation of an outward reality, ending in a creation that has been completely externalised, completely separated from the creator. And that, no doubt, the critic is bound to add, is just what artistic creations ought to be. A result of this is a quickening of the normal novelist's gifts and a revelation of how many of them Lawrence possessed. They are revealed abundantly, to be sure, in the novels; but there they tend to be overlaid by other less usual ones. Lawrence professed himself uninterested in character in the conventional sense; and it is true that many of his major personages live in our minds chiefly as depersonalised representatives of certain states of mind. Incident and circumstance are present less for their own sake than for their part in revealing some train of development quite independent of them. In the short stories character of the self-subsistent, recognisable kind comes into its own again. There are very few of these disguised representations of Lawrence himself that we have learnt to recognise in the novels. The Prussian captain, Banford and March,

Countess Hannele and Mrs. Witt assume the status of people that we know, as Miriam, Birkin, Lilly and Don Ramón hardly do. And since the short story must inevitably have a discernible incidental focus of some kind, we see them more completely involved in action.

The next group of stories, the *England, My England* volume, illustrates these points well enough. They are competent, undoctrinaire and spring more from a response to the outer world than from any inner necessity. The title-story was almost a transcript from life, and even Lawrence felt himself to blame for employing an actual situation so crudely. Its motive is the critical response to English society that is found also in *The Rainbow* and *Women in Love*. In the early Midland novels Lawrence had portrayed, analysed but hardly criticised the society around him. After all, he had never known anything else; for him it was the normal world. Travel and widening social horizons were to change all this. Extended contact with the intelligentsia, the educated middle and upper class (Lawrence probably had more of it at this period than at any other) made him increasingly aware of his own difference from them, of the different scale of values in which he had been brought up. The note of rather strident class-awareness, soon to become familiar throughout his work, makes its first appearance in "England, My England". It is disagreeable in itself; but like so much that is disagreeable in Lawrence, it is intimately connected with his strength. We notice at first in his sharp touches of observation the nagging voice of the outsider; only afterwards is it observed how unerringly the details have been selected, and how they all spring from a deep underlying disquiet at the whole tone of bourgeois life.

> There was a sound of children's voices calling and talking: high, childish, girlish voices, slightly didactic and tinged with domineering: "If you don't come quick, nurse, I shall run out there to where there are snakes." And nobody had the sang-froid to reply: "Run, then, little fool." It was always: "No, darling. Very well, darling. In a moment, darling. Darling, you must be patient."

Only a fragment, and a fragment chosen probably in resentment at the contrast between this kind of childhood and his own; yet a sharp, prying little searchlight on to a whole ethos. And that, on a more extended scale, is what the whole story is. "England, My England" is concerned with an individual man; but also with a family, and with the family as typical of a whole social world. Egbert the protagonist is a young man of good birth who lives in the country, partly on a small private income, partly on his father-in-law, and potters about doing nothing. His character degenerates under this regime; so do his relations with his wife; one of the children is crippled through his carelessness; his futility and alienation increase; when the war comes he drifts into the army and is killed. Energy and will have burnt so low in him that it seems the only thing left. His character is contrasted sharply with his father-in-law's. The old man has been an active, stirring person—one of the makers of this society that is fizzling out in the younger generation, and a certain vigour and authority still cling to him; Egbert has charm and distinction of manner as his only weapons; and life rolls over him like a wave over a piece of wreckage until he is lost. The whole story is told with a pitiless directness that has in it a considerable element of cruelty. Its virtue is in the fineness of its texture and the delicate discrimination of detail. None of the characters is a stereotype, the physico-moral individuality of each is etched with the last precision. And though the title of the story is a rueful, half-despairing cry over England, comparable to some of those in *Lady Chatterley's Lover*, the temptation to let a lugubrious symbolism overpower the specific situation is completely resisted. As in "Daughters of the Vicar", the Laurentian message is allowed to express itself only through the concrete events.

The rest of the stories in the volume are a mixed bag. They show Lawrence's powers working freely and with ease, but none are in the first rank. "Monkey Nuts" and "Tickets, Please" do not attempt any great seriousness; and "The Primrose Path" and "Fannie and Annie" come to less than they promise at first. The most considerable are "You Touched Me", "Samson and Delilah" and "The Horse-dealer's Daughter". All are on English themes; for some of them Lawrence returns to the Midlands, but not at all in the old spirit. There is no trace of autobiography, and the new interests of *Women in Love* have succeeded those of *Sons and Lovers*. Relations between men and women are always relations of conflict, and lovers rarely seem ever to have any ordinary human understanding of each other; all the stress is on bonds other than the conscious ones. In "Samson and Delilah" a man comes back to claim the wife he deserted fifteen years before. He has a very tough reception and is violently thrown out. But he comes in again, and in the end is tacitly accepted. There is a pull between the two of them stronger than the conscious emotions of either. In "The Horse-dealer's Daughter" a doctor rescues a girl from drowning in a pond, warms her and brings her back to life. He has never taken any notice of her before, in any ordinary sense he does not love her; yet suddenly they know that they are inevitably bound together. In "You Touched Me" a young man is accidentally touched in sleep by his foster-sister, who in normal relations dislikes him. Yet he is convinced that this touch gives him the right to claim her in marriage, a right which he proceeds to exert, against all her opposition. The situations described would not in themselves seem odd or out of place in any ordinary short story. Their peculiarity in Lawrence is that in every case a claim, a bond or an attractive force exerts itself in flat opposition to the normal sentimental disposition of the characters. Of course it is no new thing in fiction for the odious man whom the heroine cannot abide in the first chapter to become the accepted lover in the last. But then the greatest pains are taken to make the overt sentimental sequence correspond to the operation of the unconscious forces. Any experienced novel-reader can see at the start that Elizabeth Bennet is going to marry Darcy; but the latter part of the book is largely occupied in explaining the process that makes it psychologically possible for her to do so. No such explanations can be given in these stories of Lawrence—or, indeed, in most of the personal relations in his works. It is this in part that gives them their disconcerting air of harshness and cruelty. People are always being driven to do just what they do not want to do—women marry the men they hate without apparently modifying their hatred; men marry women who are certain to make them unhappy. Lawrence feels the primacy of unconsciousness and unrecognised forces so strongly that he must show them harshly victorious over all opposition. A harmonious accommodation between conscious and unconscious would not serve his end, however frequently this occurs in normal experience. It is often said in consequence that he fails to portray normal experience, and there is something in it. In life, after all, there are calms between the storms, and Lawrence is apt to pass over them in a paragraph; he is little interested in the flavour of ordinary daily intercourse. Yet the violent oppositions, the abrupt changes of front that abound in his stories, are rarely hard to credit; they are probably more disconcerting to the amateur of conventional fiction than they are to the observer of life as it is lived.

The two long-short stories "The Fox" and "The Captain's Doll" must be counted among Lawrence's most important work of the *Aaron's Rod* period. In fact, at this stage the subordination of tales to novels disappears. *Aaron's Rod* is a short and scrappy novel; "The Fox" and "The Captain's Doll" are both stories of considerable scope and substance, and beautifully constructed. However, the distinction we made earlier remains valid: *Aaron's Rod* is, in its fashion, a voyage of exploration; and these two stories are not. Lawrence preferred "The Ladybird" to both of them, on just that account. But here surely he is mistaken. When Lawrence sets out to survey some new relationship or some new way of feeling that he himself has not completely understood, above all he needs time—time for his curious method of alternating incident and exhortation to break down resistance, for his repetitions to make their effect; time for the concealed pattern of psychic development to become apparent beneath the surface incoherence; time for revisions and indecisions to be made and to be overcome. A shorter piece cannot afford so much; it needs a predetermined procedure and a predetermined end. And the very quality for which Lawrence preferred "The Ladybird"—that it had "more the quick of a new thing in it"—in fact establishes the superiority of "The Fox" and "The Captain's Doll".

As a matter of fact, it is doubtful whether there is anything so very new in "The Ladybird". The theme is the typical Laurentian one of the fascination of a woman by a man outside her normal sphere. This time it is not a man of another class who is the representative of the unknown forces, but a foreigner, an enemy, a prisoner. The symbolism could hardly be more explicit. Count Dionys is a Bohemian, discovered desperately wounded in a prisoner-of-war hospital in England. Lady Daphne is a beautiful young woman, wife of a rising politician, now in the army. She and her husband are meant to be typical representatives of the English governing class, with its virtues and its defects. But alas, we have met them before, the reserved, adoring, idealistic but passionless upper-class Englishman, and the cool, remote beautiful wife with an untapped layer of passion underneath. We have met them in too many novels, novelettes and society dramas for Lawrence's quite competent evocation of them to affect us much. And Count Dionys—yes, I am afraid "there is something remote and in a sad way heroic in his dark face. Something primitive". As could be foreseen, Lady Daphne at first regards him with kindly indifference, and then finds herself dominated by him. When her husband returns, she finds that he is only her day-time husband and that Count Dionys is her master in the dark. The situation is left so. The bond between them remains a purely mystic one, and Count Dionys goes away, telling her to be loyal and true to her own husband, but to remember that she is always his night-wife.

I suppose that the only thing Lawrence can have regarded as new in this tale is the introduction of such an explicitly symbolical figure as Count Dionys into a story of war-time England otherwise conceived in naturalistic terms. As usual with such mixed intentions, it is a failure. The pseudo-mystical vapouring in which Count Dionys expounds his philosophy to Lady Daphne is totally out of key with the rest of the story, and suffers from the same kind of misplaced explanatory fervour as Ramón's Quetzalcoatl preaching in *The Plumed Serpent*. Lawrence's aim is to emphasis the difference between two worlds. But the result of his procedure is to remove Count Dionys from the world of reality altogether, and to reduce the other characters to novelist's stereotypes.

"The Fox" is certainly one of Lawrence's masterpieces of straight-forward naturalistic narrative. His besetting vice is the tendency to present his vision of life unconditioned, or insufficiently conditioned, by specific time and place and circumstance, to allow it to work loose from the particular setting of the story he has in hand. Now "The Fox" can be interpreted quite easily in terms of Lawrence's prevailing ideology. The two girls trying to run a struggling farm do not at first suggest any of the obvious Laurentian types; but after a little it becomes easy to see the frail, affectionate, spectacled Banford as a representative of "white" passionless love, and the ruddy, physically effective March as natural energy unawakened or misdirected. The fox who preys on the chickens is a bit of wild nature hostile to their way of life. When the young soldier appears on the scene he is partly identified with the fox. He, too, is an intruder on the girls' life together; he is like the fox in appearance; March once even mistakes him for the fox. So he also represents an outside natural force, more dangerous than the fox, for he introduces discord: he is inimical to the March-Banford combination, and he is not inimical to March herself. He does not yet realise that he is to break up the girls' alliance; he appears as a friend, and kills the fox; a hostile natural force is replaced by an apparently friendly one. Then he comes up against Banford's hostility, and realises that he can never marry March while she is still about. Then he sees that it was not enough to kill the fox, he must also kill Banford. And when he has done so we reach one of those typical endings which is no ending; there is no future for him and March in their present surroundings, they must go out to Canada—they must pass on, that is to say, to somewhere outside the confines of the story altogether. The characteristic solution for Lawrence—to move on and start again somewhere else.

It is easy enough, then, to see the story as another Laurentian parable if we wish. But this interpretation is far from forcing itself on our notice. The æsthetic surface is never broken by symbols that call attention to themselves. Everything is expressed through the concrete and the realised—the atmosphere of the dank unsuccessful little farm; the sympathetic picture of the girls; their rather brave and not unhappy life, yet a life with no real foundations and no real future. The young man resists all temptation to become one of Lawrence's garrulously symbolic figures. He seems at first almost an irrelevance, with no particular charm or character or force. He just is. Yet when his course leads to an act of half-deliberate and brutal violence, we feel this to have sprung naturally, almost inevitably, from his being. There is no great variety of scene or character in this story, and few of the typically Laurentian flashes. It is classically perfect in its unforced development of a single unitary theme.

"The Captain's Doll" is a very different matter. It has, it is true, a rather raw Laurentian maxim undisguisedly at its core; it is not a woman's business to love a man unless she is prepared to honour and obey him as well. But this theme is presented in the vein of comedy, at any rate with an unusual and engaging lightness; and it leaves us free to be pleased and even a little dazzled by the brilliance of the execution. The setting is in occupied Germany, and the protagonists are the Countess Hannele and the Scottish officer Captain Hepburn. They have formed one of those post-war friendships with a very uncertain future, and it means more to her than to him. The Captain is married, and shows little inclination to make up his mind about the situation. Hannele is clearly in love with him, though disturbed and irritated by his indecisiveness. Hannele has been impoverished by the war and earns a living by making dolls and puppets; we discover her in the opening scene making a doll which is the exact portrait of the Captain. With very little actual description, the oddly provisional nature of this society is excellently brought out; and how compelling its personal relations can be, although they have no past and apparently no future.

In the midst of this, Hepburn's wife appears—a pretty, silly little elderly woman who has already suspected something amiss. She is one of Lawrence's few brilliantly comic characters—her half-shrewd half-silly chatter, her self-important good nature, and the sort of domination she exercises over the Captain are done in a vein of accomplished social comedy that Lawrence undoubtedly possessed but did not often care to exercise. With a firm belief in her womanly intuition, she completely misinterprets the situation, tries to buy the doll-portrait, believes that the Captain is in love with Hannele's friend, and makes the position of these two German ladies excessively uncomfortable. Just as a considerable complication is developing—she falls out of her hotel window and is killed. This hardly fits in with the notion that the piece is a comedy, and it may be said that Lawrence is making too convenient a use of a brutal coincidence. Not more irrelevantly, however, than life sometimes does, and the effect in the context is neither brutal nor improbable. It is not unlike "Exit Antigonus pursued by a Bear"—a character that has served its purpose is simply removed. Deeply shocked, the Captain and Hannele talk things over; he describes the odd, undeveloped nature of his wife with sympathy and insight. It becomes clear to Hannele, however, that his wife has never really touched him deeply—perhaps no one can. She can do nothing with a man like this, she even begins to find him slightly ridiculous; so they part and lose touch with each other.

The Captain goes home, realising that all his human relations have been abruptly severed. He, nevertheless, remains haunted by the recollection of Hannele, though she does not represent rosy romantic love to him; indeed, rather a hard destiny. Suddenly he takes the train back to Munich. Inquiries for Hannele have proved fruitless, but it turns out that his doll-portrait has acquired a certain minor celebrity as an *objet d'art*, and through that he is able to trace her. She is apparently going to marry an Austrian official, and the latter part of the story includes some extremely vivid and lively pictures of post-war Austria. The Captain is no more 'in love' with Hannele than he ever was. He wants her, but he will have her only on his own terms—only if she will honour and obey him as well as love him. Hannele displays a spirited indignation at this, and the process by which these uncomfortable lovers finally and inevitably come together is as good an example of human, unsentimental comedy as we are likely to find in modern fiction. Lawrence's gift of evoking the atmosphere of a place and a society is at its best, and this is one of the works where his powers are working most freely and happily, without doctrine or *arrière pensée*.

But this state with Lawrence never lasts long. If it had he might have been a less imperfect artist; but he would have been something different from the complete Lawrence that we know. He returns in a more familiar guise in the Mexican stories. There are three of them—"The Princess", "The Woman Who Rode Away" and "St. Mawr"—all longish tales and all belonging to the *Plumed Serpent* period. "The Woman Who Rode Away" is so clearly an offshoot of *The Plumed Serpent* that we have dealt with it already in discussing that novel. It is perhaps Lawrence's masterpiece in the fabulous-symbolic kind, but it belongs more to his dealings with the mythology of Mexico than to his stories as such. "The Princess" can be fairly quickly dismissed. It is a product of the sort of doctrinaire cruelty that possessed Lawrence for at least a part of this period; a more distasteful variant of it is found in the later story "None of That". Its theme is the white woman and the dark man—a theme that evidently had a persistent importance for Lawrence, and one which he often pushes to the point of dreary obsession. He comes very near to it here. "The Princess" of the title is a rich American woman who takes Romero, a Mexican guide, for a long trip in the mountains. She is unconsciously stirred and attracted by him but is sexually frigid, and when he interprets her demeanour in the obvious way she is disgusted. This maddens him, and he rapes her and keeps her prisoner—till he is shot and she rescued by a search party. It is all done with power and conviction, but leaves behind a sense of disquiet. Apart from a mere social distaste for the theme, it is not at first clear why. The contrast between the inhibited sexuality of the woman and the natural sexuality of the man is valid enough. And the not unknown situation in which a rich cosmopolitan woman half consciously exploits a poorer and more primitive man for his sensation value is a legitimate object of Laurentian satire. Yet there is something repellent about the treatment of this story, as about the treatment of similar themes elsewhere in Lawrence. I believe it is an impurity of motive, perceptible but hard to pin down. Lawrence is often implicated in his stories in the wrong way; and often he overcomes the difficulty by putting himself or a representative of himself into the fiction. This is not the most refined artistic method, but as often as not it works. "The Princess" is handled differently. Romero's motive in the story is sexual revenge; and without admitting it, Lawrence seems to participate in this sentiment. He does not, it is true, sentimentalise Romero, who remains a most disagreeable specimen. But it is hard to get rid of the feeling that the author, not only his character, also wants to revenge himself on all cold white women, especially if they are rich; and it is this suspicion of a suppressed sexual malice in the tale, rather than the subject itself, that makes it offensive.

A similar suspicion, spreading equally over the sexual and the social sphere, affects the flavour of "St. Mawr". This story has been very highly praised by Dr. Leavis, and indeed in some of its characterisation and description it is among Lawrence's most brilliant performances. I am, none the less, persuaded that it is not an authentic piece of work, that there is a falsity in the motive and the conception that fatally affects the whole. Let us first note some external and circumstantial features. Although it is vitally conditioned by Lawrence's American experiences, and its conclusion is one of his most beautiful evocations of the New Mexican scene, it is not for the most part a Mexican story at all. It is an attack on modern civilisation; other things besides, but if it is not that it is nothing. Its setting is mostly English, and the type-specimens it deals with are the phenomena of English social life. Mexico comes in only as a contrast and a counterpoise. Elsewhere Lawrence has recorded the impression made on him by Mexico for its own sake. It is something *sui generis*, unlike all his other experiences, separated from them in time and place. However, in the middle of his American sojourn he made a short trip back to England. It was one of the most dismal episodes

of his career. He hated everything, the attempt to pick up old relationships was a failure—in fact, his whole connection with his own country
seems to have been violently dislocated. He kept exhorting his
associates to join him in a settlement in New Mexico; they responded
in various unsatisfactory ways. Several people made nauseous fools
of themselves, including Lawrence. His appearance as a sort of
resurrected prophet and the *schwärmerisch* or half-hearted reactions
to it, at any rate as recorded by his disciples, form one of the least
edifying phases of his life. "St. Mawr" was written on his return to
Taos. It is the only work where England and Mexico are brought
sharply into the same focus; it seems therefore that we must take it as
an attempt to come to terms with his recent experience. The American
south-west had impressed him more deeply than any other place he
had ever known. The atmosphere of England now disgusted him. Yet
he was of England, irrevocably; worry about it, concern with it,
pervades his writing; it was an obvious necessity for him to bring
the new experience and the old into some kind of relation. Anyone
who has lived much abroad and then returns to his own country can
testify to this need. But the trouble with "St. Mawr" is that Lawrence
is not using his real knowledge of England; he is not drawing on the
wealth and weight of experience used in *Sons and Lovers*, *The Rainbow*
and *Women in Love*. It is not, indeed, written out of experience at all,
but out of a need and a mood that are too partial and too close; the
nerves are still too much irritated, the prophetic pretensions too
much affronted; the trivial social irritations to which Lawrence was
always subject (and New Mexico had put to rest) were too recently
reactivated. These are the outward and biographical reasons, I
believe, why "St. Mawr", in spite of its passages of intensity and
power, remains a failure.

But it is a failure which is typical of all Lawrence's failures, and
for that reason it needs a closer and more internal examination. And
first we must reckon with its success. It is in the first place a superbly
concentrated work. About a third the length of one of the full-length
novels or twice as long as "The Fox", it has great variety of scene
and character. It lives in the memory as a novel rather than a short
tale, and in spite of its brevity nothing is scamped or hurried. Lou,
the unrooted cosmopolitan American girl, is established as a person
with the lightest, briefest, most economical of strokes. Her husband

Rico, the artistic, rather effeminate, 'charming' young Englishman, is less surely done, but we see what he stands for. And Mrs. Witt, Lou's mother, is one of Lawrence's most unforgettable characters. For all that he says in other places about his lack of interest in character in the usual novelist's sense, Mrs. Witt lives in just that sense. Strange, unclassifiable being as she is, she makes all the impact of a person met in real life, has just that quality of pressing actuality that most novelists value and Lawrence commonly neglects. Her Texan laconic bluntness, her hideous virility, her nihilism, her irony combine into a massive and uncomfortable whole. The group is completed by St. Mawr, the untamable stallion that Lou buys as a mount for her husband.

Here the doubts begin to assert themselves. The magnificent chestnut horse, quivering with pride, beauty and power, is surely too obvious and unmodulated a symbol of primitive energy. And he immediately begins to conflict with the carefully conditioned social reality that Lawrence is trying to establish for his human characters. The marriage of Lou and Rico is a sexual failure, but at the beginning of the story they get on well enough and remain good friends. Rico is a poor rider, Lou is an amiable girl, St. Mawr is a stallion who has already killed two men. Yet Lou insists on buying him for Rico as a nice mount for the Park, and insists on his riding him against his will. Allowing full weight to her unconscious dissatisfaction with Rico and her rationalisation of her action as a desire to see him in a picturesque light, surely this is crazily impossible. And in spite of Mrs. Witt's sullen contempt for people in general and her son-in-law in particular, that she should deliberately scare the horse to make him bolt with Rico in the Row is an excessive gesture even for a Texan mother-in-law. Unless, as has been suggested, the story is of a plot to kill Rico by the two women, which is fairly obviously not the intention. It would, I suppose, be too petty a cavil to point out that no one rides stallions in the Park; but since niggling objections of this kind keep raising themselves, let us see where they lead.

Rico going for a ride in the country "dressed himself most carefully in white riding breeches and a shirt of purple silk crape, with a flowing black tie spotted red like a ladybird, and black riding-boots. Then he took a chic little white hat with a black band." This is a grotesquely impossible get-up for even the most flower-like young man; but what

is far more impossible is that Rico in this outfit should be admired
and worshipped by the conventional hunting young woman Flora
Manby. In reality she would never speak to a man who could be seen
in such a costume. Other bits of nonsense intrude themselves. Lewis,
the Welsh groom, is set up against the gentry as a survival of the
ancient inhabitants of Britain, mysteriously uncorrupted by modern
decadence. He supports his rôle by several pages of imitation Celtic
twilight about the moon-people, which we are asked to accept as
folk-lore. There is a similar falseness about the values of nearly all
social types whom Lawrence has undertaken to represent. Lou gets
progressively more tired of men and more devoted to St. Mawr, and
is supposed to be distinguishing herself from her country neighbours
by this. But in fact the English countryside is full of young women
who like horses better than men, and Lou sinks herself into the picture
by the very attitudes which are intended to take her out of it. Similarly
with Mrs. Witt. After Rico has had an accident with St. Mawr, she
firmly takes the side of the horse; Rico's equestrian incompetence is a
moral and vital failing which deserves no sympathy. And this of
course is entirely true to a certain type of horsy mentality; the hunting
neighbours whom Mrs. Witt is so anxious to distinguish herself
from would actually react in just that way, blame Rico for being fool
enough to ride a horse he can't manage. Yet Lawrence attributes
to them a grandmotherly solicitude that is ludicrously out of character.
As these objections accumulate, we begin to see that they are not
trivial—for, after all, the force of all these incidents depends on their
being what they profess to be—a picture of a real society. And
gradually we come to realise that this whole elaborately painted
English scene is pure pasteboard, a stage set done with nothing
deeper than a scene-painter's knowledge. Compare it with the earlier
chapters of *The Rainbow* or the colliery chapters of *Women in Love*,
and its shallowness and falsity become immediately apparent. The
village out of a come-to-Britain poster, the stage country rector, the
bouncing young people out of an Aldwych farce, are thinner than the
paper they are printed on.

This is to some extent obscured by passages of great insight and
truth. The scene where Mrs. Witt proposes marriage to the groom
Lewis is hard to credit in itself, but it is redeemed by the crusty
dignity of Lewis's reply:

"No, Mam. I couldn't give my body to any woman who didn't respect it."

"But I do respect it, I do!"—she flushed hot like a girl.

"No, Mam. Not as I mean it," he replied. There was a touch of anger against her in his voice, and a distance of distaste.

"And how do you mean it?" she replied. . . .

"No woman who I touched with my body should ever speak to me as you speak to me or think of me as you think of me," he said.

Some of Mrs. Witt's reactions to English country life are also excellent.

"How strange these picturesque old villages are, Louise!" she said, with a duskiness around her sharp, well-bred nose. "How easy it all seems, all on a definite pattern. And how false! And underneath, how *corrupt*!"

This is shrewd, penetrating and in character. And Lou's gradual realisation of Rico's hollowness is also excellently done. It almost leads us to forget the vapidity of her doctrinaire conversation and the impossible jeering vulgarity of her letters to her mother after Rico is hurt.

And what is the end of it all? Of course there is nothing to be done. Society is irredeemable; England cannot change. As so often in Lawrence, the only thing to do is to move on. So Lou and Mrs. Witt go back to America, back to the South-west, with St. Mawr. And though this gives rise to one of the most magnificent pieces of description in all Lawrence's work, it is here that the weakness of the story as a whole becomes most evident. After the comprehensive indictment of modern society outlined in the first part, the solution is inadequate. If you don't like men any more, go and live in New Mexico with a horse. There is no suggestion that human life there takes on any new quality. For a little time Phœnix, the Indian groom, looks as if he is to be a symbol of unfallen or regenerated mankind; but he turns out to be a presuming servant who would be glad to play the part of Romero in "The Princess" if he could. All that remains is St. Mawr and the magnificent landscape of Lou's ranch (actually Lawrence's own ranch near Taos). St. Mawr has never been able to bear the symbolic weight that has been put upon him; he is too overworked and generalised an image to be more than a bit of shorthand notation for what Lawrence wants. But the landscape of Taos is different. A uniquely powerful experience in Lawrence's life, it can become the concrete embodiment of a vast, impersonal force, beyond good and evil, the power of life itself that seems gone from contemporary civilisation. The ten pages or so describing the place and its history are superb: individual, realised to the last detail, yet with the great authentic wind blowing like a spirit through each particular thing.

But it is not what Lawrence or the story really needs at this point; not, at any rate, if it is to stop there. Lou's solution has no general validity. An attempt is made to give it some general human reference by recounting, most movingly and impressively (as Dr. Leavis has been alone in pointing out) the life of the previous owners of the ranch, their triumph in building a little outpost of civilisation in the heart of a splendid wilderness. But Lou is doing nothing of the kind, and we cannot suppose that her bit of make-believe ranching, supported by money from the corrupt civilisation she has deserted, can mean anything more than a few weeks' exaltation and refreshment. In any case, to point out, however powerfully, that the creative struggle with wild nature can be a valid way of life throws no light, however indirect, on the problems of a complex civilisation where this particular struggle has long ceased. Lou is alone with a magnificent landscape that, as far as human existence is concerned, is cruel at worst, at best splendidly indifferent. Like others who are left alone with the universe, having found nothing better to attach themselves to, she tries to cheer herself up: "And I am here, right deep in America, where there's a wild spirit wants me, a wild spirit more than men." But what Lou and Lawrence really want is something else—a way of bringing the wild spirit into relation with men again, a way of letting the great wind blow through human society. To make a cardboard model of human society, and then to set up in opposition to it a magnificent image of wild natural power is too easy and too unhelpful. How is the spirit of Taos to be led down into the world of men? All Lawrence's Mexican writing is the record of his failure to find an answer. *The Plumed Serpent* attempts to embody the spirit of Mexico in ritual and institution. It fails—and ends in indecision. "The Woman Who Rode Away" finds the answer in the death of the whole white consciousness. And that is the response of an honest despair. "St. Mawr" provides a fake solution; and in spite of its scattered insights and splendours, this strain of falsity runs through the whole work.

Of course it is a weighty tribute to "St. Mawr" that it demands discussion in these terms; and in turning to the stories of the last phase we are aware, for the most part, of an abrupt decline of seriousness and intensity. There is one exception, "The Man Who Died", and that is an exception to the general run of the stories in other ways as well. And there is an admirable *novelle*, "The Virgin and the Gipsy". The volume, including "The Woman Who Rode Away", published under this title in 1928, includes a number of post-Mexican stories, and it was the last collection to appear in Lawrence's lifetime. Several other stories were written about the same time for various periodicals, and they may all be dealt with together. Two new features become prominent in them—a strong element of personal satire and the use of the supernatural. Neither is particularly beneficial. As for the first, Lawrence had always used his friends and acquaintances, often too directly, as material for his works; but generally for some creative purpose. A real figure may have been used unscrupulously, but he takes his place in a pattern that goes beyond malicious portraiture. But in several of these late stories—"Smile", "Jimmy and the Desperate Woman", "The Man Who Loved Islands", "Things", perhaps others—the dominant motive seems to be irritation, contempt or amusement inspired purely by individual characters and their behaviour. Though the vigour and aptness of the writing is as great as ever, the effects are specialised and negative. The wine has gone thinner and sourer in the time from "The Fox" and "The Captain's Doll". And as for the supernatural, in "The Border Line", "The Last Laugh" and "Glad Ghosts" it becomes too easy an evasion of the story-teller's problem to work out a theme through the medium of character and action. Ghosts should be raised in fiction by people who believe in them or by those whose aim is to produce a shudder of the nerves. Lawrence belongs to neither of these classes, and his ghostly visitants only produce effects that in his more vigorous moods would have been achieved through the conflict of character and circumstance.

These qualifications do not deny the appearance of a hard, shrewd perception and an easy executive power. The opening description in "Jimmy and the Desperate Woman" is a brilliant, acid piece of character-drawing.

"I am not," he said to himself, "a poor little man nestled upon some woman's bosom. If I could only find the right sort of woman, she should nestle on mine."

Jimmy was now thirty-five, and this point, to nestle or be nestled, was the emotional crux and turning point.

He imagined to himself some really *womanly* woman, to whom he should be *only* "fine and strong", and not for one moment "the poor little man". Why not some simple uneducated girl, some Tess of the D'Urbervilles, some wistful Gretchen, some humble Ruth gleaning an aftermath? Why not? Surely the world was full of such!

The trouble was he never met them. He only met sophisticated women. He really never had a chance of meeting "real" people. So few of us ever do. Only the people we *don't* meet are the "real" people, the simple, genuine, direct, spontaneous, unspoilt souls. Ah, the simple, genuine, unspoilt people we *don't* meet! What a tragedy it is!

And Jimmy's actual meeting with a hard-bitten miner's wife is a triumph of ironical imagination. The sardonic dexterity Lawrence shows here, and in "Things", for instance, would be the making of an ordinary satirist. But with him it is hard to avoid the feeling that an imagination meant for other ends is being used in an almost petulantly destructive way. Or, if more is attempted, it is not employed wth a sufficiently sustained intensity to penetrate the structure of the tale. This is the trouble with "The Border Line". It tells of a woman of German birth formerly married to a vigorous raw-boned Scottish soldier who has been killed in the war, now married to a gentler, weaker man. Immediately after the war she travels from France into Germany to meet her present husband. The description of war-weary Europe and of the atmosphere on the Franco-German border has all the sombre penetration of the contemporary "Letter from Germany", reprinted in *Phœnix*. Though based on the merest glimpses obtained on the Lawrences' short return to Europe in 1924, these passages are the most striking examples of his intuitive power. But there is not enough of it, or it is not of the right kind, to inform the plot. As the woman penetrates into Germany the ghost of her former husband comes to claim her, finally defeating his successor in a scene of grisly and cruel power. If Lawrence's energies had been working at full stretch it would have been presented as a psychological process, a change in the woman's mind by which the old scenes, the landscapes and towns where her life was really rooted also reactivate the old love that had really dominated her life. The bit of ghostly machinery evades this necessity; and this means that the job is not really done, the story becomes far less serious than it promised to be.

"Glad Ghosts" compels a similar judgment. Here the appearance of a family ghost brings back fertility and warmth to a group of people whose life has for long been dried up and withered. Some of the characterisation here is complete enough to demand a more genuine solution. And as for "The Last Laugh", it describes one of those embarrassing visitations of Pan to Hampstead that illustrates emphatically the way not to evoke the chthonic powers. "The Rocking-Horse Winner" is an exception among the supernatural tales. It is not at all a Laurentian story—fancy rather than imagination—this tale of a small boy who by riding his toy rocking-horse can spot the winners of real races. The supernatural element is boldly and properly left unexplained, and is not made the substitute for a psychological reality that could be presented without it. The theme develops into a hectic and pathetic tale of gambling fever that destroys the boy himself as it reaches a successful climax; most skilfully done, but quite outside the range of Lawrence's usual work.

In other stories he is rather laboriously calling up old themes. "Sun" is a dreary tale of an unsatisfied American woman with a pallid business-man husband who finds a kind of fulfilment by living in Italy, sun-bathing all the time, and looking at a hard brown peasant. And "The Lovely Lady" returns to the equally worn subject of possessive maternity and frustrated manhood. In fact, in many of these stories Lawrence went nearer to popularising his gospel on the magazine-story level than he had ever done before. His energies were limited by illness; the best of them were absorbed by *Lady Chatterley* and exhausted by the subsequent controversy; so that the full force was rarely available to turn into the minor works.

Before writing *Lady Chatterley* Lawrence wrote a long tale, "The Virgin and the Gipsy". It is an independent work, with a complete imaginative integrity of its own, but it does in many ways suggest a preliminary working over of *Lady Chatterley* material. It marks a change in the direction of Lawrence's interests—a return to England, foreshadowed in "The Flying Fish" and reaching its full development in *Lady Chatterley* itself. Of course "St. Mawr" had been about

England, and so are many of the late short stories. But the country of "St. Mawr" is a cardboard affair, put up to be knocked over; and the other stories only happen to be in England because they have to be somewhere. In "The Virgin and the Gipsy" we feel a return to a long-neglected source of Lawrence's power—the profound feeling for certain aspects of English life, seen at its best in *The Rainbow* and *Women in Love*. The sisters Lucille and Yvette reveal a half-conscious desire to revive Gudrun and Ursula, to go back to an imaginative construction firmly based on knowledge and understanding. "The Virgin and the Gipsy" is set vaguely in the north country; but its actual scenery seems to be the Derbyshire that Lawrence knew well. Instead of the thin social caricatures of "St. Mawr", we have the dank, uncomfortable but infinitely real presentation of a family from which all the life has departed, leaving only the strain of rival egotisms. The story tells of the constantly frustrated struggle of the girls to find some sort of life for themselves; and at least the glimpse of salvation for Yvette through her love for the gipsy. Besides *The Rainbow*, reminiscences of "Daughters of the Vicar", "The Horse Dealer's Daughter" and *The White Peacock* come to mind. The tale of the lady and the raggle-taggle gipsies is so little novel that this version of it has perhaps attracted less attention than it might. It is characteristic of Lawrence to go back again and again to a familiar theme. In "The Virgin and the Gipsy" he not only does this but also goes back after a long interval to a setting where all is familiar, where he has little need for the intuitions and projections that help him to build up the unfamiliar Mexican scene. The freshness and completeness of the tale, the absence of hate and intrusive bitterness, show how reviving the return to his native roots could be.

With the last of Lawrence's tales, "The Man Who Died", we pass again into another world—the world of *Apocalypse* and *Last Poems*. As his hold on life slackened he forgot about England, forgot about Mexico and lived more and more in the actual Mediterranean present, or imaginatively in the Mediterranean past. *Etruscan Places* and some of the later poems reveal the abandonment of strange gods, weariness of the wrestle with modern civilisation, and a dream-like relapse into the life of pre-Christian Europe, whose survivals he could still detect, or imagine he detected, in uncorrupted parts of Italy and the south. But whatever Lawrence might be, he could never become a pre-

Christian. A paganism haunted by Christianity is something inevitably different from a paganism that has never known it. And Lawrence is haunted by Christianity. Time and again we have seen how his own religious intuitions can become clear only when set in opposition to a Christian background. So, in his last story, when he is approaching death and knows it, the Christian myth forces itself again on his mind, and he makes a last effort to come to terms with it.

But in doing so he deserts the limits of ordinary fiction. More decisively than in "The Woman Who Rode Away", we enter the sphere of the mythopœic imagination. By accepting the gospel story of the Resurrection as his theme even as far as he does, he acknowledges a remoteness from the temporal and the conditioned. And by departing from it, removing it to another plane, adding to it, he acknowledges an attempt to reinterpret one of the central myths of our culture. This makes the story incommensurable with his other tales. There is no way of considering "The Fox" and "The Man Who Died" in the same context. In a sense this last story belongs more with the philosophy than the fiction; at any rate, it is in "The Man Who Died", if anywhere, that Lawrence transcends the limits of the philosophy he has been arduously hammering out in fiction and exposition all his life. We shall therefore postpone consideration of it till his thought and its limits have been examined more fully. Though it is not his most perfect work of art, there is a sense in which "The Man Who Died" represents the consummation of Lawrence's work, and the place to consider it is at the end.

Chapter IV

THE POEMS

Lawrence's poetry is rarely read as a whole. Perhaps it should be, for it is poetry rather than poems—a body of work poetically felt and conceived whose individual units rarely reach perfection or self-subsistence. If, neglecting the smaller accidents of bibliography, we simply read the three volumes of the collected verse straight through, they assume the status of a running commentary to the course of development outlined in the novels. This seems the wrong thing to say about any poetry, but it is, in fact, what Lawrence says himself, in the preface to the *Collected Poems*.

It seems to me that no poetry, not even the best, should be judged as if it existed in the absolute, in the vacuum of the absolute. Even the best poetry, when it is at all personal, needs the penumbra of its own time and place and circumstance to make it full and whole. If we knew a little more of Shakespeare's self and circumstance, how much more complete the Sonnets would be to us, how their strange, torn edges would be softened and merged into a whole body!

And he asks the reader "to fill in the background of the poems as far as possible with the time, the place and the circumstance"; and in the rest of the preface from which these words are taken gives us a brief chronology that enables us to do so. Richard Aldington, in the preface to *Last Poems*, comments to the same effect.

There is perpetual intercourse with the Muse, but the progeny is as surprising to the parent as to anybody else. Lawrence's writing was not something outside himself, it was part of himself, it came out of his life and in turn fed his life. He adventured into himself in order to write, and by writing discovered himself. From the first sentence in *The White Peacock* to the last broken utterance:

> Give me the moon at my feet
> Set my feet upon the crescent like a Lord!

written by a dying hand, all this mass of writing forms one immense autobiography.

Now, claims of this sort cannot be imputed to any poetry as a merit. At worst they are an invitation to us to do the work that the poet has failed to do; at best they subordinate the poetry to some chain of circumstance outside itself. In either case, they are a limitation. With Lawrence, however, it is probably necessary to accept the limitation, at least provisionally, if we are to see how far and on what occasions he transcends it. There is an admirable formalist criticism of Lawrence's poetry by R. P. Blackmur.[51] From its own point of view it leaves nothing more to be said. Yet at the end the essence of Lawrence's poetry is no more discernible than it was at the beginning. Mr. Blackmur's close argument is quite incontrovertible, so let us not waste time trying to controvert it. Let us outline it, in all its imposing simplicity, and then try to worry our way round it to another point of view.

The title of the essay is "D. H. Lawrence and Expressive Form"; and the burden of the argument is that Lawrence regarded his poetry as fragmentary biography, and refused to use the resources of the art that he was practising. His art lacks the support of a rational imagination and fails to couch itself in a rational form. Lawrence declines to impose a form on his insights; he relies on the structure of the experience itself to provide the structure of the work. When he does adopt a conventional and symmetrical form, it is incompletely and without art. The exigencies of rhyme and normal accentual verse are allowed to interfere with his expression without ever becoming a formal principle in themselves. When he does not use such a form his only principle of organisation is hysteria—the abnormal heightening of an intensely perceived reality. When Lawrence talks, as he does in the preface quoted before, of the failure of some of his early poems "because the young man interfered with his demon", he is wrong. The young man of the quotation is the poet as craftsman, and the demon, as Mr. Blackmur puts it, is "exactly that outburst of personal feeling which needed the discipline of craft to become a poem". The situation is the reverse of what Lawrence supposes—in fact, the craftsman did not interfere with the demon enough. And the result is that Lawrence left us only "the ruins of great intentions".

One would be hard put to it to deny much of this; and yet "Snake", "Bavarian Gentians" and "The Ship of Death" remain, and the strong odour of "Pansies". When poetry succeeds formally its

quality can be fully exposed by formal criticism; all has been mani-
fested in form. When poetry partly fails from a formal point of view,
yet something impressive remains, formal criticism can never be
enough. There is something lingering beyond the threshold of
realisation. The purist may regard it as inadmissible because, in fact,
it has not succeeded in gaining admission; yet by a more generous
interpretation of the critic's duty, it ought as far as possible to be
examined, its relation to what has been fully realised should be made
plain. And for that we must abandon the purely formal procedure, and
admit expressive and biographical aims to some share of our consideration.

Taken in rough chronological order, Lawrence's poems fall into
five groups. There are the early poems, mostly connected with
Miriam or his mother and written in Eastwood or London; there is
the series called *Look! We Have Come Through!*, all connected with
the early days of his marriage, written in Germany, Italy and England
again; there are *Birds, Beasts and Flowers*, nearly all written in Italy,
but a few in Mexico. There are *Pansies*, which are perhaps doubtfully
poems at all, but then they are not prose either, and they are certainly
something. They were written after Lawrence's return from America,
and the later ones overlap with *Last Poems*, written under the shadow
of approaching death. All these groups can be more or less closely
related to the prose works. The early poems belong with *The White
Peacock* and *Sons and Lovers*; *Look! We Have Come Through!* is equally
closely linked with *The Rainbow* and *Women in Love*; *Birds, Beasts
and Flowers* covers a longish stretch between *Aaron's Rod* and *The
Plumed Serpent*, but they are not obviously connected with the fiction,
they are nearer to the travel essays *Sea and Sardinia* and *Mornings
in Mexico*, and nearer still to being something quite on their own,
embodying insights and apprehensions that do not find expression
elsewhere. *Pansies* are close in mood to *Lady Chatterley's Lover* and
the pamphleteering that surrounded it; and the last poems have an
obvious kinship with *The Man Who Died*. Each of these collections of
poems has its own special phase of life to express.

Many of the early poems are filled with exactly the same awareness
of an omnipresent natural vitality as *The White Peacock*. Indeed, this
vivid poetic sense of a quivering responsive life running through
everything is habitual and pervasive, almost independent of particular

193

occasions. With Wordsworth, for example, this habitual sense is precipitated into separable formal units by particular scenes and incidents; with Lawrence this hardly seems to occur. And an all-pervading, unconcentrated mode of perception is perhaps better used as the presiding spirit of a novel like *The White Peacock* than in short lyric poems. Much of the verse of this period is formally indistinguishable from prose except for the intervention of the rhyme; and since there is hardly any discernible verse rhythm the lines have no existence as separate units, the rhymes mark nothing and seem curiously irrelevant.

> Rabbits, handfuls of brown earth, lie
> Low-rounded on the mournful turf they have bitten down to
> the quick.
> Are they asleep?—are they living?—Now see, when I
> Lift my arms, the hill bursts and heaves under their spurting
> kick.

At other times a rough rhythmic parallelism begins to give the sense of a controlled form, and odd lines tremble on the verge of regular metric. In any case, complete success is only occasional, and so far we must grant all that Mr. Blackmur has said.

There are a good many townscapes and landscapes in the Georgian mode—a natural, unaffected but at the same time rather diffuse response to the outward scene. After the prætorian cohorts of romantic verse had been disbanded, there was no doubt a certain fresh honesty in descriptions like that in "Flat Suburbs":

> The new red houses spring like plants
> In level rows
> Of reddish herbage that bristles and slants
> Its square shadows.
>
> The pink young houses show one side bright
> Flatly assuming the sun,
> And one side shadow, half in sight,
> Half-hiding the pavement-run.

But it is neither very intense nor very workmanlike. One suspects that the first stanza just came, and is just right; while the rest of the poem is genuine observation indeed, but versified in a very perfunctory fashion.

Combining freely with this poetry of response to the outer world is a young man's love poetry. The substance and the feeling behind it are all to be found, translated into another medium, in the early novels. Lawrence writes in his preface "The poems to Miriam, and to my Mother, and to Helen, and to the other woman, the woman of 'Kisses in the Train' and 'Hands of the Betrothed', they need the order of time, as that is the order of experience." And anyone who has read *The White Peacock, Sons and Lovers* and *The Trespasseer* with an eye to their autobiographical background will know where to place these pieces. They tell the familiar story of Lawrence's early life: the love for the mother; the love for a girl, always frustrated and unsatisfying; experimental loves with other girls, equally unsatisfactory; the death of the mother, and the long pain of reminiscence. How many of them would make their own effect without such external reference? Probably not many. A short poem is expected to be all poetry, and to subsume everything into a close-knit unity. Few of these short poems succeed in that way. But a long poem is permitted a unity of a laxer kind; we do not expect it to be all poetry; and it can have separate beauties whose connection with the whole is undefined or merely contingent. I want to suggest that that is the way to save Lawrence's early poems—to read them as a long verse-journal, in which we are to expect neither completeness in the parts nor an Aristotelian plot, but simply the development of an intelligible train of feeling through a number of fragmentary occasions. It may be said that we should not try to save them—that the lapses into banality of diction, the perfunctory gestures towards verse form, the uneasy compromises with conventional poetic expression, should involve all in a common oblivion. But why should any moments of pleasure or truth be lost? Why should we give up so many fragments of honesty, poignancy and direct power of expression?

Let us first extract a few poems that could stand without their context—"Dog Tired" and "Cherry Ripe" from the earliest group. "Dog Tired" is a haymaker's idyll; and it has a balanced, symmetrical, yet quite unforced construction. The first two stanzas run parallel to each other—"If she would come here . . ."; "If she would come to me now . . ." The middle verse breaks this pastoral reverie with recollections of "the chattering machine", the strenuous bustle of the day that is past. And in the last two stanzas the repetitive parallelism of longing is resumed: "I should like to drop . . ."; "I should like to lie still . . ."

"Cherry Ripe" is remarkable for its controlled symbols of richness and generosity in love, contrasted with pain and death; the crimson cherries and the dead birds who have been shot for stealing them; the laughing girl offering cherries and the knowledge that what will be demanded of her is tears. There are some small pieces in the Imagist manner, like "Apple Blossoms"; and the school poems deserve a rank among conversation pieces, *sermoni propriora*; "Discipline" especially is a moving poem, with its intelligence and tenderness surviving a brutalising weariness. The poems on the death of the mother belong mostly to the class that cannot stand on their own; without their biographical context they are painful and eccentric; but there is one exception among the poems of reminiscence after the mother's death—the much-quoted "Piano". The added strength and objectivity given by distance is shown chiefly in the rhythm—so shifty and uncertain in many of the poems, but here so consistent and controlled, from the slow opening, the dawn of recollection, through the accelerated pace of the second verse, as the journey backward through time becomes more urgent, to the full powerful movement of the compelling flood of memory in the last stanza.

Even here, in one place, the diction relies on a range of reference outside the poem itself; most of it is unobtrusively accurate and sufficient; but "hymns in the cosy parlour, the tinkling piano our guide" is flat and banal, risks a dreary suggestion of petty-bourgeois pietism where the intention is to convey the warmth and security of home. Of course to anyone familiar with *Sons and Lovers*, where the gaps left by these words are filled in so solidly and fully, this suggestion disappears; and in any case the poem is strong enough to overcome it. In other places—in "Letter from Town" and "Scent of Irises", for example—in "Coldness in Love", "Last Words to Miriam" and the poems on the mother's illness—the reader is inevitably, I think, driven back to his knowledge of Lawrence's biography, if he has it; or if not, to an imaginary biographical setting which he constructs to take its place. I cannot persuade myself that they are therefore without value. The biography is, as it happens, real; even supposing it were not, the pieces could take their place in a loose fictitious biographical sequence, and gain strength and significance from each other; poetry, not separate poems; poetry of an unequal intensity and purity, but of a quality one would not willingly forgo.

THE POEMS

There is of course another class of poems altogether in the early work—the dramatic and fictitious pieces. These include some admirable dialect poems, where strangely enough the rhythm, a rough ballad metre, seems to come more naturally and cause less difficulty than anywhere else. The first of these, "The Collier's Wife", is simply a ballad on the familiar theme of the miner hurt in a pit accident. In others, "Violets", "Whether or Not", "The Drained Cup", Lawrence takes bitter eccentric situations, such as might have served him for short stories, and treats them in acrid, concentrated verse, with a sure command of the vernacular. The influence of Hardy is strong here, though the dialect and the situations are all Lawrence's own; and the Hardy of *Satires of Circumstance* is seen more obviously behind "Turned Down", "Lightning", "Reading a Letter", "Two Wives". In none of these is Lawrence as sure as in the dialect poems. The other ostensibly dramatic poem, "Love on the Farm", is in a different class. Though dramatic in presentation, it is composed of motives obvious in *The White Peacock* and *Sons and Lovers*—and these the most directly concerned with Lawrence's intimate personal life. It is thus the transmutation of a subjective confession; and the necessity for transmutation brings an immense accession of art. It is a pity that Lawrence's personal poems were not more often subjected to such a process. The poem is spoken in the person of a gentle, timid girl (the Muriel of *The White Peacock*, the Miriam of *Sons and Lovers*), and describes her reactions to her roughly bucolic lover, who enters carrying a snared rabbit with the smell of death on his hands. The girl in his embrace is like the rabbit he has killed; love is like death. It is an old trope, but presented here as a fact, with a weight of powerfully observed circumstance. An idyllic, almost Tennysonian opening, representing the girl's dreams, is contrasted with a second, less lyrical passage, where the actual man makes his appearance, casually startling the timorous natural life around him.

> Into the yellow, evening glow
> Saunters a man from the farm below;
> Leans, and looks in at the low-built shed
> Where the swallow has hung her marriage bed.
> The bird lies warm against the wall.
> She glances quick her startled eyes
> Towards him, then she turns away
> Her small head, making warm display

Of red upon the throat. Her terrors sway
Her out of the nest's warm, busy ball——

After the swallow's fears come those of the rabbit and the girl;
yet the man's unperceptive kindliness is hardly disturbed. She dies
in his embrace, and finds death good. Readers of *The White Peacock*
need not seek far for the subjective roots of this piece. The lover of
the poem is manifestly the George Saxton of the novel. The girl in
the novel is his sister; she shrinks from him in just this way, but it
is not an amorous shrinking. In the novel it is Cyril, the young, girlish
representation of Lawrence himself, who feels the fascination of
George's crude strength. The poem transfers Cyril-Lawrence's feeling
to the girl, and the effort of doing this gives it an element of dramatic
tautness that Lawrence's personal poetry so often lacks. The poem,
in fact, is a reconstructed and dramatised version of the "Poem of
Friendship" chapter in *The White Peacock*. This in itself would be
without interest, except that it illustrates how the labour of construction, of making an emotion into a fiction, can improve and tighten
Lawrence's poetic method.

Some indifferent poems of the war period must be passed over.
The next phase opens with *Look! We have Come Through!*. We may be
permitted to take the early poems as a biographical sequence, but
we are actually enjoined to take these so. The story they tell is of
course that of Lawrence's early marriage; and he provides a brief
prose argument.

> After much struggling and loss in love and in the world of
> man, the protagonist throws in his lot with a woman who is
> already married. Together they go into another country, she
> perforce leaving her children behind. The conflict of love and
> hate goes on between the man and the woman, and between these
> two and the world around them, till it reaches some sort of con-
> clusion.

But, as before, the series is discontinuous, and some of the best
poems are quite detached from the main theme. Much therefore that
was said about the early poems applies to these also. There is the
same formal failure or incomplete success; some brilliant flashes of
insight and presentation; while as for the total impression, though it
arouses neither sympathy nor admiration, a gap would be left in our
experience if it were lost. However, there are differences. Lawrence

apparently regarded these poems as formally different from the early ones, for he classifies them as Unrhyming Poems, as against the Rhyming Poems of the first series. As a matter of fact, a number of the pieces in *Look! We Have Come Through!* are in rhyme; but it is true that in the bulk of them Lawrence develops for the first time his own particular kind of rhymeless "free verse", whatever that may mean. Secondly, the experience behind *Look! We Have Come Through!* is more concentrated and more intense than that of the early poems. These two circumstances conspire to produce a result of doubtful benefit to the verse, which on the whole shows a decline from the earlier work.

The sheer urgency of the experience makes Lawrence feel, even more than was his wont, that all that is necessary is to get it down somehow while it is hot, that his job is expression not making. This is probably the reason for the abandonment of rhyme—even the very slight hurdles presented by Laurentian rhyming are now felt as an obstruction to the direct flow of emotion. Yet what, after all, is rhymeless free verse? I have never seen the matter properly examined, but surely it is always one of two things—on the one hand, a relaxation of or an approximation to some conventional form, usually blank verse; or, on the other hand, mere rhythmical prose, verse only by courtesy and typography, and poetry, if at all, in virtue of its purpose and method, or of some special concision of imagery or evocativeness of language. Lawrence's free verse is clearly in the latter class; and all too often the language is of a flatness and banality that fails to create a structure satisfying in itself, and even at times fails to evoke the underlying experience.

> I hold the night in horror;
> I dare not turn round.
>
> To-night I have left her alone.
> They would have it I have left her for ever.
>
> Oh my God, how it aches
> Where she is cut off from me!
>
> Perhaps she will go back to England.
> Perhaps she will go back,
> Perhaps we are parted for ever.

In this poem, "Mutilation", there is not even anything individual or characteristic in the experience. To utter the time-worn lover's complaint in this shoddy dialect seems the most hopeless of literary enterprises. In other places, however, a strangeness and unconventionality in the experience itself survives the formal deficiencies, and makes, if not a good poem, at least some quite unique fragment of literary expression. Mr. Blackmur has pointed out that in "She Said As Well to Me" Lawrence manages to present "merely by the intensified honesty of the observation", the dignity of individual isolation. So he does, we might add, in other places. In "Loggerheads" he presents equally successfully the exhaustion of a lover's quarrel; in "In the Dark" the sheer intrinsic conflict of personalities; and in "A Bad Beginning" the longing, not for love or pleasure, but (something far less often expressed in poetry) for a real marriage relationship. The general direction of the series is that of the honeymoon chapter in *The Rainbow* and the Birkin and Ursula parts of *Women in Love*; and the personal poetry adds little to what is done under the guise of fiction in the prose. The destination, what we have come through to, is supposed to be revealed in "Manifesto", a doctrinaire piece of the *Women in Love* period exalting the virtue of communion in separateness. In its formal nonentity, its mere blank assertion of something that remains finally only half-formulated, it is the measure of the failure of *Look! We Have Come Through!* as a whole. The series survives as a biographical document; otherwise only by a few beautiful and incidental poems.

These particularly successful poems are hardly connected with the whole except by contiguity of time and place. The "Hymn to Priapus" could take its place among the dramatic pieces in the early group, with the same moments of rich sensuous vividness:

> I danced at the Christmas party
> Under the mistletoe
> Along with a ripe, slack country lass
> Jostling to and fro.
>
> The big, soft country lass,
> Like a loose sheaf of wheat
> Slipped through my arms on the threshing floor
> At my feet.

And the same lapses into slackness of expression. The situation is imagined, but this meditation on fidelity to a dead love and renewed sensuality is very close in spirit to the poems about the love for the dead mother, and probably has its root in this complex of emotions. If so, the poem is a deliberate and successful transmutation of a personal emotion, like "Love on the Farm". "Everlasting Flowers" is addressed directly to the dead mother, and is a straightforward poem of personal love—too little stiffened by the tension of art to be a very good poem, and too directly felt and expressed to be other than moving. More remarkable are the pieces where Lawrence takes intuitive, divinatory glimpses into the life of people quite unconnected with him, among whom he merely happens to be living. "A Youth Mowing" is a slight example. A better one is "Sunday Afternoon in Italy", with its admirable objective portrayal of the distant, bitter courtship of the rustic lovers, modulating into an invocation to the warring male and female principles. "Giorno dei Morti" is similarly objective; it is grave and restrained, without the flash of peculiarly Laurentian insight, but with an unusual formal delicacy.

But for the most part it must be said that these poems are by-products. They are small facets of topics that have been more comprehensively worked out in the novels. It is in *Birds, Beasts and Flowers* that Lawrence for the first time uses his poetry to express a special sense of life that can hardly find its place in the prose. They were mostly written in Italy, a few in Ceylon, Australia and Mexico. The novels contemporary with them are *Aaron's Rod* and *Kangaroo*, and these are both books where Lawrence's powers are working at something less than full stretch. It is a period of interim and abeyance in his dealings with human experience, and much of his insight and energy flows into communion with the natural world, a communion of a highly original kind. There has probably been too much nature poetry in English since Wordsworth. A merely passive sense of natural beauty as a comforting, sustaining, more rarely an exciting influence became too easy an indulgence for poets and poetically minded persons. Lawrence's nature poetry breaks sharply with this tradition. It is not passive appreciation; it has not much to do with beauty as such; it does not use natural objects as stimulants to generalised and habitual emotions. Instead it makes an energetic and intuitive attempt to penetrate into the being of natural objects, to show what they are in themselves, not how they can sustain our moral nature. Or it presents encounters between man and the non-human, the perpetual mystery of the animal and vegetable creation. Of course it is radically subjective; who can know what it is to be a pomegranate or a kangaroo, what one meets when one meets a snake or a bat? But it has little to do with common human subjectivity; it is more an attempt to put common human subjectivity in its place by showing the myriad of queer, separate, non-human existences around it.

There are other modes of apprehension than ours, other gods than our gods. We can know our own; we can seize intuitive glimpses of some of the others; and so by these fragmentary separate approaches we can reach towards the common mystery that is at the root of all of them. But only reach towards it; it remains always beyond. Linnæus, who saw God as order, could write *Deum sempiternum, immensum, omniscium, omnipotentem, expergefactus transeuntem vidi, et obstupui.* For Lawrence there is no such bright systematic vision. He is too aware of the dark underworld that can never be known, that can never bear witness to anything in human consciousness, the world from which his snake has come and towards which his kangaroo yearns.

Of course these glimpses of other worlds than ours suggest parallels and contrasts with our world, and of course these associations are often arbitrary. We used to go to the ant for lessons in industry; now we go to it for warnings against totalitarianism. He who finds sermons in stones, books in the running brooks is apt to find that they preach his own doctrine. When Lawrence finds in Tuscan cypresses an emblem of the mysterious inward life that he believes to have gone on among the ancient Etruscans, he is using an imposed and personal symbolism; in quite a normal poetic way, to be sure, but there is not anything in the nature of cypresses to require them to stand for that rather than anything else. Some of his associations are fanciful, half-playful, confessed by the diction to be such. In the "Bare Fig-Tree" poem the way the twigs bud sideways and then turn vertically upwards is seen as the effort by each twig to assert its individual identity, "to hold the one and only lighted candle of the sun in his socket tip". And this gives rise to some reflections on fig democracy, with analogical sidelights on human democracy.

> O weird Demos, where every twig is the arch-twig,
> Each imperiously over-equal to each, equality over-reaching
> itself. . . .
> Still, no doubt every one of you can be the sun-socket as well
> as every other of you.

THE POEMS

Physically the fig branches do behave in this way; the attribution
of any such moral intention to them is merely humorous, as the language confesses; and the implied reflection (that we cannot each be
superior to everyone else, but we each have a unique faculty for holding
up the lighted candle of the sun and a unique right to bear witness to
it) is something that Lawrence profoundly believes. And in a sense
the fig tree, by its living form, does say just that. The spirit of these
poems is in this respect not unlike that of the seventeenth-century
emblems, in which anything may be used to typify anything else, and
no association is too improbable. All, indeed, are in some sense real,
for to Lawrence as to the *seicentisti*, the world is really emblematic,
every fragment of reality bears witness to the nature of the whole.

Where the revelation is of absolute otherness, the element of
arbitrary subjectivity disappears. The attempt is at objective presentation of the nature of things that can never fully form part of our
awareness.

But sitting in a boat on the Zeller lake
And watching the fishes in the breathing waters
Lift and swim and go their way——

I said to my heart, who are these?
And my heart couldn't own them. . . .

A slim young pike, with smart fins
And grey-striped suit, a young cub of a pike
Slouching along away below, half out of sight,
Like a lout on an obscure pavement. . . .

Aha, there's somebody in the know!

But watching closer
That motionless deadly motion,
That unnatural barrel body, that long ghoul nose, . . .
I left off hailing him.
I had made a mistake, I didn't know him,
This grey, monotonous soul in the water,
This intense individual in shadow,
Fish-alive.

I didn't know his God,
I didn't know his God.

Which is perhaps the last admission that life has to wring out
of us.

Other Gods
Beyond my range . . . gods beyond my God.

The superb Tortoise series is probably the most sustained attempt
in literature to penetrate the mysterious life of a remote part of the
brute creation. From the naked, solitary independence of the baby
tortoise to the weird cry of the male tortoise in the extremity of coition
a small organic unit of non-human existence is brought as far as it
can be within human imaginative apprehension. I know of nothing
else in art to express this intimate and joyful observation—unless it
is some small Han sculptures, where like Lawrence the Chinese
craftsman can summon up by a supreme effort of identification an alien
animality, and yet retain at the same time his faculty for human
delight and wonder.

The motive of other poems is to present the encounter between
animal and man. An easy natural piety has used faithful dogs, spiritual
skylarks, as opportunities for extension of the normal sympathetic
emotions. Lawrence sees the strangeness, the real antagonism. Yet
a profounder kind of natural piety is present all the same—profounder
because it does not reduce everything to the anthropomorphic, because
it recognises otherness and difference. This is Lawrence's theme in
"Snake". He is frightened of the snake and throws a log at it.

> And immediately I regretted it.
> I thought how paltry, how vulgar, what a mean act!
> I despised myself and the voices of my accursed human educa-
> tion.
>
> And I thought of the albatross,
> And I wished he would come back, my snake.
>
> For he seemed to me again like a king,
> Like a king in exile, uncrowned in the underworld,
> Now due to be crowned again.
>
> And so, I missed my chance with one of the lords
> Of life.
> And I have something to expiate;
> A pettiness.

It is even the theme of "Man and Bat", where the dominant
feeling is one of hostility and repulsion.

> What then?
> Hit him and kill him and throw him away?

Nay,
I didn't create him.

Let the God that created him be responsible for his death . . .
Only, in the bright day, I will not have this clot in my room.

Let the God who is maker of bats watch with them in their
  unclean corners. . . .

It will already have become apparent that I regard these as the most striking of Lawrence's poems up to now—the most striking because they express a unique sense of life, not expressed anywhere else in his works or anywhere in anyone else's. If this arresting quality is the index of a real superiority, it should be confirmed by a strengthening and completion of form, an overcoming of the formal insufficiencies that we have so often had occasion to note in the earlier poems. I think this confirmation can be found; and this is perhaps the place to try to suggest the formal rationale of these rhymeless irregular free-verse pieces. Poems of personal emotion, like most of those in *Look! We Have Come Through!*, above all need the discipline of outward and predetermined form. The temptation is always to too lax an outflow from too wide an orifice; and even the alternative discipline of exact honesty of observation that Lawrence so signally employs is rarely sufficient in these cases to overcome it. When observation is of the self, and of the self acting and suffering, it is never quite pure; never, therefore, a real principle of control. But observation, if it reaches a sufficient intensity, can become a true discipline when it is of something objective, outside the self. And in pieces like the "Snake" and the "Tortoise" poems, I think it does so.

But what kind of poems are they? They are so independent of literary tradition that the ordinary categories will hardly serve us. Clearly they are not lyrics, in any of the several senses of that difficult word; they are not verse as song, and we are not overhearing the poet communing with himself. They are things related and described, but their interest is not narrative. Even when they tell a story, their ultimate mode of existence is not the narrative one of something extended in time, but of something presented for timeless contemplation. They are closely related to a prose form, the imaginative essay, in which fragments of external reality—things, people, places—

appear, and the effort is to present them with the maximum of objectivity and vividness—yet to offer them as objects of contemplation in themselves, not as elements in a narrative or exercises in self-revelation. In that case, why are they not presented as prose essays, why assume the guise of poems at all? Because their method is poetic, even if verse is absent. The essay tends towards exposition, poetry towards direct presentation—and towards the symbolic kind of presentation in which the part can stand for the whole. The essay is tentative and fragmentary; that is its essence; its name suggests as much. But when poetry presents glimpses or lights up facets of an object, these glimpses and facets do not appear as fragments; they appear as parts of an organic whole that can be discerned through and around them. The "translucence of the special in the individual, or of the general in the special, or of the universal in the general" as Coleridge puts it, is a poetic quality. These poems of Lawrence possess that quality in a high degree. They begin with close and delicate observation—an observation so intent and so submissive to the real nature of the external object that all mere subjective effusion is burned away. They select certain aspects of the object for presentation, and at first it seems that these aspects are arbitrarily chosen fragments; but as the poem completes itself they become merely the visible portions of an imaginative whole. And this makes them something utterly different from the dispersed meditations, the assemblage of fragments of which the essay is composed.

This organic quality is sufficient to justify their status as poems; and as for their conventional and typographical presentation, the printing in a kind of verse form—this has its justification, too. The solution of normal prose syntax, the descriptive phrases without principal verbs, the general atactic quality, correspond to the mode of vision—in rapid intuitive glimpses—and is represented on the page by the arrangement of the lines. But again to quote Coleridge, everything in a poem must "contain in itself the reason why it is so and not otherwise". That the line arrangement gives a rough graphic representation of the mode of thought is not really enough. By dividing his discourse into lines instead of presenting it in a homogeneous undifferentiated prose slab, the poet tacitly asserts that this arrangement has meaning, that it represents a rhythmic organisation essential to his total effect. The just objection to many of Lawrence's earlier poems is that this assertion is not true. The arrangement of the lines means nothing; there is no rhythmic organisation, or if there is it is partial, fragmentary and incomplete. In the best of *Birds, Beasts and Flowers* this is no longer so. In "Snake", for instance, no one sensitive to the rhythms of English speech can fail to observe the lovely fluidity of movement (like that of the snake itself):

> He lifted his head from his drinking, as cattle do,
> And looked at me vaguely, as drinking cattle do,
> And flickered his two-forked tongue from his lips, and mused
>   a moment,
> And stooped and drank a little more,
> Being earth-brown, earth-golden from the burning bowels of
>   the earth
> On the day of Sicilian July, with Etna smoking.

The rhythm trembles on the verge of regular iambic for a line or two, then relapses into a looser conversational run; yet the two are not inharmonious but united; just as the mood of the poem oscillates between the apprehension of a strange Orphic life and the prosaic voices of "accursed human education". And a formal articulation is provided by the punctuating of the longer passages of description or reflection with short two-line sentences.

> Someone was before me at my water-trough,
> And I, like a second comer, waiting.

"Snake" is one of Lawrence's finest achievements; but the same sort of argument would apply to many of *Birds, Beasts and Flowers* and to most of the *Last Poems*. There are of course other poems, still successful, in which the rhythmic arrangement is more fortuitous— a convenient kind of discourse that suits Lawrence's way of thought, but is not its necessary or inevitable expression. This is particularly so in the next group—*Pansies*. *Pansies* belong to a different stage of Lawrence's development, they have a different *raison d'être*, and demand on the whole a different kind of consideration. They were written after the return from Mexico, are contemporary with *Lady Chatterley* and the last stories, and for the most part are epigrammatic precipitations of ideas that are floating about in all Lawrence's later work. In them we return to the relations of men and women; indeed, their central theme is the social and personal relations, the interaction between them, and the distortions to which they have been subject in the modern world. So for the first time Lawrence's poetry becomes mainly critical, and finds its substance in the critical and doctrinal matter that has so far been mainly confined to prose. The title means *Pensées*; but prose *pensées* or aphorisms are not to Lawrence's taste.

> Pascal or La Bruyère wrote their *Pensées* in prose, but it has always seemed to me that a real thought, a single thought, not an argument, can only exist easily in verse, or in some poetic form. There is a didactic element about prose thoughts which makes them repellent, slightly bullying. "He who hath wife and children hath given hostages to fortune." There is a thought well put; but immediately it irritates by its assertiveness. It applies too direct to actual practical life. If it were put into poetry it wouldn't nag at us so practically. We don't want to be nagged at.[52]

I think there is something in Lawrence's claim that there is a didactic, assertive element in the prose *pensée*. These massive generalisations are meant to stand in all weathers, to be impersonally and permanently true. Lawrence has no such aim; he wants to capture the mood or impression of the moment, whose only claim to truth is that it is actually felt at the moment, not that it is a permanent guide to life. "So I should wish these *Pansies* to be taken as thoughts rather than anything else; casual thoughts that are true while they are true and irrelevant when the mood and circumstance changes."

> I know no greater delight than the sheer delight of being alone.
> It makes me realise the delicious pleasure of the moon
> that she has in travelling by herself; throughout time,
> or the splendid growing of an ash-tree
> alone, on a hill-side in the north, humming in the wind.

Obviously a passing thought. Can it be claimed that it is in verse or "in some poetic form", and that the form modifies its mode of being in the way that Lawrence suggests? Certainly this could be written out in quite normal and respectable prose; but it may be noticed that one rhythmic order is suggested by the punctuation, another by the line arrangement: and the slight tension between the two makes the experience of reading these four lines rather different from that of reading two prose sentences. This slight formal tension justifies the two images (not very obtrusive, it is true, but perhaps a little assertive for prose)—the moon travelling by herself, and the ash tree humming in the wind. And the ensemble of rhythm and images makes the whole something different from a plain, declaratory prose statement, something justified by its own completeness, not by reference to some outside state of affairs. Surely it is here that we are to find the essential difference between prose *pensées* and Lawrence's *Pansies*. It is not primarily that the thoughts are passing thoughts. A thought of Pascal or La Rochefoucauld is judged by its correspondence to our experience of life; a Laurentian Pansy—if it is one of the good ones—by its own self-subsistent being. And that in the end is Lawrence's justification for calling them poems, and making it clear that they do not claim the same kind of truth as prose statements.

Of course the thoughts are about something; as we have said, they are largely critical, and in fact they cover a wide range of topics which arouse immediate interest and curiosity. If they did not refer to a wide and varied world and reveal an alert and lively mind, they would be made of dull material; and the workmanship itself would not be sufficiently curious or elaborate to save them. As it is, Lawrence has invented a combination of form and matter that is both satisfying in itself and ideally suited to his purpose. The pieces vary greatly in mood, interest and merit. Some are brilliantly intelligent and well worked-out observations on the contemporary world—like "Now It's Happened", quoted on page 8. Some are mere explosions of temper. The poems on the English, and those on the middle class— in fact, nearly all that have to do with the class system—are Lawrence at his worst; not because what he says is not true (it is, as far as it goes), but because of the snarling gracelessness of the expression, the reflection of a dreary immature class-consciousness. The best are those on direct human relationships. They represent the momentary intuitive flashes of insight out of which Lawrence's doctrine was made —and the insight is commonly better than the doctrine. Some are bitterly satiric:

> Don't you care for my love? she said bitterly.
> I handed her the mirror and said:
> Please address these questions to the proper person!
> Please make all requests to headquarters!
> In all matters of emotional importance
> please approach the supreme authority direct!
> So I handed her the mirror.

And she would have broken it over my head
but she caught sight of her own reflection
and that held her spellbound for two seconds
while I fled.

Some have a touch of tenderness under the satire:

Will no one say hush! to thee,
poor lass, poor bit of a wench?
Will never a man say: Come, my pigeon,
Come an' be still wi' me, my own bit of a wench!
And would you peck his eyes out if he did!

Occasionally we find a late-Yeatsian gnomic compactness:

Desire may be dead
and still a man can be
a meeting place for sun and rain,
wonder outwitting pain
as in a wintry tree.

Nearly all, even those that are roughest and least memorable in expression, are filled with an inspired, angry common sense. At this late stage of his career most of Lawrence's doctrinal eccentricities have been shed; he is content to rely on the naked truth and certainty of his contact with people, events and scenes. It rarely fails him; and beneath the exasperation, the despair of the current social scene, what shines out is wisdom. There are even glimpses of fulfilment and ecstasy, as in "For a Moment" and "Who is This?", moments when the gods who seem to have vanished from the modern world return.

Who is this that softly touches the sides of my breast
and touches me over the heart
so that my heart beats soothed, soothed and at peace?

. . . . .

I tell you it is no woman, it is no man, for I am alone
And I fall asleep with the gods, the gods
that are not or that are
according to the soul's desire
like a pool into which we plunge, or do not plunge.

By this time Lawrence was near his death; and this is very near the mood of the posthumously published *Last Poems*, which were all written under its shadow. Of course he had been ill, fatally ill, ever since the return from Mexico; but he had refused to recognise it. Now he is quite consciously building his ship of death, making a vehicle in which his last journey can be undertaken in peace and confidence. They are filled with images of autumn and sunset:

> Now that the sun, like a lion, licks his paws
> and goes slowly down the hill.
>
> . . . . .
>
> Now it is autumn and the falling fruit—
>
> . . . . .
>
> In soft September, at slow, sad Michaelmas.

Always death is seen as a natural process; its pathos and mystery are not reduced, but there is no sense of fear or intolerable anguish. It is in these poems, in fact, that Lawrence's sensuous mysticism reaches its maturity. Even on the point of the "long journey towards oblivion" there is no decline in sensuous acuteness and intensity; and no feeling of unbearable contrast between this living power and the forgetfulness that is at hand. At this period—the period of *Last Poems*, the Etruscan essays and *Apocalypse*—Lawrence could have written like Yeats:

> never had I more
> Excited, passionate, fantastical
> Imagination, nor an ear and eye
> That more expected the impossible.

But Yeats felt acutely the opposition between the life of the sensuous imagination, which he associated with youth and bodily vigour, and the life of spiritual contemplation which he felt old age impose upon him, a life in which he had "to bid the Muse go pack, Choose Plato or Plotinus for a friend". Of course Lawrence was not old; he was facing death in early middle age; yet bodily decrepitude and the approaching end of all he had lived by were to be met just the same. His way of confronting them is quite different from that of Yeats. The whole direction of *Last Poems* is precisely to avoid the Yeatsian opposition, to refuse to make any *volte face*, to absorb the fact of death into the mode of consciousness that is already his own.

All compromise is avoided. A denial of the physical and a relapse into the traditional spiritual wisdom of old age might have been a possible solution. But Lawrence refuses to take it. The God of *Last*

Poems is as emphatically the God made flesh as ever—made flesh
not only in man and woman but in all things that have their special
or individual mode of being. Lawrence reverses the Christian order
as emphatically as in the preface to *Sons and Lovers*. The ultimate
Godhead is the creative force as actualised in substantial, physically
existent things: the logos or the Idea, or whatever pre-existent force
there may be is only an inchoate demiurge who has not yet found his
actual existence. In Christian and Jewish thought God creates by
withdrawing some of his reality from a portion of being, so giving
it a purely contingent separate identity. In Hindu thought he creates
by establishing the mere illusion of separate identities. In Lawrence's
thought God only comes into being by actualising himself in the
separate identities of the visible and tangible world. This is the motive
of "Red Geraniums and Godly Mignonette", "The Rainbow" and
"The Body of God".

> There is no god
> Apart from poppies and the flying fish,
>   men singing songs, and women brushing their hair in the sun.
> The lovely things are god that has come to pass, like Jesus came.
> The rest, the undiscoverable, is the demiurge.

Only man can fall away from God; the beasts can never fall into
the self-conscious knowledge of themselves apart from God. Even for
man it is difficult.

> It is not easy to fall out of the hands of the living God
> They are so large, and they cradle so much of a man.

But man can fall:

> And still through knowledge and will, he can break away
> man can break away, and fall from the hands of God
> into himself alone, down the godless plunge of the abyss,
> a god-lost creature turning upon himself
> in the long, long fall, revolving upon himself
> in the endless writhe of the last, the last self-knowledge.

And this is the only final vacuity. Lawrence ends "The Hands of God"
with the prayer:

> Save me from that, O God!
> Let me never know myself apart from the living God!

THE POEMS

To know oneself as individual and separate, yet never apart from the living God that is in all other living and separate things—that is the paradox by which alone man can be saved.

What are the consequences of this philosophy for a man who is facing death? An accidental and superficial one for Lawrence was a heightened consciousness of a transient physical being, especially the vanished life of the old Mediterranean world, whose relics were actually around him, which he had lately come to see again as the fullest flowering ever granted to man. We see this consciousness in *Etruscan Places*, in *The Man Who Died* and in such poems as "The Argonauts" and "The Man of Tyre"—the man of Tyre who sees a woman wading in the sea ("Oh lovely, lovely with the dark hair piled up, as she went deeper, deeper down the channel, then rose shallower, shallower") and clasps his hands in delight and cries out:

> lo! God is one god! But here in the twilight
> godly and lovely comes Aphrodite out of the sea
> towards me?

There is a likeness to Keats here—the Keats of the odes, finding his absolute in these moments of actual yet transient fulfilment. Keats attempts to go beyond this, in the second *Hyperion*, by a transition to the life of moral struggle. Lawrence has long ago rejected that course. The only way is to accept the fact of transience, the passage into oblivion—to accept it fully, for oneself as much as for the Argonauts and the man of Tyre. If God only exists as embodied in transient things, then transience must be a part of his nature:

> The breath of life is in the sharp winds of change,
> mingled with the breath of destruction.

Lawrence has too much natural piety to speculate explicitly on the possibility or the nature of a life beyond. Perhaps there is one of some kind; perhaps the self continues to exist in some sort of unforeseeable mingling with the body of God, the actual created world. I would not try to paraphrase "Shadows", where this intimation of immanence appears most plainly. Like Lawrence's God, these final intuitions of his exist fully only when they are embodied in specific form.

> And if to-night my soul may find her peace
> in sleep, and sink in good oblivion,
> and in the morning wake like a new-opened flower
> then I have been dipped again in God, and new-created.

But this 'if' finds no certain resolution, and in any case it is not the immediate human problem. The immediate human problem is to find the courage and the calm to transcend these speculations, to accept the coming darkness with tranquillity and joy. This is the motive of the most famous and most beautiful of *Last Poems*—"Bavarian Gentians" and "The Ship of Death". Both are a sort of incantation, almost an initiation ritual. They seek, by the use of symbols, to fit the mind for an utterly unknown experience, so unknown, so unimaginable, that it can only be prefigured as darkness—the negation of all experience. The symbol in the first is the gentian itself, the flower that seems to glow with darkness, like a torch of Pluto. It is to act as a torch in Pluto's realm, a light within the absolute darkness, the absolutely unknowable into which the spring and all the bright things of the world must pass.

> Reach me a gentian, give me a torch
> let me guide myself with the blue, forked torch of this flower
> down the darker and darker stairs, where blue is darkened on
> blueness.
> Even where Persephone goes, just now, from the frosted Sep-
> tember.

Lawrence is without Yeats' passion for empirical certainty on these matters; he has the Keatsian Negative Capability—"capable of being in uncertainties, mysteries, doubts, without any irritable reaching after fact and reason". In these poems he is beyond conceptual statement, in a realm to whose existence only symbol and image can bear witness. In "The Ship of Death" the symbol is an anthropological one—the little ship which many peoples make to convey the soul on its passage to the other world. The time has come for it.

> Now it is autumn and the falling fruit
> and the long journey towards oblivion.

And this poses a question.

> O let us talk of quiet that we know,
> That we can know, the deep and lovely quiet
> Of a strong heart at peace!
> How can we this, our own quietus, make?

There is only one answer, to accept our own destiny:

                        all we can do
          Is now to be willing to die, and to build the ship
          of death to carry the soul on the longest journey.

We are not told how to build it; the poem is only a stilled, almost
ecstatic acceptance of its necessity. We are not told how to build
the ship within the confines of this poem, for though in one sense the
building of it is the immediate preparation for death, in another sense
it is the task of the whole later part of life; and the task is impossible
unless the necessary materials have been gathered in earlier life. The
ship is "the ship of courage, the ark of faith"; it is to be provided
with "oars and food, and little dishes and all accoutrements"; and
these provisions are the relics and memories of our life, the experiences by which we have attained our being, without which we can
never be ready to change into something else, for without them we
would never really have been at all. So, in a still wider sense, all our
life is a preparation for the building of the ship, though it must never
be lived with that as its overt purpose. Where the ship is to sail we
cannot know; we only know that we are launched:

          upon the sea of death, where still we sail
          darkly, for we cannot steer, and have no port.

It is the ultimate darkness, it is the end, it is oblivion, and must be
accepted as such in all its fearfulness. And yet:

          And yet out of eternity a thread
          separates itself on the blackness,
          a horizontal thread
          that fumes a little with pallor upon the dark.

                  .   .   .   .   .

          A flush of rose, and the whole thing starts again.

"E'en in our ashes live their wonted fires"; and even at this extremity Lawrence, after all the acceptance of the dark, sees a tenuous
and partial glimpse of a purged and calcined body, like a worn sea-
shell, reunited with the frail soul again.

There are many ways of contemplating and writing about death,
and Lawrence has avoided almost all the traditional ones. He has not
accepted the Christian dilemma—neither its terrors nor its consola-
tions. He is without trace of that denial of humanity, the Stoic
apatheia, and has even less interest in the Roman compensations of

after-fame and human respect. Whatever genuflexions to strange gods he may formerly have made, by this time he has entirely abandoned death-worship, and he was never much tempted by the varied canon of Romantic fantasies and evasions. All that remains for him then is to face death with naked human simplicity ; and in these poems he has presented more fully than any other what must always be for man the inescapable paradox—the necessity to accept death as absolute darkness, and the impossibility of accepting the darkness as absolute. Various ways have been suggested of taking Lawrence's earlier poetry in all its varied phases. Now that we have come to the end, we may suggest another one—that his poems which we have regarded as an adjunct and a commentary to his life receive their final justification as successive stages in the building of his ship of death.

Chapter V

THE DOCTRINE

I. FICTION AND PHILOSOPHY

IT can plausibly be said that an imaginative writer's philosophy of life exists only in his imaginative works, and should not be examined outside them. Modern criticism, strongly committed to the unity of form and content, tends to take this point of view. We remember all the sad expository essays on Shakespeare's philosophy and Browning's thought. I am now about to write one on Lawrence, but I hope with more excuse. In the first place Lawrence has not yet suffered from systematic exposition; he has suffered rather from vulgarisation, which would boil down his extensive and complex vision into some simple maxim. Secondly, Lawrence's case is very different from that of, say, Browning. Browning resolutely refused to extract a message from his dramatic presentations; he lives in them alone. Lawrence began the process of distillation himself. "The novels and stories come unwatched out of one's pen. And then the absolute need one has for some sort of satisfactory mental attitude towards oneself and things in general makes one try to abstract some definite conclusions from one's experience as a writer and a man." So he wrote in the preface to *Fantasia*. There is little danger therefore that the "definite conclusions" will be something read into the work by the commentator, for it is Lawrence who has drawn them. They, too, are a part of his vision, and an essential part of it; for in the same preface, while asserting the priority in time of his fiction, he goes on to say "that even art is utterly dependent on philosophy: or if you prefer it, on a metaphysic. The metaphysic may not be anywhere very accurately stated, and may be quite unconscious, in the artist, yet it is a metaphysic that governs men all the time."

There are difficulties of other kinds. The first is the rather trivial one of terminology. One is tempted to talk about Lawrence's philosophy because he does so himself; but ideally the word 'philosophy' should always be in quotation marks. For of course Lawrence is not a philosopher. At the back of every philosophy is a vision, but the philosopher's claim is that the vision has been corrected—checked for internal consistency and for consistency with the reports derived from other modes of experience than his own. Lawrence could make no such claim; what he offers is a *Weltanschauung*, his own vision of life. But we have no convenient word for this; so we must make do with philosophy, bearing in mind that it is philosophy only in a loose sense of the word; or fall back on 'doctrine', which sounds repellent but is not inappropriate, for among other things Lawrence is very much a doctrinaire.

It may still be said (and sometimes is) that Lawrence's philosophy is a confused affair, that whatever is of value in it is, in fact, in the imaginative works in which it first came, and that Lawrence himself was misguided in trying to extract theoretical conclusions from them. It is true that most of Lawrence's consummate successes are in immediate intuition, and that the shifting kaleidoscopic pattern of his intuitions must always be a richer thing than any fixed doctrine that could be deduced from it. But the two modes are actually mixed at most stages of his career. Fiction and doctrine co-exist in most of the major novels. Pure fiction is separated out in some of the tales, pure doctrine in the frankly expository works; and when this happens each has its claim to separate consideration. Fiction was Lawrence's way of arriving at doctrine; and since fiction is necessarily immersed in the immediate and the contingent, so the doctrine most closely linked with the novels will be tinged with the same contingency, coloured by the particular autobiographical or fictitious problem with which he is wrestling at the time. From this arises diversity of symbolism, diversity of immediate aims, apparent inconsistency. But the inconsistency is more apparent than real. From all Lawrence's divers prophesyings, on whatever themes, a pretty steady and coherent system of ideas does, in fact, emerge. His own expository works are an attempt to outline it more clearly. They are often eccentric, but in general they are remarkably successful. One comes out from a reading even of *Fantasia* with a pretty clear idea of what Lawrence is driving at. There is a kind of writer who covers an inner uncertainty by an illusion of clarity, an illusion produced by the surface qualities of his style. Lawrence is at the opposite pole from this. He sometimes becomes obsessed by some minor irritation and laboriously worries it to death; he sometimes employs fantastic or misleading symbolism; and he generally prefers a method of incremental repetition to first-shot precision; but to anyone who reads to understand rather than to contradict and confute, the effective drift of his thought is not in doubt.

It might therefore seem enough to leave Lawrence to do his own exposition without commentary. But the situation is not quite as simple as that. Lawrence's expository writings are scattered, written in different phases of his career for different immediate purposes. And he employs a variety of terminologies and symbolisms. There is a good deal to be gained by carrying the process begun by Lawrence one stage further, and trying to abstract from his abstracts some central conclusions. Then, if contradiction and confutation are needed, we can at least be sure whether we are attacking the centre of his beliefs or merely skirmishing about some inessential outpost; or worse still, wasting energy on some hot-headed or careless bit of formulation which Lawrence himself corrects elsewhere. It would be possible to do this by taking the doctrinal writings—essays, criticisms and longer treatises—in order, and trying to extract the core from each. But it would be an unprofitable way to work. It would involve much repetition, chasing the same idea through half a dozen formulations that are only superficially different; or chasing the ideas on half a dozen different subjects only to find that they are easily deducible consequences from a few central positions. We shall therefore abandon here the method used in the rest of this book—the separate examination of individual works—and try first to establish these few central positions, with due reference to the places where they are most prominently displayed.

First a brief survey of the material. Lawrence's earliest important assertion of his *Weltanschauung* is the letter to Ernest Collings of 1913—"My great religion is a belief in the blood . . ."; and this is followed a few weeks later by the foreword to *Sons and Lovers*. These have both been discussed in connection with *The Rainbow*, and they are both explicit enough, though in the second Lawrence adopts the unhappy scriptural-prophetic style that was to haunt him for some years to come. From this time on there is a steady series of attempts, extending over the next seven years, to formulate a philosophy. On his return to England in 1914 he wrote a study of Thomas Hardy.

Little of it was published at the time, but the whole is printed in *Phœnix*. I agree with Dr. Leavis that Lawrence is an admirable critic— with the qualification that he is generally more concerned with himself and his own ideas than with his ostensible object. And the *Study of Hardy*, though excellent on Hardy whenever it talks about him, is for the most part an important step in the development of Lawrence's own thought. At this time Lawrence, shaken by the war, was half-seriously trying to affect the political development of England by working on people with influence and position. Among them were Bertrand Russell and Lady Cynthia Asquith; and in the letters to these two is to be found a good deal more of the intended application of Laurentian doctrine. Lawrence talks much about his "philosophy" at this period, but it was apparently never formulated as fully as he hoped. The most considerable document that survives is the essay "The Crown", written in 1915 for a short-lived periodical called *Signatures*. This is an important piece, for it represents a widening of the metaphysical range from the largely sexual preoccupations of the earlier pronouncements. But it is written in Lawrence's most portentous-symbolic style; it often fails to achieve the poetic force that was intended; and some areas of it remain obscure and themselves need to be interpreted by more lucid statements elsewhere. It was followed in 1917 by the essay. "The Reality of Peace" (printed in *Phœnix*), to which Lawrence was at this time deeply committed. Happier in its symbolism than "The Crown", it attains a lyrical exaltation, but it lacks directness of attack. Lawrence is trying to move from ethics and psychology to metaphysics, and some of his virtue is lost in that more rarefied air.

There is an abrupt change in "The Education of the People" (1917, printed in *Phœnix*), a series of essays which were intended, odd though it may seem, for the *Times Educational Supplement*. This, besides including the distinct outlines of a corporate state, with classes hierarchically graded according to function, is full of explicit injunctions about the training of children, their relations with their parents and of parents with each other. It is thus a clear illustration of how the Laurentian doctrine to date is to be expressed in actual human relations, and it leads directly to the two key books *Psychoanalysis and the Unconscious* and *Fantasia of the Unconscious*. The first of these is a short, admirably written book, containing some shrewd criticisms of the new psychology, and Lawrence's own estimate of the rôles of conscious and unconscious in the psychic life. The *Fantasia* is an almost indescribable work, developing the same ideas more fully, with the aid of a good deal of pseudo-scientific symbolism, which Lawrence may or may not have taken half-seriously. Roughly contemporary with these were the *Studies in Classic American Literature*, begun in 1917 but not published till 1922. They are brilliant critical essays, but the criticism is also an important exercise in clarifying Lawrence's own ideas. Here, as in *Fantasia*, he abandons his early vaticinating style and evolves the slangy, casual, hard-hitting manner which was his most effective polemical weapon.

By this time Lawrence's philosophy was virtually complete and the spate of expository writing slackens. During the years in America (1922-5) anything of this sort that he has to say is combined with fiction or with travel essays. After his return to Europe there are only the *Assorted Articles* of the *Lady Chatterley* period, and the posthumously published *Apocalypse*. With these we must take *The Man Who Died*. *Assorted Articles* contain nothing new; they are a brilliant vulgarisation of what he had said more challengingly and obscurely already. The fact that they appeared as ordinary newspaper pieces in The *Evening Standard* in 1928-9 is striking evidence that some at least of Lawrence's ideas had become generally presentable towards the end of his life. *The Man Who Died* seems out of place in this context. Formally it is fiction, but in fact it is a philosophic fable that reflects the closing phase of Lawrence's lifelong worry about Christianity and the relation of his own doctrine to it. *Apocalypse* is a last attempt, written at the point of death, at uttering his thoughts on the same subject, and at summing up his message.

The doctrinal writing, then, is mostly concentrated in the middle of Lawrence's career; and we can now make some indication of its place in his work as a whole. Before it come *The White Peacock* and *Sons and Lovers*—and they are pure experience. If any general conclusions are reached, it is by living through the experience again rather than by deliberate abstraction from it. From *The Rainbow* on there is growth in experience certainly, but also a purposeful effort to draw deductions from it and to formulate a doctrine. The principal documents are the Hardy study, "The Crown", the education essays and *Fantasia*; and the contemporaneous fiction is *The Rainbow*,

Women in Love and *Aaron's Rod*. By this time the doctrine was pretty well complete, but it had not yet been shown in action. The creative effort of the next few years is to show it at work—in the political and religious spheres as well as in individual life. *Kangaroo* is a preliminary attempt at this. In *The Plumed Serpent* and the Mexican writing generally there is an agonised struggle with the problem—ending in failure. And the struggle is conducted largely in fiction, the doctrine itself being unchanged. After the end of the Mexican experiment, there is a period of relapse and uncertainty. *Lady Chatterley* simply falls back from the public to the personal side of the philosophy, and there are no new ideas. *The Man Who Died* and *Apocalypse* between them form a last testament.

II. LEADING IDEAS

We must look, then, for Lawrence's leading ideas in the expository writings between 1914 and 1923. They form a pretty consistent body of work, for they are on the whole successive shots at saying the same thing, or at applying the same set of ideas to different fields of experience. So we can draw on them eclectically for our evidence.

The central field of Lawrence's philosophy is always the study of man. Occasionally it passes over into a theosophy, which is a study of God; more often into a sort of nature-philosophy—a study of life in all its manifestations. But Lawrence only makes these temporary excursions in order to survey the boundaries of his proper territory. Lawrence certainly felt that the nature of man is of a piece with the nature of the world in general. But he would be quite opposed to any attempt to *deduce* conclusions about the nature of man from *a priori* metaphysics or natural science. Both are abstractions, serviceable for their own particular purposes, but something less than the totality of human experience and incapable of taking us very far. The field that is really open to our investigation is living human experience, the totality of human experience—with such brief glimpses into other realms—the realm of non-human life, of unliving matter (if there is any unliving matter), of the greater and more general forces that direct the whole—as analogy and intuition will permit us to make. Lawrence's attacks on science are sometimes silly, but they are really attempts to by-pass it rather than to confute it. (One is reminded sometimes of Coleridge's revulsion from the eighteenth-century "universe of death".) His attacks on *a priori* metaphysics are precautions against allowing partial abstractions from experience to forbid the possibility of further experience. His effort is always to grasp the totality of human experience. Criticisms of Lawrence are commonly criticisms of his psychology, his morals or his politics; and these are all indeed open to criticism. But such attacks must remain partial and inconclusive unless it is seen how all these particular doctrines arise from a few central ideas.

Lawrence's philosophy is basically naturalistic. This is obscured by his use of Biblical language and a religious exaltation of tone; but for him God is in nature. He flames in the poppy, darts in the snake, ripens and bursts in the fig, loves and becomes self-conscious in man. God only transcends these things in the sense that he is more than any one of them. But he has no being outside them.

> There is no god
> apart from poppies and the flying fish,
> men singing songs, and women brushing their hair in the sun.
> The lovely things are god that has come to pass.[53]

God, then, is the whole natural order seen in the mode of reverence and delight. Any creator or creative force behind this is something less than God, not an ultimate source, but something struggling into being. Of course man may, in idea and feeling, deify any aspect of his experience or any part of the natural world. Lawrence himself often does so, and talks in polytheistic terms. "Beware of absolutes, there are many Gods."[54] But this is only a manner of speaking. God is the whole natural order, and all creatures, including man, must find their fulfilment in their natural being, in harmony with the whole natural order. If your eye offends you, you are not to pluck it out; you must learn to live with both the eye and the offence. "For man, as for flower, beast and bird, the supreme triumph is to be most vividly, most perfectly alive. Whatever the unborn and the dead may know, they cannot know the beauty, the marvel of being alive in the flesh."[55] And the only ultimate failure, of which man alone is capable, is voluntarily to cut oneself off from this all-pervading miracle, to break the connection.

We can, if we wish, collect labels to describe this faith. It is pantheism—every part of the universe is a manifestation of God. It is animism, in more than one sense—everything is endowed with its own particular soul, its own principle of life; and further (I am less certain of this, but I think it is what Lawrence intends), soul is the vital principle which produces all things. Sometimes Lawrence seems to talk in materialist terms; but, then, for him matter is always living matter, always inhabited by a soul. Certainly he is a vitalist, if we are to use such terms; but it is hardly appropriate to use modern analytical terminology at all: his apprehension of the world is far closer to that of primitive religion, which had not thought to distinguish clearly between organic and inorganic, spirit and matter, but saw the whole universe and all parts of it as simply and obviously alive.

Secondly, Lawrence's naturalism is radically dualistic. Reality exists only as a pair of opposites. "If there is universal, infinite darkness, then there is universal, infinite light, for there cannot exist a specific infinite save by virtue of the opposite equivalent specific infinite." "Life itself is dual." And this is a part of the doctrine that Lawrence has considerable difficulty in expressing. He is obviously concerned with ideas of a very high degree of generality, and he can never find any one satisfactory formula for the antinomy that he sees. The method he adopts is probably the only one for an unprofessional philosopher—that of multiplying instances; and he recurs again and again to his dichotomy, under a great variety of names. Here is a selection of them.

Light	Dark
Sun	Moon
Intellect	Blood
Will	Flesh
Male	Female
Love	Law
Spirit	Soul
Mind	Senses
Consciousness	Feelings
Moon	Sun
Knowledge	Nature
Motion	Inertia
The Son	The Father

This will serve as a preliminary diagram. The parallel to the Yin and the Yang of Chinese philosophy at once suggests itself—the masculine, active, conscious principle opposed to the feminine, passive, unconscious principle. Lawrence identifies the first with the spirit, the second with the flesh; the first with the light, the second with the darkness. The sun and moon symbols often change places. Sometimes the sun is the active masculine intellect and the moon passive feminine comprehension; sometimes the moon is the cold light of abstract knowledge and the sun the warm knowledge of the flesh. There are two misunderstandings to be avoided. The first is to see the contrast as the old one of spirit and matter in which matter represents the natural world and spirit some supernatural reality set over against it. Lawrence's contrast is not of this kind. Both constituents of his dual reality are part of the natural world. The other mistake is to take the common view of Lawrence's beliefs and see the opposition as a merely sexual one. Of course it is not. The Male-Female opposition is an instance of this duality, but only an instance; and Lawrence is not constructing the world on the model of sexual duality. The Father, for example, is on the same side as the female. Another possible confusion is that between 'soul' and 'spirit'. Lawrence distinguishes between them. Soul is an attribute of the flesh, and is associated with nature and the senses. Spirit is opposed to it and is associated with intellect and consciousness. 'Soul' is the soul of primitive animism: 'spirit' is what Plato in the *Phædo* concludes to be the immortal part of man, though Lawrence of course does not share his valuation of it.

The next step is to see that this dualism is not a mere dichotomy, it is a conflict. The two sides are not merely contrasted with each other, they are in active opposition; and here Lawrence's symbolism becomes less uniform. In the early essay, "The Crown", and intermittently thereafter, the opposition is seen as strife, as an actual combat. Later other terms are used, to suggest opposition but not necessarily hostility. However, the metaphors of combat are pervasive; the first one used is that of the lion and the unicorn fighting for the crown. And the fight is life itself.

> And there is no rest, no cessation from the conflict. For we are two opposites which exist by virtue of our inter-opposition. Remove the opposition and there is a collapse, a sudden crumbling into universal darkness.[56]

> But think, if the lion really destroyed, killed the unicorn: not merely drove him out of town, but annihilated him! Would

not the lion at once expire, as if he had created a vacuum around himself? . . . They would both cease to be, if either of them really won the fight which is their sole reason for existing.[57]

The lion, the mind, the active, the male principle must always be at strife with the unicorn, the senses, the passive, the female principle. A victory for either side brings life to an end. A crude physical clod-dishness which refuses the responsibilities of intelligence brings one kind of collapse, illustrated in George of *The White Peacock*. A Christian-Platonic idealism which subjugates the senses to the reason brings another kind of collapse, illustrated *passim* through Lawrence's fiction. If this second error is more insisted on than the first, it is because after twenty Christian centuries it is the error to which our civilisation is prone.

But the lion and the unicorn were fighting for the crown. What then is the crown, the object of the conflict? The crown is in the first place the symbol of victory: each side wants complete victory, the annihilation of his opponent. The intellect wishes to be alone and supreme, and so do the senses. Yet if either of them succeeds, life is at an end. So in the royal arms the crown belongs to neither; it is alone, above and between the combatants. It is then, secondly, the symbol of the eternal balance between the two forces—a prize that is only worth having as long as it is never won.

And here straightforward expository language necessarily fails. It is not for nothing that among the terms for the Laurentian opposites are the dark and the light. For at any given moment, in any individual person, one of the two forces is in the light, the other in the darkness. One, that is to say, is recognised, self-aware, identified with the ego; the other is—radically other, obscure, disowned, seen only as some-thing to be fought against—sometimes seen as an outside force, not as part of the psyche at all. And the balance or reconciliation between the conscious and unconscious forces is not to be accomplished by any means open to conscious inspection. One of the purposes of Jung's therapy is to effect this reconciliation, and one of the reasons for the obscurity of his writing is the virtual impossibility of explaining it. In the end Jung is reduced to using the symbolism—dream-images, pictorial or diagrammatic representations—that his patients them-selves employ, and to assuring us that such a process cannot be described, only lived through. It will already have become apparent that I find a close resemblance between Lawrence's thought and Jung's. I do not want to force the parallel—only to show that Lawrence is facing the same cardinal difficulty. And being an imaginative writer first, he deals with it by varied, repeated attempts to find an adequate "objective correlative" for this integration or balance of forces that for him is the key to the whole vital process. Many of these we have traced in the novels. It may be that none of them was wholly satisfactory because Lawrence never completed this complex integration himself. However that may be, let us now try to say what little can be said of it in plain expository terms.

First, as we have seen, the reconciliation cannot be effected by the victory of either side. It is not achieved by giving the victory to the Spirit and making the Flesh its willing subject, as Platonism and Christian morals enjoin. But neither can it be achieved by giving the victory to the Flesh and allowing it to lead the Spirit captive—a procedure of which Lawrence is often accused. One way of doing this would be for civilised man to return to a primitive tribal life before the Spirit, the Logos, had yet emerged from the womb of the Flesh. And Lawrence, however stirred by the primitive, always insists that this is impossible; developed man must stick by the responsibilities of consciousness. "I can't cluster at the drum any more." The woman who rode away rode to her death. Another way of doing it would be by deliberate, peripheral sensuality. This is the way of Gerald Crich, and it is anathema to Lawrence. Secondly, integration is not the result of a simple cessation of conflict, or agreement to differ or compromise. The lion and the unicorn are not to make up their quarrel. "If they made friends and lay down side by side, the Crown would fall on them both and kill them." Benjamin Franklin, who "uses venery" for health and procreation, is an exceptionally well-ordered person; but his tensionless, platitudinous ethics are the especial object of Lawrence's derision. Tommy Dukes in *Lady Chatterley's Lover* knows all about the relative positions of intelligence and sensuality in life, but like the rest of Clifford Chatterley's friends can hardly generate enough steam to live at all.

The proper relation between the opposites is later described by Lawrence as polarity—a word that obsesses him, both in fiction and expository writing. It may be achieved, both between individuals and between psychic forces within the individual, as the result of prolonged conflict; but when achieved, it is a state where conflict is transcended, a state of still tension, life-sustaining and life-creating, forbidding for ever the merging of the opposites, and maintaining both in a state of mutual complementary balance. When Birkin wants of Ursula something more than love, it is this that he is looking for. When Somers and Harriet are not fighting, when they are rightly together, this is what they achieve. I have heard it said that this is no great matter, that it is simply the we-love-one-another-but-we-live-our-own-lives that is one of the commonplaces of a certain type of modern marriage. But that is not what Lawrence meant at all. His married men and women most emphatically do not live their own lives: they are indissolubly bound and irrevocably dependent on each other. But they never merge; each recognises at the core of the other's being an eternally separate spark. And the two poles are eternally opposed, the whole fruitfulness of the relationship depends on their opposition, yet its whole integrity depends on moments when the sense of opposition has vanished.

To illustrate the polarity within the individual psyche is more difficult. The attempts at formal exposition of polarity as an interior psychological phenomenon are apt either to take refuge in a bogus physiology, as in parts of *Fantasia*, or to tremble on the brink of the inexpressible. But something is communicated. The first step is to see that this intense polarity is never a fixed relation; it is a matter of momentary revelations, like the momentary resolutions of conflict in Keat's odes. Yet they must not be seen as short-lived or transient, but as timeless.

> Only perpetuation is a sin. The perfect relation is perfect. But it is therefore timeless. And we must not think to tie a knot in time, and thus to make the consummation temporal or eternal. The consummation is timeless, and we belong to time, in our process of living.[58]

> God is gone, until next time. But the next time will come. And then again we shall *see* God, and once more it will be different. It is always different.
> . . . When the flower opens, see him, don't remember him. When the sun shines, be him, and then cease again.[59]

In "The Crown" it is only these momentary illuminations that are celebrated; though even here we should perhaps see them as the index of a permanent state. Sometimes Lawrence sees the right relationship as a perpetual travelling from one pole to the other and back again· Complete consummation in the flesh for the moment annihilates spirit and transcends all duality. And at the same moment a new movement begins, towards the opposite pole, to be concluded by a complete consummation in the spirit. And it is only when man has had full experience of both that he can become himself or reach God. This is not a recommendation to an alternate series of orgies and repentances. The spirit is not to repent of what the flesh has done, nor the flesh to deny the spirit. Fullness of being, the subjective realisation of God, is the simultaneous recognition of unity in duality.

> In the beginning, the light touches the darkness, the darkness touches the light, and the two embrace. They embrace in opposition, only in their desire is their unanimity. There are two separate statements, the dark wants the light, and the light wants the dark. But the two statements are contained within the one: "They want each other."[60]

And from that statement it is not difficult to conceive of integration as a durable condition, extended in time, a continued recognition of unity in duality, valid and present whatever happens to be the immediate situation between the poles. To this state, or to the power that brings this state about, Lawrence gives many names—the crown, the rainbow, the rose. He even calls it the Holy Ghost; for in one formulation of his mythology the Father is the fleshly or material ground of all being, the Son is the Logos, the spiritual emanation from this, and the Holy Ghost is the reconciler between them.

> These two halves I always am. But I am never *myself* until they are consummate into a spark of oneness, the gleam of the Holy Ghost. And in this spark is my immortality, my non-mortal being, that which is not swept away down either direction of time.[61]

But the Holy Ghost is also the comforter, and Lawrence sometimes calls the result of its operations simply "peace".

> Where then is peace if the primary law of all the universe is a law of dual attraction and repulsion, a law of polarity? . . . There is peace in that perfect consummation when duality and polarity is transcended into absorption. . . . And this is peace. The lion is but a lion, the lamb is but a lamb, half and half separate. But we

are the two halves together. I am a lion of pride and wrath, I am a lamb with Christ in meekness. They live in one landscape of my soul.[62]

I have used the word integration for this state not because Lawrence uses it; he does not; but because what Lawrence is trying to express is so close to the widely known integration concept of Jung. I do not think there can be any question of direct influence from that source. Lawrence knew something of Jung, probably rather vaguely, at the time he wrote *Fantasia*, and rather more after his association with Mabel Luhan. At the time he wrote "The Crown" and "The Reality of Peace", it is unlikely that he knew anything about him. In any case, Jung's dealings with this problem are of a later date. But both, of course, are drawing on a tradition that is widespread in esoteric religious literature. There is a parallel in the Tao, the way, of Chinese thought, by which the universe is governed and the individual is fulfilled. Lawrence's aim in the writings that have just been discussed is undoubtedly to become a teacher of wisdom. In spite of his great fertilising power I think he was both too isolated and too involved to succeed—too isolated from any really nourishing stream of thought in his own day, and too involved in the immediate and the personal. The prophet can only utter his mature message when his personal problems have been transcended, as Lawrence's never were. After all, he died at forty-five. Nevertheless, the closing words of Jung's *Integration of the Personality* are an apt comment on the rôle for which Lawrence cast himself, and on the aim of this part of his work:

> When all is said and done, the hero, leader, and saviour is also the one who discovers a new way to greater certainty. Everything could be left as it was if this new way did not absolutely demand to be discovered, and did not visit humanity with all the plagues of Egypt until it is found. The undiscovered way in us is like something of the psyche that is alive. The classic Chinese philosophy calls it "Tao", and compares it to a watercourse that resistlessly moves towards its goal. To be in Tao means fulfilment, wholeness, a vocation performed, beginning and end and complete realisation of the meaning of existence innate in things.

Aspirations in this direction are very lofty ones, and we cannot be surprised that Lawrence's were incompletely fulfilled. We must add that he is one of the few modern writers in whom such aspirations do not appear absurd.

THE DOCTRINE

III. PRACTICAL APPLICATIONS

To descend from these cloud-wreathed heights. A good deal more can be learnt of the nature and bearing of Lawrence's ideas by showing their consequences in action—an activity to which Lawrence himself devoted more time than to attempts at abstract psychology or metaphysics. Detailed illustration is less necessary here, for so much has appeared in the novels themselves. The prime example of polarity in human affairs is the polarity between the sexes. What is the consequence of this for Lawrence's sexual ethics? Not pan-sexualism, as we have already said. The sex-relation is only an instance of the polarity that runs through the universe—but it is primary for man. His very being is the result of a sexual encounter, and in the sexual encounter he returns to his origins and finds his completest fulfilment. God the Father is the Flesh, the physical, and is primary; the antithetical Son, Logos, spirit, is his secondary emanation. And our completest means of realising primary reality is in sexual experience. This is a bald statement, but there is no need to recapitulate the many passages where it is lyrically or prophetically enforced.

If it be objected that for many people this is simply not true, that their sexual experience is incomplete or unsatisfying, certainly not the central one of their lives, Lawrence replies that this is due to a radical perversion of human nature which has been going on for over two thousand years. Of this in its social and cultural aspect there is more to be said hereafter. All the great pagan cults, before the advent of the "higher religions", were cults of fertility and generation, and it is the genial influence of the phallus that alone can produce active and happy forms of human society. If sex is not our primary fulfilment, it is due to a cultural failure in which we are nearly all involved. Nevertheless, it is the business of a free man to fight against the failures of his culture; and the implication of this is that sexual failure in the individual is always in part a failure of character. Whether this belief is true or not, I do not know; but it is one that Lawrence shares with many men and nearly all women. In some places, mostly early, he suggests that there should be a special place, like that of the Vestals or the religious orders, for those rare beings for whom sexual life is not and cannot be the real fulfilment. He writes of Sue Brideshead in the *Study of Hardy*: "Sue had a being, special and beautiful. Why must she feel ashamed if she is specialised? . . . If we had reverence for what we are, our life would take real form, and Sue would have a place."[63] But in later work this tends to disappear, and deviations from the Laurentian sexual norm are treated with cruelty or contempt.

Although Lawrence lays a good deal of stress on the ancient fertility religions, he says very little about the instinct for procreation. It is decidedly not the motive behind the sexual relations between man and woman. For him the experience of the participants in sex is always primary, and the child is a by-product. And this, no doubt, however false genetically, is true to subjective experience; there can be few people, like Benjamin Franklin, who "use venery" consciously for the sake of procreation. Lawrence does, however, seriously underrate the power of parental feeling and the desire for children; and he seems to have no concrete idea of the completion of a sex relation in children and the family. He fought against these things in life, and he pays the penalty by a yawning incompleteness in his sexual doctrine. Though he spends a great deal of energy on the relations between parents and children, it is nearly always on its perversions, and there is scarcely an instance in his novels of normal parental love.

Since the central fact of human experience is the polarity between the sexes, the difference between men and women is to be maintained and emphasised as far as possible. "The great thing is to keep the sexes pure. And by pure we don't mean an ideal sterile innocence and similarity between boy and girl. We mean pure maleness in a man, pure femaleness in a woman."[64] The ideal of comradeship, of "being pals", is the target of some of his most acrid denunciation. We may imagine what he would have said of Margaret Mead's thesis that the traditional differentiations of the sexes are largely social and conventional. For Lawrence they are essential; and it should be noticed that it is precisely the age-old, traditional differences that are valid for him. The man who allows himself to become too gentle, tender and sensitive is denying his own manhood. The woman who tries to dominate others by the will, instead of drawing them to her by her essential nature, is a parody of *das ewig weibliche*. She is the object of some of Lawrence's most scarifying satire, and if she is raped and killed by six Mexican bullfighter's assistants, we are left to infer that this is what she deserves. Woman finds her true fulfilment in sex, and after that in being queen of her own realm—the home and children. Here her sovereignty is assured and indisputable, far more so than any that is open to the male. "Hensure is so much surer than cocksure." Man finds his fulfilment in sex, and beyond that, outside the family altogether, in outward creative activity, in politics and the arts. Certain aspects of the current Anglo-American world, with all the men clucking like hens and all the women crowing like cocks, provide Lawrence with object lessons in support of his thesis. They become more numerous in the tales after his visit to America.

Although the man's and the woman's rôles are essentially complementary, opposition and conflict between them is to be expected. It should be admitted, indulged, never shirked or avoided. Any attempt to deny its existence or to suppress it in support of a preconceived moral or social ideal simply destroys emotional integrity and poisons the springs of life.

> If you hate anything she does, turn on her in a fury. Harry ner, make her life a hell, so long as the real hot rage is in you. Don't silently hate her, or silently forbear. . . . Never repent of your real hot rages, whether they're "justifiable" or not . . . and if your heart weeps tears of blood afterwards, tell her you're thankful she's got it for once, and you wish she'd had it worse.
> The same with wives and their husbands. If a woman's husband gets on her nerves she should fly at him. If she thinks him too sweet and smarmy with other people, she should let him have it to his nose, straight out. She should lead him a dog's life, and never swallow her bile.[64]

This rousing programme for domestic life calls up images of slammed doors and packed suitcases. It is intended, however, as a recipe for monogamy. Lawrence never wavered in the belief that a mate once chosen was chosen for life. His own wife was a divorcée and so were many of his friends, but this did not prevent his asserting, in season and out of season, that marriage was marriage, once and for all—not from any principle of external law, but from the nature of genuine human sexual relations in themselves. Undoubtedly he made the reservation of hopelessly mistaken or inauthentic matches, as all who are not restrained by some overriding religious precept are likely to do. The remarkable thing, however, is his certainty that his principles of action would lead to durable, indissoluble alliances. Perhaps he generalised too widely from his own experience. No doubt an occasional row is better than suppressed resentment; but had Lawrence not been by nature a monogamous man, and Frieda a woman of singular longanimity, these convictions could hardly have been sustained so vigorously.

At any rate, he sees marriage as permanent, and the permanence as a part of its *raison d'être*. As well as giving fulfilment, it is to give stability, a fixed centre to life. Woman indeed finds a large part of her satisfaction in providing this stability, in being herself the fixed centre—as long as she is satisfied sexually. If she is not she has the right—sometimes it seems the duty—to reject the unsatisfactory mate and find another. On what grounds the man has the right to make a similar rejection does not become apparent. Here, as often, Lawrence tends to write from the woman's point of view. In any case, man needs for his fulfilment a life of physical or otherwise creative enterprise outside the sex-relation altogether. The success of the sex union itself depends on this. A man who has not a vigorous and independent creative life of his own will never be any use to a woman. And for this, the man needs a positive emotional relationship with other men. This is a notion that haunted Lawrence, as we have seen, from *Women in Love* to *The Plumed Serpent*. He never worked it out satisfactorily, and never indeed seems to have understood man-to-man relationships at all well; but it led to the various attempts at ritualised male comradeship, *Blutbrüderschaft* and so forth, both in his fiction and in his life.

Remarkably little is said, either in the doctrinal writing or the fiction, about what writers like Havelock Ellis call sexual selection in man. Many of Lawrence's characters, like Lou Carrington or the Ursula of *The Rainbow*, make what turn out to be bad choices; some make good ones. But all that lingering analysis of the growth and vicissitudes of sexual attraction that forms the substance of so many novels is almost absent in his work. And the absence is not without reason. For it is the undifferentiated fact of sexual polarity itself that is vital for Lawrence—the attraction between man and woman, rather than the attraction between this particular man and this particular woman. This massive undifferentiated attraction in which personality is almost extinguished is to him the only secure basis of marriage; and the intense individual specialisation of romantic love is regarded with suspicion. It is not always easy to see in his fiction why the bad pairs of lovers are bad or the good ones good; but a basic reason is that the love of the bad ones springs from the ego, from all that is most individual and idiosyncratic about them; while the love of the good ones is something more (or less) than personal, often in contradiction to the overt demands of the personal life. The whole romantic concept of the heart finding its happiness in another heart delicately attuned to it is either absent or is rudely attacked. The typical Lawrence lovers fall in love (if that is the right name for it) with people that they rather dislike, in an ambience of violence or cultural or personal antagonism. To the poets of the *dolce stil nuovo*, the central truth is that:

> *al cor gentil ripara sempre amore.*

Such a love would find little hospitality in Lawrence's world. There are not many gentle hearts about.

Of course throughout the whole Platonic-Romantic love tradition of Europe (Plato, *amour courtois*, Dante, Petrarch and all their varied modern progeny), it is always a question of moulding and refining the basic sexual instinct into some exquisite and artificial form. It is a matter, to use modern psychological jargon, of some kind of sublimation, or some postponement or diversion of the sexual aim. To all this Lawrence is violently opposed. His attacks on idiosyncratic, individualist and personal love pass over into attacks on 'spiritual' love—by which he means all forms of love in which the basic sexual energy has been diverted or delayed or sophisticated into something other than its primitive form. (It is perhaps unnecessary to add that most of those who have practised such refinements have thought that they were doing something radically different—that they were finding in sexual love an echo and an analogy of a love that was in origin divine. Without prejudice and for the sake of the argument, we will continue to stand at Lawrence's point of view.) A further development of this first attack is the attack on that whole Platonic process by which love of physical beauty becomes love of mental beauty, and passes over into the love of ideas—abstractions, as Lawrence would call them and Plato would not. He finds this (as he believes) perverse idealisation at the root of Christian love, of modern democratic and humanitarian sentiment, and of many of the accepted norms of personal relationship in modern life. To any reader of Lawrence detailed illustration of the destructive fervour with which he attacks these targets is unnecessary. And it should be said at once that no one else has exposed with such surgical penetration the corruptions to which ideal love is subject—the sterile cultivation of an ideal that has no longer any roots in the real being, the rottenness of a love that is kept going by the will alone, its transformation into a peculiarly poisonous kind of high-minded bullying. There is more to be said of this hereafter; but we must also say now that if we are to follow Lawrence in his rejection we are rejecting all that culture of the heart which is one of the major streams of European civilisation. Lawrence knew this perfectly well, and his readers should know it, too.

The application of Laurentian doctrine to society and the body politic need not detain us long. The specific practical recommendations are sometimes brilliant, sometimes obstinately irresponsible, and never quite serious. They are never quite serious because Lawrence had no capacity for co-operation with his fellows and no idea how men in the mass are really moved. Witness the grotesque comedy of his relations with Bertrand Russell and the schemes for the ideal colony of Ramanim. So when Lawrence recommends the closing of all schools or the establishment of a corporate state under a dictator, it is with the lack of commitment and the partial insincerity of a man who knows that there is not the slightest chance that his ideas will have any effect. We can therefore afford to skip much of the detail.

As we might expect, the burden of Lawrence's educational doctrine is an attack on premature intellectualisation. He uses a good deal of pseudo-physiological mumbo-jumbo to demonstrate what, I dare say, we should have been willing enough to accept without it—that a diffused instinctual somatic activity, with both volitional and sympathetic aspects, is prior to the development of consciousness. The great offence is to awaken the child's consciousness too early; and in the modern world parents and teachers do it all the time. The mother is not content with the child's simple physical response to her presence: she tries to awaken its 'love' for her, as a conscious personal thing, at an age when the infant has no business to be loving anybody. A small child is not capable of any genuine emotional life beyond a simple positive response to warmth, security and animal tenderness; and an equally simple negative response of anger and rejection. To try to force a mental awareness of its processes on the child—to make it do things because it loves mummy, or not do them because they are naughty—introduces a note of falsity into its life at the start. It is the beginning of that prolonged dependence on maternal stimulation of which Lawrence himself knew too much. The positive physical response to the mother is the true beginning of the sympathetic life; the impulse of rejection and independence is that of the volitional life; and they should be trained and developed with no more consciousness or moralising than we use in training puppies.

Lawrence writes this in a strain of bitter resentment against all emotional and moral tenderness. *À bas les mères.*

> Seize babies away from their mothers, with hard, fierce, terrible hands. Send the volts of fierce anger and severing force into the child. Volts of hard, violent anger, that shock the feeble volitional centres into life again. Smack the whimpering child. . . . Quick, quick, mothers of England, spank your wistful babies. Good God, spank their little bottoms; with sharp, red anger spank them and make men of them. Drive them back. Drive them back from their yearning, loving parasitism; startle them for ever out of their pseudo-angelic wistfulness; cure them with a quick wild yell of all their wonder-child spirituality.
> . . . Kick the cat out of the room when the cat is a nuisance, and let the baby see you do it. And if the baby whimpers, kick it after the cat.[65]

Teachers are as bad as mothers; they try to develop the child's power of self-expression long before it has any self to express, and the result is the posturing humbug of recited poetry and child-art. This was in the twenties, the early days of liberalism in child-rearing; and Lawrence is knocking the heads off the idols of the time with a vengeance. That enemy of the child-cult, and of Lawrence himself, the old right-wing ogre Wyndham Lewis, could hardly have done the job with more macabre gusto. He might have been surprised, had he read these essays, to find so close an approximation to his point of view.

There is no doubt a complex psychological history behind the almost hysterical temper in which Lawrence is writing these passages. His real point is that the constant over-stimulation of faculties that are not ripe for development etiolates the instinctual forces and introduces a deep strain of falsity into all contemporary culture. The remedies proposed need hardly concern us in detail. They are all directed to awakening the instinctual and physical life of the child first; and proceeding to the culture of the intellect and the emotions only when they are ready for it, and carried only so far as the individual is really capable of it. This involves the abolition of all schooling before the age of ten, and leaving the child to itself as much as possible. After that, mental education is to begin, dividing the time with handicrafts. The mental training is to be confined to reading, writing and arithmetic; and the crafts are to be real ones—cobbling and carpentry, not finger-painting and model-making. A thorough technical mastery is to be achieved of whatever is attempted. The main job of headmasters and senior educators generally is to manipulate a constant selection process by which children with intellectual or artistic gifts are picked out for further education, and the others drafted out in due time to various grades of manual and clerical labour. Only a few will go on to higher education. So, Lawrence believes, each will become what he really is, not a poor imitation of some standard cultural ideal.

Lawrence's own experience as a teacher had shown him the sufficiently obvious truth that the majority can never be educated beyond a certain point. Yet it is hardly to be supposed that he would have been satisfied by the 1944 Education Act, the eleven-plus examination and the secondary modern school. The grading system occupies a large place in his educational machinery; but its fundamental aim is not the reformation of the class system for its own sake; it is the recognition that the physical and instinctual life is the primary one, the common substratum of all human existence. Its right development matters more than anything else, and the intellectual culture of the few can be easily superimposed on it. If the reverse is the case, intellectual culture made a universal ideal and superimposed on weak instinctual and physical foundations, the result is humbug, stunting and distortion. Inequality is a necessary consequence of this programme, and Lawrence is bluntly anti-egalitarian. Men are not equal, and the kind of democracy founded on the assumption that they are is a lie. Like all social lies, it is a source of poison and corruption. But, he adds, men are only unequal if you compare them with one another; and you have no business to compare them at all. Ultimately there is no basis for comparison, for each one is unique. The class system and the graded education are only the means by which each one is to become what he is really capable of. A contempt for egali-

tarianism often implies a contempt for the individual as such, a glorifi-
cation of hierarchy and the social order for their own sakes. Needless
to say, this is far from Lawrence's intention. His anti-democratic
sentiment consorts with an almost religious veneration for the
individual human person.

The most compendious account of Lawrence's politics is given in
two letters, one to Russell and one to Lady Cynthia Asquith, both of
July 1915. He writes to Lady Cynthia:

> I hope, after the war, we may have a real revolution. I want
> the whole form of Government changing. I don't believe in the
> democratic (republican) form of election. I think the artisan is
> fit to elect for his immediate surroundings, but for no ultimate
> Government. The electors for the highest places should be the
> governors of the bigger districts—the whole thing should work
> upwards, every man voting for that which he understands through
> contact—no canvassing of mass votes. And women shall not vote
> equally with men, but for different things. Women must govern
> such things as the feeding and housing of the race. And if a
> system works up to a Dictator who controls the greater indus-
> trial side of the national life, it must work up to a Dictatrix who
> controls the things relating to private life.[66]

And to Russell:

> This existing phase is now in its collapse. What we must
> hasten to prevent is this young democratic party from getting
> into power. . . . The deadly hydra now is the hydra of Equality.
> Liberty, Equality and Fraternity is the three-fanged serpent.
> You must have a government based upon good, better and best.[67]

As Anthony West has written: "The stench of this particular brew
of poison has become so familiar that it is easy to overlook Lawrence's
prescience in 1915, when Mussolini was still a Socialist and Hitler
nothing very much in the German Army."[68] It might be added that
the brew was not even self-evidently poisonous until it was used by
the witch-doctors of the thirties for their own peculiarly noxious
purposes. There is good cause in the writings of this period for calling
Lawrence a potential Fascist, but a Fascist *avant la lettre*. The belief
that Liberalism and democracy were in collapse was shared by much
of the intelligentsia of Europe, and Lawrence died too early to be put
to the only really diagnostic test. We do not know how he would
have reacted to the new anti-democratic forces when they began to

reveal their true colours. Speculation is idle, but my own belief is that his swift intuitive penetration into the real nature of men and movements would have saved him from any prolonged complacency towards Fascism in action.

A last curious point about Lawrence's politics is that they contain what at first sight seems a major inconsistency. In his educational and social pyramid, the highest government responsibilities go to those with the highest education—to those, that is to say, most capable of the conscious intellectual activity that he has apparently been at most pains to dethrone. There is no suggestion that the inarticulate somatic awareness that is the common foundation of life shall be the administrative *magister vitæ*. The rulers are to be the self-conscious and articulate mouthpieces of this diffused, unexpressed wisdom, a kind of priesthood.

> Hence we shall see that the system is primarily religious, and only secondarily practical. Our supreme judges and our master professors will be primarily *priests*.[69]

A race, in fact, of philosopher kings—Laurentian philosophers, of course. And so, by an ironical twist of his not very developed political thought, Lawrence goes near to rejoining the Plato he has rejected.

IV. THE QUARREL WITH CHRISTIANITY

Further discussion of detail is hardly called for. Lawrence's practical recommendations for the reform of society vary between the politics of cloud-cuckoo-land and the politics of the sergeants' mess. But the defect is largely a defect of executive power, and his most incondite or ill-considered practical precepts turn out to be linked with ideas of fundamental importance. The history of his political ideas is really an eccentric and not very significant branch of his ideas about religion—especially the great historical and institutional religion of his own culture, Christianity. And to trace Lawrence's relation to Christianity genetically, from the first tentative agnosticism of his letter to his sister to *The Man Who Died* and the *Last Poems*, would be to trace the whole course of his work again from another and more specialised point of view. Let us here attempt something more summary, a synoptic view, neglecting chronology, a composite photograph made up of many shots, not all wholly compatible with each other, but still capable of fusion into a comprehensible whole. We might start at any one of a number of points—so let us start at the one we have in any case reached—his anti-democratic political doctrine.

After innumerable attempts at defining the basis of his objection to democracy, scattered through his work from *Women in Love* onwards, Lawrence gets it out most clearly at the eleventh hour in *Apocalypse*:

> The mass of men have only the tiniest touch of individuality, if any. The mass of men live and move, think and feel collectively, and have practically no individual emotions, feelings or thoughts at all. They are fragments of the collective or social consciousness. It has always been so, and it always will be so.[70]

Which has not prevented him saying earlier that the end of all education and social life is the development of the individual. So it is—but only so far as the individual exists. And in most men the individual exists very little, the rest of them being realised in their share of the collectivity.

Most men are largely citizens, members of the community, collective men. And "as a citizen, as a collective being, man has his fulfilment in the gratification of his power sense". A man may wish to be a unit of pure altruistic love, but since he is inescapably a member of the political community, he is also inescapably a unit of worldly power. A man must be both a unit of love and a unit of power; he must satisfy himself both in the love-mode and the power-mode. This theme, appearing in almost the last words Lawrence wrote, goes back to a far earlier period of his career. It is expressed in almost similar terms in the last chapter of *Aaron's Rod*.

> I told you there were two urges—two great life-urges, didn't I? There may be more. But it comes on me so strongly, now, that there are two: love and power. And we've been trying to work ourselves, at least as individuals, from the love-urge exclusively, hating the power-urge and repressing it. And now I find we've got to accept the very thing we've hated.
> We've exhausted our love-urge, for the moment. And yet we try to force it to continue working. So we get inevitably anarchy and murder. It's no good. We've got to accept the power motive, accept it in deep responsibility.[71]

And this is as good a point as any to enter Lawrence's long quarrel with Christianity. For Christianity as Lawrence always sees it is the attempt to live from the love-motive alone—to make love, *caritas*, pure altruism the only motive in life. "The essence of Christianity is a love of mankind." Of course this takes no account whatever of historic and doctrinal Christianity in all its developed complexity; still worse, from the Christian point of view, it takes no account of the *source* of that love, which should be the motive of all faith and all action. Still, in a thousand places in his fiction and expository writing Lawrence makes the identification between Christianity and the doctrine of pure, universal, altruistic love. It is against this doctrine of Kangaroo's that Somers revolts, exalts his own dark god and preserves his integrity. It is against this doctrine that Don Ramón revolts and triumphs over in the person of Doña Carlota. It is against this doctrine that the Ursula of *The Rainbow* revolts when she shakes the little sister who has slapped her face, and feels the better for it—"unchristian but clean". On every level from the prophetic to to the trivial Lawrence sees Christianity as the love-ideal and rejects it.

Two thousand years ago Western man embarked on the attempt to live from the love-motive alone. Sometimes Lawrence puts it a few hundred years earlier, with Platonism and the rise of the higher religions. He refers to this momentous step in the history of humanity in at least two different ways. Sometimes he sees it as a great rejection, a failure of courage, a refusal of the responsibility of life, sometimes as a necessary development, living and valid for its time and for centuries to come, but now at an end. Perhaps the second judgment represents his steadiest and most central belief.

> I know the greatness of Christianity: it is a past greatness. I know that, but for those early Christians, we should never have emerged from the chaos and hopeless disaster of the Dark Ages. If I had lived in the year 400, pray God, I should have been a true and passionate Christian. The adventurer.
> But now I live in 1924, and the Christian venture is done. The adventure is gone out of Christianity. We must start on a new venture towards God.[72]

In either case, the love-mode is exhausted. Christianity is kept going by a barren effort of will, it has no longer any connection with the deep sources of life; and the consequences of this continuing will-driven automatism of love is to be seen everywhere in the modern world.

The psychological and personal consequences have been touched on sufficiently often already. The withered and fluttering figure of Doña Carlota is supposed to represent the etiolation of spiritual love; and the unsleeping will behind it has strained her relation to Don Ramón beyond the breaking point. When Kangaroo proposes to love Somers, Somers reflects: "He doesn't love *me*, he just turns a great general emotion on me, like a tap. . . . Damn his love, he wants to *force* me."[73] Hermione wants to love Birkin spiritually, and when Birkin, to preserve his integrity, has to reject her, she tries to knock his brains out. Farther back still, the unhappy Paul of *Sons and Lovers* is in the toils of a 'spiritual' love which should have been a happy physical relation, but can never become so because of Miriam's fixed spiritual will; and his situation is complicated because there is another woman, his mother, who also wants to possess his soul. The common element in all these admittedly complex and varying situations is a love which is cut off from the natural carnal roots of love, and continues to exist simply as a function of the will. It is sterile in itself and becomes life-exhausting to whoever exercises it. Since it is something imposed on the object of love, not a reciprocal relation, it becomes inevitably a kind of spiritual bullying, and must inevitably be rejected by anyone who wishes to preserve his individual being. And all this in Lawrence's eyes is an inevitable consequence in personal relations of the Christian love-doctrine, the Christian discipline of the heart.

There is an analogous development in public life. The universal sentiment of love for mankind is similarly cut off from the natural roots of human comradeship, the warm, carnal physical community; known, for instance, by men working together in a common manual task or playing together in a ritual dance. These are communities of power, and have behind them the inexhaustible vitality of a common physical life. The love of mankind offers only a community of sentiment, and can be maintained only as a fixed direction of the will. So, like private spiritual love, it becomes a kind of bullying. *Sois mon frère ou je te tue.* Hence the devastating wars by which Christendom has been riven. Further, this kind of love is not a true communal feeling at all, it is a product of the individual will, of the ego, of all that is most personal and least deeply rooted in man. It demands that each man shall be an individual power-house of universal love. This has two consequences. The first, only clearly apparent late in the Christian cycle, but its inevitable and logical development, is democracy. Each individual must love all others, equally and impartially—the Whitmanesque universal brotherhood. The mysteries of power and lordship are denied—for they would be a break in the uniformity of universal love. So that universal love becomes a forcing of the same ideal sentiment on all alike; or looked at in reverse, a claim by each individual alike for the same universal consideration. And this claim is false, for all men do not possess individuality in the same measure. And this brings us to the second consequence of the demand for universal love—it involves the demand that all men shall be fully individuals, and that each shall be a separate individual source of universal spiritual love. It is a demand for the impossible, and it falsifies the whole relation of man to man.

> In democracy, bullying inevitably takes the place of power. Bullying is the negative form of power. The modern Christian state is a soul-destroying force, for it is made up of fragments which have no organic whole, only a collective whole. In a hierarchy each part is organic and vital, as my finger is an organic and vital part of me. But a democracy is bound in the end to be obscene, for it is composed of myriads of dis-united fragments, each fragment assuming to itself a false wholeness, a false individuality. Modern democracy is made up of millions of fractional parts all asserting their own wholeness.[74]

Christianity, in fact, is designed for a world of free, pure, bodiless individuals, not for a world of men—men, who exist largely in their undifferentiated physical community, most of whom are capable of very little individual spiritual development. "Christianity, then, is the ideal, but it is impossible."[75] Lawrence agrees with Dostoevsky's Grand Inquisitor, as he makes plain in an introduction that he wrote to that dialogue. Christ loved man, but loved him in the wrong way. The following words of the Inquisitor might almost have been written by Lawrence himself: "By showing him so much respect, thou didst, as it were, cease to feel for him—thou who hast loved him more than thyself. Respecting him less, thou wouldst have asked less of him. That would have been more like love, for his burden would have been lighter." Or, as Lawrence paraphrases it: "To be able to live at all, mankind must be loved more tolerantly and more contemptuously than Jesus loved it, loved for all that, more truly, since it is loved for itself, for what it is, not for what it ought to be, free and limitless."[76]

But man is not free and limitless. He needs earthly bread, the satisfaction of his physical appetites, and he needs to acknowledge that satisfaction as a divine gift. And he needs authority, someone to bow down to, the acknowledgment of power—not the spiritual power of an unseen god, but embodied power in the flesh. To restore health to the community of men it is first necessary to accept the power-motive again, to acknowledge the legitimacy of both individual authority and collective power. The mass of undeveloped mankind will find their vicarious fulfilment in this acknowledgment. Lawrence worries constantly over this problem of power from *Aaron's Rod* to *The Plumed Serpent*; and never successfully. His negative analyses of the corruptions of 'white' love and democratic humanitarianism are piercing and profound; yet the dark god of power who is to be not destructive but life-giving is never successfully evoked. The attempts to embody him in fiction produce fascist leaders or posturing mounte-banks. It might be said that this is exactly what such attempts produce in life—these are the only practical embodiments of the dark god. History since Lawrence's death might well seem to confirm the accusation. I think Lawrence could still reply that this is not so; it is precisely because the reality of power is shirked by the general "democratic" presuppositions that, like all realities that have been denied and suppressed, it reasserts itself in violent and terrible ex-plosions. If the reality had always been admitted to its rightful place, the explosions would not have been necessary.

He would in part be right. The most committed liberal democrat would be free to admit that the calamities of the last thirty years are in part a result of the decadence of his own ideals, a decadence evident in the general loss of all sense both of the proper mode of exercising authority and the proper mode of submitting to it. This decay is not yet arrested, and Lawrence is one of its sharpest analysts. He was asking a real question, though he never found an answer.

It may be that Lawrence had himself too many relics of Christianity in his heart ever to be able to cope with the problem of earthly power, or even thoroughly to accept the necessity he asserted. Certainly he knew too little of how it works and how it is obtained. What could a man who had never had an ordinary job, never had a place in a community of men, never exercised or submitted to authority, know of political reality? His characters become steadily less convincing the nearer they come to exercising political power. The only way Lawrence can realise power and convey the sense of it, unhampered by ignorance or an inner resistance, is when it is displayed in nature. Lou Carrington submits to the "wild spirit" she finds in the mountains of Taos, but it is hard to see her submitting to any human embodiment of it. Lawrence becomes aware of this failure himself, for after *The Plumed Serpent* we hear less of the power-mode. He is still equally concerned with the failure of 'Christian' love, but he is now inclined to find the alternative in "a new tenderness", a fleshly tenderness. *Lady Chatterley* is supposed to be the illustration of this tenderness, and the story which explores its relation to Christianity is *The Man Who Died*.

As Lawrence's attention shifts from power to sensual tenderness as the alternative to Christian love, the opposition becomes less intense; and it becomes easier for him to represent his doctrine as a completion of Christianity rather than a contradiction. Spiritual love and sensual love are, after all, both forms of love: and the Christian depreciation of sexuality* is an accident rather than the essence of its doctrine. *The Man Who Died*, therefore, comes nearer to being a reconciliation with Christianity than anything else Lawrence wrote. In other places sensual love is seen as the negation of 'white' love, *agape*, Christian love. Here we come near to seeing it as a transcendence, reached by death and re-birth. And this means that it represents, not the climax of his art, which it certainly is not, but a climactic point in the development of his thought.

This story of the rejected prophet, almost killed, left for dead, returning painfully to life, and finding it, not in the resumption of his mission but in the knowledge of a woman—this story of the resurrection is certainly Lawrence's most audacious enterprise. Many readers have found in it the final evidence of the arrogance, the ignorant

---

* I take it for granted that Christianity does depreciate sexuality, or at most make reluctant concessions to it; and that Lawrence was right in believing this, wherever else he was wrong; and that the Chestertonian (and post-Chestertonian) trick of representing Christianity as a robustly Rabelaisian sort of faith is a vulgar propagandist perversion.

presumption of which Lawrence has often been accused. To take a story so tremendous, so profoundly interwoven with the life of our civilisation, and "to try to improve on it", as I have heard it said, may well seem to suggest something of the kind. I think the charge can be dismissed if we are careful enough to see what Lawrence was trying to do. Although the prophet is unnamed, the identification with Jesus is not disguised. The Crucifixion, the Entombment, St. Mary Magdalen, the journey to Emmaus are all explicitly referred to. Yet what is the Jesus to whom the story refers? The "historical Jesus", the Lamb of God who takes away the sins of the world, the Christ who shall come again with glory to judge the living and the dead? Surely none of these. Lawrence had believed since he was twenty that Jesus was "as human as we are"; but he is not trying to provide a demythologised historical version of his end, more acceptable to positivists than a supernatural resurrection. George Moore attempts something of the kind in *The Brook Kerith*; but not Lawrence. And the cosmic and eschatological bearings of the Gospel story concern him even less. There is no suggestion anywhere in his tale that the death and resurrection of Jesus is a mystery of redemption or that it affects the destiny of mankind. Lawrence is concerned with two aspects of the Christian myth, and two only: one, the value of Christian love; the other, the personal destiny of Jesus the teacher. What he has done is not to vulgarise or reduce the splendours and mysteries of traditional Christology; he simply leaves them on one side. He has taken Jesus as what he believed him to be, a human teacher; he sees what he believes to be the consequences of his teaching, and tries according to his own lights to push beyond it. Certainly an audacious attempt, possibly a misguided one, but to anyone who cares to read what Lawrence wrote, not to rest on a conceptual summary, it will not, I think, appear as an attempt made without due reverence.

The story was originally called *The Escaped Cock* and ended at Part I, with the prophet setting out alone to walk through the world, vividly aware of life in the flesh, but as yet without any active participation in it. The central symbol of this part of the story is the cock itself, tied by the leg by the vulgar peasant, released by the prophet. The first act of his re-born existence is to let it fly free; and its new-found freedom is a symbol of his own sensuous faculties, imprisoned during the years of his mission and almost extinguished during his passion and death. For it has been a real death. With great discretion Lawrence avoids the question of a miraculous resurrection. What does it matter? One who has suffered, as the prophet has done, the extremity of physical and spiritual torment has in effect died; and if his vital powers should, miraculously or unmiraculously, return, it is a real re-birth. In the concentration-camp world that we have produced after twenty centuries of Christian civilisation there are many people who know this. At first the prophet walks in the world like one who is still not of it.

> He felt the cool silkiness of the young wheat under his feet that had been dead, and the roughishness of its separate life was apparent to him. At the edges of rocks, he saw the silky, silvery-haired buds of the scarlet anemone bending downwards. And they too were in another world. In his own world he was alone, utterly alone.

He can feel no kinship with the tender life of the young spring; and this may serve to remind us how different Lawrence's nature religion is from the Wordsworthianism of the nineteenth century. Lawrence is more aware of the tormenting complexity of human experience, of the indirectness, even the contrariety of the relation between man and external nature. Man cannot learn of man by passively receiving impulses from a vernal wood, but only by adventures in the world of men. The prophet awakens to the new life of the body only when he realises that the peasant woman desires him. He does not desire her; he has died and does not desire anything; anyway, he knows that she is hard, short-sighted and greedy. But the knowledge of her desire awakens in him a new realisation.

> Risen from the dead, he had realised at last that the body, too, has its little life; and beyond that, the greater life. He was virgin, in recoil from the little, greedy life of the body. But now he knew that virginity is a form of greed; and that the body rises again to give and to take, to take and to give, ungreedily.

So he does not reject her harshly—"he spoke a quiet pleasant word to her and turned away".

But he has another and a sterner rejection to make, the rejection of his own former mission, and of Madeleine, the woman who had believed in him. They meet, and she wishes him to come back to her and the disciples. But he only replies that the day of his interference with others is done, the teacher and the saviour are dead in him. In a sense he accepts this death: betrayal and death are the natural end of such a mission. "I wanted to be greater than the limits of my own hands and feet, so I brought betrayal on myself." This is what happens to the man who would embrace multitudes when he has never truly embraced even one. On his second meeting with Madeleine he again rejects her entreaties, saying that he must ascend to the Father. She does not understand, and he does not explain; but the reader will remember that in Lawrence's mythology the Father was also the Flesh.

Madeleine, who wants to devote everything to him, is also under the spell of a hard necessity. In her life as a carnal sinner she had taken more than she gave. Now she wants to give without taking, and that is denied her. The prophet prefers the society of the peasants, for their earthy inert companionship "would put no compulsion on him". He dreads the love of which he had once been the preacher, the love that compels.

The central symbol of the second part of the story is the priestess. She is a priestess of Isis, Isis in search of the dead Osiris, and like the prophet she is virgin. She had known many men in her youth, Cæsar and Antony among them, but had remained always cool and untouched; and an old philosopher had told her that women such as she must reject the splendid and the assertive and wait for the re-born man.

The lovely description of her temple and its setting is a delicate Mediterranean landscape, nature at its most humane, friendly and responsive. At the moment when the stranger lands on her shores—the stranger who is the prophet on his travels—she is idly watching two slaves, a boy and a girl. The boy beats the girl, and in a moment of half-frightened excitement copulates with her, scared and shame-faced. The priestess turns away indifferently. These are the loves of slaves; whatever fulfilment she is to find has no more in common with these vulgar couplings than with the loves of Cæsars. When the stranger-prophet asks for shelter he is given it, indifferently and impersonally. A slave suspects that he is an escaped malefactor, and the priestess goes to look at him as he sleeps.

She had no interest in men, particularly in the servile class. Yet she looked at the sleeping face. It was worn, hollow, and rather ugly. But, a true priestess, she saw the other kind of beauty in it, the sheer stillness of the deeper life.

. . . There was a beauty of much suffering, and the strange calm candour of finer life in the whole delicate ugliness of the face. For the first time, she was touched on the quick at the sight of a man, as if the tip of a fine flame of living had touched her. It was the first time.

Both the prophet and the priestess are separate, cut off from the common life around them. She is surrounded only by slaves, and she found slaves repellent. "They were so embedded in their lesser life, and their appetites and their small consciousness were a little disgusting." And as for the prophet—"He had come back to life, but not the same life that he had left, the life of the little people and the little day. Re-born, he was in the other life, the greater day of the human consciousness." Both are aristocrats of the spirit and both are incomplete—she because she is the living representative of Isis in search of Osiris; and he because he has died and come back to the world and still dreads its contact. She realises that she has not yet found her Osiris, and he realises that there is the whole vista of a new life before him that he has not yet been able to touch.

And when she becomes Isis to his Osiris (for there are no surprises in this story), we are to see it not only as the satisfaction of a long-denied bodily hunger (it is that, too), but as the consummation for each of them of a solitary life of spiritual exploration—a spiritual journey that can never be complete until it has reached carnal fruition that will alter its whole meaning. She who has played out her life as a drama of search has now found. "And she said to herself, 'He is Osiris. I wish to know no more'." And he who has died, returned to the world, but not yet felt himself to be living again, knows that he is risen from the dead when he feels desire for the woman and the power to satisfy it. When the life of the little world, in the shape of the slaves and the Roman soldiers, breaks in upon these Christian-Osirian mysteries, the prophet takes a boat and slips away, healed, whole, risen in the body, content to take what may come on another day.

Æsthetically, no doubt, the story was more satisfying in its first form, when it ended with the prophet's rejection of his old mission and his yet unfulfilled knowledge that a new life awaits him. The temptation to be explicit about what cannot properly be explained is always the *ignis fatuus* for which Lawrence is content to lose his way. The attempt to *present* the experience of one who has stepped inside the gates of death and come out again seems foredoomed to failure. As it turns out, the failure is of a different kind from that which might have been expected. It is a breakdown of continuity, not a breakdown of expression. The idyll of the stranger and the priestess is beautifully done; the balance between fabulous remoteness and concrete sensuous realisation is delicately held; and Lawrence convinces us as he rarely does that the conjunction he describes is that of two rare beings, each with an exquisitely specialised individual life, yet satisfying each other completely by meeting on a ground which is beyond the personal life of either. And over it all is shed like sunshine the warm tolerant beauty of the ancient Mediterranean world—a beauty which may be partly the product of Arcadian fantasy, but still forms a real and living part of European experience.

All this is true. But it is also true that it is hard to accept the stranger of the second part of the book as identical with the prophet of the first. In the first part the broad, unspecific outlines of fable are filled out with what we know of the Gospel narrative, which is still very close to us. The invented myth is given density and immediacy by its dependence on the great public myth. In the second part the invented myth stands alone, and like all products of the pure personal imagination, it is thinner than what history or the mythopœic faculty of a whole culture supplies. The stranger in the second part is not so much a different person as a person out of a different story; the change is a change in the mode of conception. For the tale has two kinds of significance, unequally distributed—the one more prominent in the first part, the other in the later addition.

It can be interpreted synchronically or diachronically, to borrow terms from the linguists. Synchronically, it is simply what Lawrence first called it—a story of the Resurrection, deriving much of its strength from its background of the Gospel narrative, passing over into a more rootless fantasy as this recedes into the distance. Its theme is the necessity of rejecting the Christian love-ideal for a man who has really risen in the flesh. And right or wrong, we recognise this as an integral part of the Laurentian thesis. The second part of the story is a more arbitrary invention, and as such abides our question. Should the fulfilment of the flesh, the obvious natural destiny of mortal creatures, be discovered so late and after such long wandering? Should it, for the sake of Lawrence's thesis, be a healer for creatures who have been so long estranged from the roots of life? Could it be so, for beings who have been so long specialised in other directions, one of whom has suffered to death? It would be absurd to press these questions too hard, but they do at least begin to obtrude themselves.' They can be answered by seeing the tale in the second way, diachronically; not as the story of a particular man at a particular time, but as an allegory of the course of Christian civilisation. The death of the prophet is also a symbol of the death of the Christian dispensation. Christian civilisation is dying after two thousand years. But the story of man is a continuity, and no culture ever really dies: it comes to life again, to a new life, which it is at first incapable of realising and is unable to face. The passion and death of the prophet are the death-agonies of Christian culture ("Ours is a tragic age," as Lawrence said at the beginning of *Lady Chatterley*), and the second part of the story is a foreshadowing of the new dispensation that is to come. But it is a new dispensation only reached by death and re-birth. The fleshly tenderness that is to replace Christian love in the new order can never be the pristine, unembarrassed pagan delectation. The one thing a post-Christian can never be is a pagan, C. S. Lewis has remarked; and Lawrence is showing his sense of this. Christianity may be brought into touch again with the old nature-mysteries of death and re-birth, as it is in this tale; but they will be changed in the process. The fleshly healing is painfully, almost fearfully accepted by the priestess and the prophet, after years of deprivation and a season of anguish; and so it must be in the history of Western man. It will not be among *hommes moyens sensuels* that the new apprehension of life is born. Theirs is the "little day", as it always has been, under any dispensation. But to encompass this in the greater day will be the task precisely of those who have most completely submitted to the old spiritual disciplines. True, the mission of Christianity has to be rejected, but it has been lived through before it has been rejected, and nothing can ever be the same again. If a new order is to come into being, it will in all its splendour and joy be the inheritor of the Christian abnegation and suffering.

I believe that this, or something like it, is what Lawrence is saying in *The Man Who Died*, and that this is the most developed state of his relation to Christianity. The hostility had, after all, never been unmitigated. "Give me the mystery and let the world live for me"— Kate's cry in *The Plumed Serpent* was Lawrence's own. And Christianity, at any rate Catholic Christianity, was at least a guardian of the mystery in the midst of the desert of mechanised civilisation. As Lawrence sees it, Catholicism had even preserved some of the old earthy pagan consciousness, and through the cycle of the liturgical year had kept in touch with the rhythm of the seasons, the essential rhythm of man's life on earth. As the inheritor of the sense of vital mystery which was the essence of religion, the Catholic Church seemed at times to him a vehicle of hope. It was a sympathy of sentiment only, not at all of dogma, intermittently awakened in Lawrence by his love for the Mediterranean world. Far stronger was the perpetual intellectual and moral preoccupation with Christian civilisation and Christian ethics; a preoccupation so intense that he is able to orientate himself only by taking bearings on the Christian position he had abandoned.

For of course he had abandoned it; and the Christians (there are some) who would use Lawrence's stream to turn their own mills have need of caution. He often looks at Christianity with sympathy, but to do so he always has to turn it upside down. A choice had to be made, and Lawrence, in fact, made it in early life. However he may use Christian language, he uses it to a different end. For Christianity the life of the flesh receives its sanction and purpose from a life of the spirit which is eternal and transcendent. For Lawrence the life of the spirit has its justification in enriching and glorifying the life of the flesh of which it is in any case an epiphenomenon. It is at once an older and a newer religion that he is celebrating with what were almost his last words.

For man, the vast marvel is to be alive. For man, as for flower, beast and bird, the supreme triumph is to be most vividly, most perfectly alive. Whatever the unborn and the dead may know, they cannot know the beauty, the marvel of being alive in the flesh. The dead may look after the afterwards. But the magnificent here and now of life in the flesh is ours, and ours alone, and ours only for a time. We ought to dance with rapture that we should be alive and in the flesh, and part of the living, incarnate cosmos. I am part of the sun as my eye is part of me. That I am part of the earth my feet know perfectly, and my blood is part of the sea.

My soul knows that I am part of the human race, my soul is an organic part of the great human soul, as my spirit is part of my nation. In my own very self I am part of my family. There is nothing of me that is alone and absolute except my mind, and we shall find that the mind has no existence by itself, it is only the glitter of the sun on the surface of the waters.[77]

V. CONCLUSIONS

This is an old religion because it is the pantheistic animism that we suppose to have prevailed over the world "before we pieced our thoughts into philosophy"; it is new because for the modern world it is not something that can be accepted as a matter of course; if it is found at all, it is attended with all the excitement of rediscovery. For Lawrence it was a real rediscovery, not bookish or archæological; achieved through living experience, not through grubbing in *The Golden Bough* or tracing Tibetan mandalas.

Practically there is only one choice open to the modern Western man who feels the necessity for a religious apprehension of the world. It is the choice between some kind of supernaturalist theism* and some kind of naturalist pantheism. Lawrence chose the second. Those who choose (or are chosen by) theism are likely to end up as Christians. Pure theism is not a faith with much staying power, and the attractive force of the only great historic theism of our culture is so great, and the shocks of living so numerous, that Christianity of one kind or another is likely to receive into its fold all theists except a few insulated academic philosophers. Even Lawrence felt the attraction, though he resisted it and took the other course. He took the other course; and this means that to theists, *a fortiori* to Christians, what he has to say about human destiny can never be more than peripheral. Why should they exercise themselves overmuch about a thinker who has rejected what to them is self-evident?

For Lawrence's polemics do nothing, and can do nothing, against real Christianity. Of course real Christianity is *not* what Lawrence says it is; its essence is *not* love for mankind, meaning by this as Lawrence does a merely natural sentiment, generated within the human ego. Christianity knows as well as Lawrence did that such a

---

* "Theism: Belief in a personal God, capable of making Himself known by supernatural revelation."—*Universal English Dictionary*, ed. H. C. Wyld.

love is impossible. But then the essence of Christianity is what Lawrence has rejected in advance—the faith that there is another kind of love, outside the natural order altogether, offered to humanity as grace, mediated by the Incarnation, by which all things become possible, even the subsistence of charity in the human heart. Between those who believe in the reality of the supernatural and those who do not no argument is possible; there is no common ground. Lawrence never attempts to assail the supernatural foundations of Christianity, he tacitly assumes that they are unreal and concentrates his fire on the human and ethical consequences of its doctrines. The Christian may reject his criticism altogether, though I think he would find this difficult; or he may reply that what Lawrence is attacking is only a human perversion of Christian love; and this may well be true. Even admitting this argument, it is also true that the perversion is common and widespread, and that Lawrence's polemics have a real and not insignificant object. But there is, I think, a further point. Real Christianity is an increasingly rare phenomenon in the more or less educated Western world from which Lawrence drew most of his observations; pseudo-Christianity is a much more massive and widespread affair. By pseudo-Christianity I mean an acceptance of the verbal habits, emotional predispositions and some of the ideals of conduct of real Christianity, without any profound and fundamental belief in their supernatural foundation. This is Lawrence's actual target, though he failed to distinguish its nature; and it is not impossible that real Christianity might even be helped by his searching analysis of the imitation.

Romantic love I believe to be equally immune to his attacks. Romantic love is a psychic fact; it is something that occurs, and its peculiarity is that when it occurs it is absolute and compelling. It may be an artificial channel, but it is by now so deeply worn that any waters which find their way into it flow with a force that no verbal argument can alter or modify. Lawrence can only be effective, as he is, against its vulgar or sentimental accretions. There is no need to use the historical and pragmatic argument that we *ought* not to give up the train of feeling that has been the refiner of the European heart for eight hundred years. Lawrence may be an emotional barbarian for rejecting the whole code of courtesy and chivalry, and we have the right to reject him in consequence. But it hardly matters; this particular citadel is impregnable if sparsely garrisoned. He can blow up Poe, but not the *Vita Nuova*. All he can do, and this in part he has probably done, is to create a moral climate in which it is difficult for the sentiments of the *Vita Nuova*, and all their progeny, to occur again.

In his campaign against democracy the situation is rather different. Nothing that Lawrence says is of any great moment to democracy as a convenient piece of political machinery, a reasonably handy and equitable way of getting government by consent. But against democratic egalitarianism as the ideal of human relationship he has dealt heavy blows. What is more, he has replaced it by another, and as I think more permanent, ideal, with as much respect for the human person and without the falsity and illusion—an ideal which is capable of ennobling authority, not merely of dethroning it. Men are radically unequal, if you compare them; and there are times when both intellectual honesty and personal honour demand that we should admit it. But the ideal is to stand at a point where you do not attempt to compare men at all, for each is unique. This does not so much confute egalitarianism as render it irrelevant.

Having identified the objects of Lawrence's criticism, we can now recognise its immense corrosive power. Its peculiarly devastating influence is not a matter of rhetoric; it does not depend nearly as much as has been supposed on the evocative or prophetic force of his language, and it can only lose by the frequent cloudiness and illtemper. The real weight of his criticism does not lie here at all; it is something more intellectual, in the very substance of his thought. It lies in his power to show the rotting and corrupting effect of unliving and unrooted ideals. It is not merely that they are unreal, but that their unreality is poisonous. Lawrence shows this, and does not merely talk about it. Many writers show up false patterns of life— it is the staple, for example, of an exceedingly unrevolutionary ironist like Thackeray. But there is always the tacit allowance—we are constantly tempted to make it—that a false ideal can be pragmatically useful or serve instead of a better. Lawrence's criticism is more fundamental and more penetrating largely because he destroys this comfortable compromise.

But the world has not lacked for negative and cathartic critics, especially in this century; and it is not in the end with them that one is tempted to rank Lawrence. He is indeed a destroyer of shams and falsities, but it is also necessary to discover what it is that makes him so much more than this. Those who find the best of Lawrence in the travel books and the descriptive writing would balance the destructive force with what they find there, and make the positive side of Lawrence a sort of simple natural religion. But those who do so are making Lawrence's message into a more inviting and digestible matter than it really is. The intimate and joyful contemplation of the natural scene is the consolation rather than the business of his life. Where Lawrence's powers are working most vigorously, it is the Dionysiac fervour of his destruction that is most striking; and it can be so intense that it becomes a positive value in itself. The triumphant welcome Lawrence can give to the forces which are to extinguish all ordinary personal and social values is akin, or at least analogous to, the mystic's joy in the extinction of his personality. The ecstasy with which Nietzsche in *The Birth of Tragedy* welcomes the merging of all separate entities in the Dionysian flood is the only literary parallel to Lawrence's vision, if we are really to see it as it is, not merely to extract from it those parts that are most agreeable to us.

Lawrence had read Nietzsche in youth, and through his wife he was always subject to Germanic influences. It is probable that his doctrine would not have been what it is if the Nietzschean influence had not been felt. But I am not suggesting a direct influence here, and the moment the comparison is made a vital difference is to be observed. Nietzsche sees the Apollo-Dionysus dichotomy (much like the dichotomy that runs through Lawrence's thought) as tragic. He first becomes aware of it when he is explaining the origin of tragedy— both tragedy as a literary form and the tragic sense of life. And he accepts and welcomes the necessity of tragedy. In Lawrence there is none of this acceptance. His fiction never even approaches the tragic mode; and the violence, the cruelty, the extreme situations in his stories, are never seen in a tragic light. That is why the cruelty in Lawrence's fiction so often seems naked and unresolved—there is almost a deliberate refusal of the tragic vision. "Tragedy ought to be a great big kick at misery," he wrote. Maybe so, but only when the extremes of misery and suffering have been faced, contemplated and accepted. The suffering experienced or caused by Lawrence's charac-ters is never faced with that degree of fullness and realisation. The suffering of Miriam, of Clifford Chatterley, the full horror of the mutually destructive relation between Ursula and Gerald Crich—it is hardly too much to say that they are avoided; perhaps rightly for Lawrence's purpose; but that implies a limitation of his purpose. The full human implications of the situations in which his characters find themselves are never completely realised. And his vision of the destiny of man, for all the conflict and destruction by the way, reaches its consummation not in the tragic but in the idyllic mode—in the vision of some quasi-pastoral perfection in the past or the future, with the really terrifying conflicts all vanished away.

This I believe points to the most serious limitation of Lawrence's thought. To be alive in the flesh is magnificent, and Lawrence has expressed his sense of it magnificently. But if it is the only supreme value, man is irrevocably immersed in the transitory and the contingent, irremediably at the mercy of physical accident and physical change. And however much Lawrence may hate fixity and achieve a poetic and metaphysical exaltation by glorifying the flux, man is also a being who has a passion for the absolute, the changeless, the unconditioned. This predicament is a tragic one, perhaps the root of all tragedy. Yet Lawrence fails or refuses to see it in a tragic light.

> Man is in love, and loves what vanishes,
> What more is there to say?

Yeats' stoic question, for all its laconic brevity, contains the essence of this tragedy as nothing in Lawrence does.

To inquire why the tragic sense is absent in Lawrence leads in the end to the discovery that he is not wholly free from the sentimental idealisation that he wishes to destroy. The forms of life that Lawrence condemns are all actual enough; we recognise at once their counterparts in the contemporary world. Those which he exalts all lack reality. He projects them into some imaginary future, as much a fantasy as Morris's *News from Nowhere*, where men wear red trousers on their proud limbs and hierarchically dance in celebration of the life-force. Or he retrieves them from the past—some lost Indian culture, or the Etruscan civilisation whose great advantage for his purpose is that we know almost nothing about it. The construction of such myths is probably as old as civilization itself, and Lawrence has as much right to his imaginative indulgence as anyone. But it is imaginative indulgence rather than the rigour of the whole truth.

Yet Lawrence does, after all, claim to be doing something more, and I for one wish to claim it for him. If what he does is to subject current ideals to a corrosive criticism, bring the edifice crashing down, and then sidestep from the resultant catastrophe into a fantasy world, his achievement would be less than we feel it to be. There must be something else. It has been admitted that he does not feel with the force of full commitment the tragic bearing of his doctrine. Why does the impression of personal integrity remain so strong? It can only be because Lawrence personally manages to transcend tragedy—if the paradox may be allowed—as the saints transcend it. I am not trying to predicate sanctity of Lawrence, and it is an analogy, not an identity, that is suggested. But the selfless, obliterating joy of identification with the energies of life wipes out all individual loss, limitation and incompleteness for Lawrence as the saints' all-obliterating love of another God does for them. This self-annihilating joy becomes more intense as Lawrence approaches the end of his life. We can see its effects in *Apocalypse* and *Last Poems*. As he becomes less alive in the flesh, all the ecstasy that comes, as he tells us, from being alive in the flesh becomes more real and more acute.

Then at the last we begin to wonder whether words are not slipping beneath us, and whether Lawrence has not been betrayed by his own terminology. This ecstasy that we can only experience while we are in the body becomes by a strange paradox more intense as the life of the body ebbs away. At the end of his days, at the last extremity of sickness and physical misery, when his life, in his own words, is only the leavings of a life, Lawrence finds:

> still among it all, snatches of lovely oblivion, snatches of renewal,
> odd, wintry flowers upon the withered stem, yet new, strange flowers,
> such as my life has not brought forth before, new blossoms of me.[78]

Is it possible that these moments have their source in the flesh that is now almost worn away? We are driven to believe that Lawrence has unwittingly brought the serpent into his own earthly paradise—the soul with all its maladies, but also with its central spark of unconditioned, inexhaustible life. At the end of "The Ship of Death", when everything has disappeared down the flood of darkness, "still

out of eternity, a thread of light separates itself on the blackness";
and by its light it is possible to see that the soul is still there;

> and the little ship wings home, faltering and lapsing
> on the pink flood,
> and the frail soul steps out.

And then, having followed Lawrence so far, it would perhaps be possible to go back to the beginning, to tread the same path again, tracing the same pattern, but giving a different value to the symbols—and to find that the flesh had never been the flesh in any common acceptance of the term, and that the frail soul had been there all the time.

It is the genial corollary of Lawrence's impetuous and metaphorical way of thinking, even of his capriciousness, his uncertainty of tone and temper, that new growing points are to be found in his writing where we least expect them. When he seems to have carried one train of speculation to the point of exhaustion, a new, small shoot of life unexpectedly appears. This happens throughout his work, which seen as a whole presents a picture of energies flowing and ebbing, but continually pushing out in new directions. Not least at the end of his life, when the man who had exalted the natural forces of the body as the source of supreme good surveys the prospect of these forces burnt to ashes, and finds even in the ashes a new living flame. Here, as in other ways, he has earned the right to make the phœnix his symbol.

NOTES

Page references are not helpful for most of Lawrence's works, as there are a number of editions in wide circulation. The following plan has been adopted. The provenance of quotations from the novels, tales and poems is indicated as clearly as possible in the text; for the novels, chapter references are given, in Roman figures, immediately after the quotations. Other references are given here.

[1] T. S. Eliot, *After Strange Gods*, 1934. His criticism is modified in his foreword to Fr. William Tiverton's *D. H. Lawrence and Human Existence*, 1950.

[2] "Now it's Happened", *Pansies*, 1929.

[3] "Morality and the Novel", *Phœnix, the Posthumous Papers of D. H. Lawrence*, 1936, p. 527.

[4] *Lady Chatterley's Lover*, 1928, Chap. IX.

[5] "Morality and the Novel", *Phœnix*, p. 528.

[6] "Why the Novel Matters", *Phœnix*, p. 535.

[7] *Fantasia of the Unconscious*, 1923, Preface.

[8] *The Letters of D. H. Lawrence*, ed. A. Huxley, 1932, p. 197.

[9] ibid., Introduction, p. xi.

[10] ibid., p. 65.

[11] ibid., p. 61.

[12] T. S. Eliot, *After Strange Gods*, p. 59.

[13] F. R. Leavis, *The Common Pursuit*, 1952, p. 236.

[14] Ada Lawrence and A. Stuart Gelder, *The Early Life of D. H. Lawrence*, 1932, p. 72.

[15] W. H. Auden, "In Praise of Limestone".

[16] E. T. [Jessie Chambers], *D. H. Lawrence, a Personal Record*, 1935, pp. 94–123.

[17] ibid., p. 105.

[18] ibid., p. 103.

[19] ibid., p. 57.

[20] *Fantasia*, Preface.

[21] *Letters*, p. 76.

[22] Quoted in Harry T. Moore, *Life and Works of D. H. Lawrence*, 1951, p. 94.

[23] Helen Corke, *D. H. Lawrence's 'Princess', a memory of Jessie Chambers*, Thames Ditton, 1951, p. 25.

[24] E. T., op. cit., p. 190.

[25] ibid., p. 191.

[26] ibid., p. 202.

[27] ibid., p. 201.

[28] Helen Corke, op. cit., p. 33.

[29] ibid., p. 30. *Vide* also E. T.

[30] Frieda Lawrence, *Not I But the Wind*, 1935, p. 52.

[31] Helen Corke, op. cit., p. 41.

[32] *Letters*, p. 142.

[33] Frieda Lawrence, op. cit., p. 4.

[34] Letter quoted in F. J. Hoffman, "Lawrence's Quarrel with Freud", in *The Achievement of D. H. Lawrence*, Oklahoma, 1953, p. 109.

[35] *Letters*, p. 94.

[36] ibid., p. 95.

[37] ibid., p. 64.

[38] ibid., p. 485.

[39] "America, Listen to Your Own", *Phœnix*, p. 90.

[40] "Au Revoir, U.S.A.", *Phœnix*, p. 105.

[41] "New Mexico", *Phœnix*, p. 142.

[42] ibid., p. 143.

[43] "Indians and an Englishman", *Phœnix*, p. 99.

[44] "The Mozo", *Mornings in Mexico*, 1927.

[45] Introduction to *The Woman Who Rode Away*, Penguin edn., p. 8.

[46] *Letters*, p. 711.

[47] ibid., p. 683.

[48] ibid., p. 708.

[49] Reprinted in *Sex, Literature and Censorship*, ed. Harry T. Moore, 1953, p. 265.

[50] ibid., p. 266.

[51] R. P. Blackmur, *Language as Gesture*, 1954, pp. 286–300.

[52] Preface to *Pansies*.

[53] "The Body of God", *Last Poems*.

[54] *Studies in Classic American Literature*, 1923, p. 26.

[55] *Apocalypse*, 1931, p. 222.

[56] *Reflections on the Death of a Porcupine*, Philadelphia, 1926, London, 1934, p. 6. "The Crown" is reprinted only in this collection.

[57] ibid., p. 2.

[58] ibid., p. 93.

[59] ibid., p. 97.

[60] ibid., p. 22.

[61] ibid., p. 90.

[62] "The Reality of Peace", *Phœnix*, p. 692.

[63] "Study of Hardy", *Phœnix*, p. 510.

[64] *Fantasia*, p. 171

[65] "Education of the People", *Phœnix*, p. 639.

[66] *Letters*, p. 243.

[67] *D. H. Lawrence's Letters to Bertrand Russell*, ed. Harry T. Moore, New York, 1948, p. 51.

[68] Anthony West, *D. H. Lawrence*, 1950, p. 42.

[69] "Education of the People", *Phœnix*, p. 608.

[70] *Apocalypse*, p. 215.

[71] *Aaron's Rod*, Chap. XXI.

[72] "Books", *Phœnix*, p. 734.

[73] *Kangaroo*, Chap. XI.

[74] *Apocalypse*, p. 217.

[75] *Phœnix*, p. 284.

[76] ibid., p. 285.

[7] *Apocalypse*, p. 223.

[78] "Shadows", *Last Poems*.

INDEX

INDEX

INDEX